RODOLFO GRAZIANI

THE STORY OF AN ITALIAN GENERAL

ALESSANDRO COVA

TRANSLATED BY JAMES CETRULLO

FONTHILL

Fonthill Media Language Policy

Fonthill Media publishes in the international English language market. One language edition is published worldwide. As there are minor differences in spelling and presentation, especially with regard to American English and British English, a policy is necessary to define which form of English to use. The Fonthill Policy is to use the form of English native to the author. The translator, James Cetrullo, was born and educated in the United Kingdom and now lives in Devon; therefore British English has been adopted in this publication.

www.fonthillmedia.com
office@fonthillmedia.com

First published in the United Kingdom
and the United States of America 2021

British Library Cataloguing in Publication Data:
A catalogue record for this book is available from the British Library

Copyright © Alessandro Cova 2021

ISBN 978-1-78155-851-5

The right of Alessandro Cova to be identified as the author of this work has been asserted by him in accordance with the Copyright, Designs and Patents Act 1988.

All rights reserved. No part of this publication may be reproduced, stored in a retrieval system or transmitted in any form or by any means, electronic, mechanical, photocopying, recording or otherwise, without prior permission in writing from Fonthill Media Limited

Typeset in 10pt on13pt Sabon
Printed and bound in England

Acknowledgements

The author would like to thank Doctor Mario Serio, superintendent of the Central State Archive in Rome.

Special thanks also go to Doctor Marina Giannetto, director of the study hall of the archive itself, and to Doctor Margherita Martelli, curator of the 'Fondo Graziani'.

Writing this book would not have been possible without their generous help, the lack of which would have simply resulted in a collage of already published books.

Alessandro Cova
Rome, 1987

Photo Permissions

All photographs and illustrations in the book, unless stated otherwise, are from the translator's own private collection.

Grateful acknowledgement is made to Enzo Antonio Cicchino of Erotodo TV for having supplied newspaper cuttings from the period in question.

Every effort has been made to obtain the necessary permission with reference to copyright material. The translator apologises should there be any errors or omissions.

James Cetrullo
Pescara, 2021

Contents

Acknowledgements   3

1   Disaster in the Desert   7
2   A Home in the Mountains   35
3   Postcards from Libya   59
4   Ethiopia and the Use of Poison Gas   90
5   Marquis of Neghelli and Executioner of Addis Ababa   118
6   Twenty Months on Lake Garda   150
7   A Sentence Which is More Like an Acquittal   196
8   What Remains?   215

Postscript   218
Endnotes   221
Bibliography   231
Index   235

1
Disaster in the Desert

At sunrise, the British attacked. 'It had just turned four o'clock in the morning,' Lt-Gen. Richard O'Connor, commander of the Western Desert Force, would later recall:[1]

> Behind us, from the east, the great African night was cut in half by a sliver of light. The darkness was such that only the moon could guide us. In fact, for the first 20 miles as we approached the enemy, it was the moonlight that revealed the way to the heavy armoured vehicles of the 7th Armoured Division and the light tanks of the 11th Hussars. We studied it well, yes we did indeed.

The author of this plan of attack was Archibald Percival Wavell, commander of the Army of the Nile, future field marshal and lord of Cyrenaica.[2] At fifty-seven years of age, smooth-faced, with a slim build, Wavell had a cool temperament and was little inclined to the enthusiasm of the average Englishman. He would write: 'It's typical of the British way of waging war to initiate fighting with a complete lack of preparation. But when the inevitable tragedy occurs and the return match has to be staged, British capacity both for improvisation and detailed organization asserts itself as usual—"still as Saxon slow in starting, still as weirdly wont to win"'.[3] This was not mere boasting, as Wavell had demonstrated this a few months before when the Italian 10th Army had crossed the Libyan–Egyptian border advancing as far as Sidi Barrani. Paying no attention to the jibes of the Italo-German press, on that day, the British general had limited himself to opposing the enemy advance with a thinly spread line of troops, ordering the bulk of his army to fall back on Marsa Matruh, 200 km to the rear. In any case, had it not been Winston Churchill who had declared to the House of Commons 'A soldier who retreats lives to fight another day?' And now, Monday 9 December 1940, the British were ready to fight yet again.

Without neglecting a single detail, Wavell had prepared the counterattack efficiently and methodically. He was not thinking of a decisive engagement, his only concern was to drive the Italians back across the border, where they had begun their offensive. A limited but realistic objective, considering the fact that in front of him lay twelve Italian divisions dug-in defensively and led by Marshal Rodolfo Graziani of Italy, a career soldier with many victorious African campaigns under his belt. Wavell had not underestimated his opponent. According to the Zurich newspaper *Weltwoche*, they had known each other personally. In an article of 8 October 1940, the Swiss newspaper affirmed that 'They had met in Kufra in January 1934. After the conquest of that oasis, the Italians had invited a group of British and French officers to join them. Wavell and Graziani had joked, drunk to each other's health and exchanged sabres'. On a more serious note, when people spoke of Graziani at the Supreme Headquarters in Cairo, they did so with respect. Like Wavell, who had cut his teeth in 1917 with Allenby in Palestine, even Graziani, who was almost his peer, was an officer with long colonial experience. Like Wavell, Graziani knew everything there was to know about desert warfare and believed that in the sand 'defeat can quickly turn into a disastrous rout'. However, despite sharing an affinity in military thinking, the two generals could not have been more different. Wavell had descended from a family with a long-standing military tradition, with a great-grandfather who had fallen at Waterloo and a grandfather decorated for bravery at Balaclava. In comparison, Graziani was of more humble origins: his great-grandfather having been a shepherd and his grandfather a peasant. Whereas Wavell had been the best cadet at Sandhurst and was a member of the exclusive United Service Club in London, Graziani had studied in a seminary and risen from the ranks. Whereas Wavell was calm and precise, English through and through, Graziani was impulsive and quick to anger, 'so typically Italian'. However, in the eyes of Wavell, all of this did not diminish the real or supposed strategic capabilities of the marshal of Italy and marquis of Neghelli. For all the aforementioned reasons, the British commander decided to place all his bets on the element of surprise. He would push his army forward with small and rapid offensive attacks, sowing confusion and disarray in the enemy ranks and forcing Mussolini's army to withdraw to Bardia. As the element of surprise would be decisive, approaching the enemy had to happen at night, given that during the day the ascending dust clouds of advancing armoured vehicles could be seen from miles away.

However, the element of surprise had already been lost. The Italian divisions had been in a state of alert for days. On 19 November 1940, there had been a skirmish between British armoured vehicles and mobile patrols of the Maletti Group (formed primarily of Libyan troops) and the 2nd Libyan Division. Earlier that day, an Italian fighter plane flown by Lt-Col. Revetria had taken off from the camp of Gambut and had spotted 'many armoured vehicles' behind the Bir Emba embankment, between Marsa Matruh and Sidi Barrani. Finally, on 7 December, a British sergeant, captured at Alam Rabia by soldiers of the *Cirene* Division,

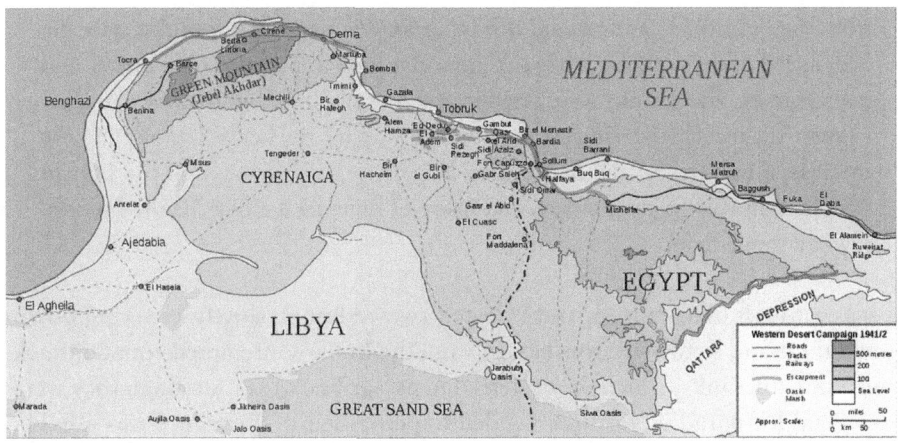

The border between Italian Libya and Egypt where the battle for the desert took place between December 1940 and February 1941. (*Wikimedia Commons*)

revealed that 'An offensive had been planned which would take place in ten days'. Despite the slow pace of military bureaucracy (three telegrams were sent by three commands to Lt-Col. Revetria 'In reply to your message of the 19th of the last month would you confirm the existence of enemy vehicles behind the embankment at Bir Emba,' forcing the poor man to repeat 'confirm,' 'confirm,' 'confirm.'), the signals were clear and unequivocal, the British were about to move.

Under a hazy sky, brutal winds accompanied a misty backdrop when the I tanks of the 11th Hussars arrived at Nibeiwa towards 6 a.m. Nibeiwa, a location essentially consisting of just four palm trees and a *wadi* to the south-east of Sidi Barrani, where the troops of the Maletti Group were quartered, the most advanced point of the Italian formation. The other Italian divisions did not form a continuous frontline. They were slightly set back at intervals between each other, so as to form a series of fortified islands protected by trenches, Friesian horses, and mine fields. The 1st Libyan Division was stationed at Maktila, on the east coast of Sidi Barrani; the 2nd Libyan Division at Alam El Tummar, towards the south-east; then, the Maletti Group, followed further to the south by the *Cirene* and the *Marmarica* divisions. In the second row, garrisoning Sidi Barrani were the Blackshirts of the *Tre Gennaio* with the *Catanzaro* Division in tow.

From the report of Lt-Gen. O'Connor:

For more than half an hour, the fighters of the RAF had been flying over the enemy, machine gunning and bombing them in order to cover up the sound of our advancing tanks. Furthermore, the Italians had the sun in their faces, and as a result of this, we reckoned that we would not be found out until the very last minute. However, things were to go differently. We were greeted by a true rain of fire; they were shooting at us with all the weapons they had. Luckily, the fire from the light field cannons did not incur any damage to our tanks, only the high-speed rounds of their anti-tank guns managed to penetrate our turrets and main frames. Five I tanks were temporarily immobilized, but the rest managed to enter the trenched perimeter, clearing the way for the heavy L tanks and the motorized infantry of the 2nd Indian Brigade. I have to say that the Libyan artilleryman were good gunners, and many of them died alongside their pieces. It was a tough fight.

It was a tough fight indeed, and it lasted twelve hours, slowly breaking down into a thousand smaller skirmishes. In vain, the Italians attempted counterattack utilising 3-ton tanks, which they referred to as 'sardine cans'. Although they were very good for parading through via dell'Impero, their performance was notably inferior in the desert. In vain, the *Cirene* Division sent a mobile column to help; however, the mobile columns were a pitiful expedient thought up by the Italian General Staff before the war. Made up of lorries with the tarpaulins taken off, they carried two 20-mm machine guns or a 47-mm light gun on the loading platform. The lorries were the same that were used to transport troops, food, and ammunition. The wobbly light guns on the loading platform were inaccurate and with a limited range, while the British artillery could fire at a distance of 12 km. Needless to say, the sighting of the *Cirene* Division's mobile columns led them being massacred by the British guns. Meanwhile, at Nibeiwa, the fight continued with bayonets. Wounded, Gen. Maletti fell, shot while manning a machine gun, and with him went approximately ten officers and hundreds of his soldiers. At 6 p.m., only Gen. Gratti's men—although surrounded—continued to hold out. Gen. Beresford Pierce's Indian Brigade finished off the last enemy holdouts, and the Libyan troops began to disengage and flee aimlessly with other soldiers towards the desert. It was as easy for the British tanks to advance and encircle the other Italian divisions as it was for the British infantry to finish the mopping up.

On paper, a counter-manoeuvre seemed possible, and the Italian High Command had made arrangements with this in mind. However, the only battalion of heavy M13 tanks was in Bardia and could not be of any help. Only about fifty lorries and some armoured vehicles could be put together on the spot, but this was far too few. There was no recourse but retreat. It was Graziani who personally gave the order: the *Cirene*, *Marmarica*, and *Catanzaro* Divisions had to fall back towards the Libyan border, on the Sollum–Halfaya pass line, a sloping ridge representing a natural defensive position. The survivors of the Maletti Group and the two Libyan divisions had to converge on Sidi Barrani and aid the Backshirts of the *Tre Gennaio* Division.

That night the Italians were in a state of utter confusion. Alongside troops marching orderly towards the west were groups of errant and disorientated soldiers who had lost their way. In addition, there were soldiers fleeing, who in order to escape more quickly, had discarded their entire kit, including their M91 rifles. Contributing to this state of disarray were 700 RAF fighters, which machine gunned the retreating troops, along with the armoured cars of the Hussars, which were firing a few volleys at the marching Italian divisions and then quickly disappearing into the dark. As an unexpected success was clearly in the making, Wavell decided to change his plans. The directive was to give no quarter to the enemy, to pursue and chase him into Marmarica, overtaking and closing him into 100 tiny pockets. Some 200 light I tanks and 400 heavy L tanks advanced, racing into the night followed by armoured cars, repair vehicles, motorised infantry, and baggage trains. 'We didn't know it,' wrote Col. Heinz Heggenreiner, German liaison officer attached to Graziani's command in a report to the Führer, 'but we were looking at the first modern battle in the desert. The Italians were fighting against fast-moving armoured forces with a rigid and antiquated military force. They were doomed from the start.'[4] It was more obvious that they had been defeated the following morning, on 10 December. At that point, the light tanks of the Hussars and the infantrymen of the 5th Indian Brigade—who had come from Nibeiwa—reached Alam El Tummar from the back, destroying the 2nd Libyan Division. Later, a regiment of Coldstream Guards and an Australian armoured column, which had left Marsa Matruh that night, shattered the defences of Maktila where the 1st Libyan Division had been lingering. Meanwhile, in the desert, the Italian divisions—which were being hammered from above by fighters and stung on land by tanks—had ceased to exist as such, having been reduced to scraps of divisions in rout. Only the *Catanzaro* Division, reinforced by a battalion of heavy M 13 tanks from Bardia, was militarily operational and was proceeding along the coastal road to Buq Buq, a small Egyptian coastal town whose name means pit in Arabic.

At Sidi Barrani, where the remains of the two Libyan divisions and the Maletti Group convened, Gen. Sebastiani Gallina decided to fight on until the bitter end. Around that desolate, dusty village, four forts had been constructed each 1 mile in circumference, complete with anti-tank ditches, concrete walls, barbed-wire entanglements, and mines. Defending Sidi Barrani were the Blackshirts of the *Tre Gennaio* Division. They were considered, even by Col. Heggenreiner, to be one of the best units of the 10th Army. 'Soldiers of the highest morale, yearning for combat,' the German officer asserted. Rhetoric aside, it was easy to believe him, as almost all of them were young volunteers raised by the regime inside the regime, trustful of Benito Mussolini and the slogans of the Fascist Party. Besides, in 1940, the fate of the war was in the Axis's favour. The German Army was undefeated, France had surrendered, and Britain, being hammered from the skies, would soon be invaded. The war seemed as good as won; why would anyone even think of defeat on the African front, on what Mussolini liked to call the 'fourth shore?' In the beginning, the besieged of Sidi Barrani opposed the enemy attack with determination. However, at midday, from the open sea, the ships of the Royal Navy began firing broadside after broadside. The Italians could not muster anything against the cannons of the British fleet. On the coast, in the absence of large calibre guns, the Italians could only make use of two bronze mortars, war booty from the First World War against Austria-Hungary with a range of little more than 2 km. Meanwhile, from the sea, shells were raining down from 22 km away and were systematically demolishing the fortifications. Towards 3 p.m., the British tanks managed to cross the minefields and enter the defensive perimeter. What happened next was a replay of the tragedy which had occurred at Nibeiwa, with bloody melees, hand grenades against tank treads, many dead, wounded, and thousands of prisoners. The Blackshirts had fought valiantly. Franz Reicher, correspondent for the *Deutsches Nachrichten Buro*, wrote: 'Many fell squashed by tanks, and others surrendered after running out of ammunition'.[5] At 5:30 p.m., Gen. Gallina sent a radio message to Graziani to inform him that 'enemy armoured forces have penetrated Sidi Barrani, taking many prisoners.' At 7 p.m., a second radio message clarified: 'This is our last transmission. We are preparing to destroy the radio. Many strongholds are silent, we have run out of ammunition. British armoured forces are advancing further and further towards us through forts reduced to silence'. Even on Sidi Barrani, the curtains had closed.

If Wavell in Cairo had reason to be satisfied with how the operation was progressing, in London, Churchill was ecstatic. For psychological reasons, Britain in 1940 needed a victory that would demolish the myth of Germany and her allies' invincibility. In his monumental history of the Second World War, the British prime minister dedicated fifteen pages to Wavell's offensive, the tone being euphoric and proud.[6]

> At home in Downing street, they brought me hour-to-hour signals from the battlefield. It was difficult to understand exactly what was happening, but the general impression was favourable. At first light on the 10th they assaulted the Italian positions on their front, supported by heavy fire from the sea. Fighting continued all day, and by ten o'clock the Coldstream battalion headquarters signalled that it was impossible to count the prisoners on account of their numbers, but that 'there were about five acres of officers and two hundred acres of ranks.' I remember being struck by a message of a young officer in a tank of the 7th Armoured Division: 'Have arrived at the second B of Buq Buq.' I was able to inform the House of Commons on the 10th that active fighting was in progress in the desert, that 500 prisoners had been taken and an Italian general killed; and also that our troops had reached the coast. 'It is too soon,' I added, 'to attempt a forecast of either the scope or result of the considerable operations which are in progress. But we can at any rate say that the preliminary phase has been successful.'

After the fall of Sidi Barrani, Winston Churchill abandoned (in private correspondence more than in official speeches) any form of restraint. He spoke openly of 'Victory', writing to President Roosevelt and the prime ministers of

Australia, Canada, and other Commonwealth countries ('as many as four Italian divisions are out of action'). His happiness was such that he signed off his letters to Roosevelt as 'Former Naval Person'. But above all, he wrote to Wavell. The correspondence between the prime minister and the commander of the Army of the Nile offered more enjoyable exchanges. For Wavell, there were ritual congratulations 'for the glorious service given to the Empire and our cause', accompanied by the reaction of the House of Commons 'which was stirred when I explained the skilful staff work required and daring execution by the army of its arduous task;' but there was also a curious exchange of biblical quotations, which according to Anglo-Saxon custom, are considered necessary for exceptional occasions. These quotations are reproduced in full here:

> Prime Minister to General Wavell. Saint Matthew, chapter 7, verse 7. Ask, and it shall be given to you; seek, and ye shall find; knock, and it shall be opened unto you.

> General Wavell to Prime Minister. James, chapter 1, verse 17.... Every good gift and every perfect gift is from above, and cometh down from the Father of lights, with whom is no variableness, neither shadow of turning.

Evidently, Churchill did not limit himself to invoking the saints, he was also a marvel of imperious suggestions: 'Forward, forward onto the chase. We need to maul the Italian army and rip them off the African shore as soon as possible, at least as far as the border of the desert of Marmarica. These people are like grain ready to be reaped'. In conclusion, besides being a statesman, the prime minister also had a wry sense of humour and was careful to pay attention to minute details, as he observed here:

> I have learned that our brave soldiers, whilst advancing, are singing a song brought over from Australia which is becoming very popular even here in England. It goes like this:
>
> > *We're off to see the Wizard,*
> > *The wonderful Wizard of Oz,*
> > *We hear he is a Whiz of a Wiz,*
> > *If ever a wiz there was.*[7]

Churchill's conclusion from this was: 'This song doesn't mean much. But I like it, I often think about it and I will keep thinking about it always. Occasionally, I find myself singing it'.

Rodolfo Graziani's headquarters were located at the Italian Supreme Command based in Cyrene. Located on top of a plateau, it was surrounded by the villages of numerous colonists, most of whom were Venetians sent by the

Fascist regime to cultivate Cyrenaica. Some 500 km away from Sidi Barrani and 1,300 from Tripoli, Cyrene had been chosen for its elevated position. At 700 metres above sea level, it guaranteed a more tolerable climate compared to the scorching temperatures of the desert, and because of its distance from the coast (30 km), it was safe from the Royal Navy's guns. The officers were lodged in a small hotel, and the marshal was housed nearby in a small four-roomed villa, connected by a spiral staircase to a 30-metre-deep Ptolemaic tomb, which had been turned into an air raid shelter and emergency command post by military engineers. Cyrene is one of the vastest necropolises of the ancient world, rich in all kinds of tombs: Phoenician, Greek, late Egyptian, and Roman. Some of these artefacts were preserved in a small museum situated among the palm trees. In the entrance hall, there was once a bronze bust of Graziani. An old photo, which testifies to its existence, had this written on the base: 'Wavell, for you we shall make a bust out of tuff, and it will be your tombstone'.[8]

From Embaie Tekle-Haymanot, who was the marshal's devoted Ethiopian *shumbashi*, (according to Graziani's autobiography, he was his 'loyal companion in good and bad times'. Once he even reprimanded a journalist who dared call him a 'black servant'), we learn that since the previous July, the marshal had been 'nervous, in a foul mood, and more distracted than usual'.[9] Noting further to his preoccupation, 'His Excellency lit forty cigarettes a day even though afterwards he would only smoke five or six, covering the entire ash tray and the edges of his work desk in cigarette butts.' 'His Excellency asked for a bottle of olive oil to season his buttered beans and forgot to put the oil into his salad.'[10]

To be frank, Rodolfo Graziani had always been hot-tempered and distracted, and was not known to have a friendly demeanour. To those whom he mistrusted, he often appeared brusque, moody, superstitious, and misanthropic, everything that was typical of a man who felt disdain for simple day-to-day life and mundane chitchat. Perhaps he was naturally shy, or perhaps that was the natural behaviour of a peasant torn from his land. Be that as it may, after returning from Libya, the marshal had good reason to be 'nervous and in a foul mood'. After the war, Graziani's personal diary from this period—found with its pages ripped out—was made public by the Roman daily *L'Indipendente*.[11] In it, we can see that Graziani blamed 'the scheming manoeuvres of the Roman clique' for his having ended up in this position. He suspected that 'Marshal Badoglio had given him the slip,' and he cursed himself and bad luck for not having had the strength to show his worth.[12]

Unlike most Italians who had cheered on the declaration of war on 10 June, Graziani knew perfectly well how things stood. In November 1939, the *Duce* had made him chief of staff of the army, and in the few months that followed, he was certainly not able to modify the situation, although he had had plenty of time to see things as they really were. His first observation was that the Italian army was practically unarmed, with some divisions lacking up to 92 per cent of their equipment. Even the famous 8 million bayonets only existed on paper. There were

'The *Duce*'s new collaborators'. The front page of the *Corriere della Sera* on 1 November 1939. As a result of Hitler's invasion of Poland, there had been a major government reshuffle in which Graziani (top row, third) was made chief of staff of the Army. (*Erodoto TV*)

actually only 1.3 million bayonets in use by various branches and units, including the youth section of the Fascist Party. Thirdly, the modernisation plan for the artillery, which had been started in January 1939, was expected to be completed 'by 1950'. Fourthly, the very new M11 and M13 tanks were, in February 1940, 'unique specimens', and according to technicians, mass production would only begin in June. His final observation was that, with the government's blessing, the Minister of the Exchequer and Currencies, Raffaelo Riccardi was selling Italian industrial goods (anti-tank weapons, 45-mm and 81-mm mortars) to the highest bidder, including—until March 1940—France and Britain. On 25 May 1940, with a 121-page memorandum under his arm, the marshal asked to be received by the *Duce*, with the intention of telling him the whole truth. But during their meeting, Mussolini seemed irritated and stopped him short with the following brusque remark: 'Don't worry. The next war will be a purely naval-aerial affair, the Army won't do much'.[13] The conversation died before it had even begun. The two men did not understand each other. Mussolini had been giving Graziani the cold shoulder ever since the end of the Ethiopian campaign, and the marshal could not understand why the dictator's attitude towards him had changed. As a result, he refrained from insisting and airing his grievances, and in the future, he would justify his attitude by saying that the first duty of a soldier is to obey. Titta Madia, a lawyer who wrote a sympathetic biography on the marshal, advanced the hypothesis that Graziani 'was in awe of Mussolini, although he occasionally broke out into unpredictable and recriminatory outbursts, typical of introverted people'.[14]

One fact is clear: no dialogue was possible regarding his transfer to Libya. From Graziani's account:[15]

> On the 10th of June, at the beginning of hostilities, I was transferred to the French front. On the 28th, returning from the Alps, I took a day off to go to my holiday home in Piani di Arcinazzo, not far away from where I was born. There, the following morning, I received a telephone call from Badoglio telling me that, due to a tragic error, the *quadrumviro* Italo Balbo, Governor of Libya, had been shot down by our own anti-aircraft guns in the skies over Tobruk. I was called to replace him. I was nominated Commander-in-Chief in North Africa with the added position of Governor and I also retained, nominally, the post of Chief of Staff of the Army. I was to leave immediately. 'What do you mean immediately?' I asked Badoglio. 'I need more information; I need an orientation meeting.' He replied: 'You will find all the necessary directives in Tripoli. You will leave tomorrow.' I rushed to Rome, where I learned that Mussolini was in Turin. I asked to speak to him personally on the phone. 'What do you want Graziani?' the *Duce* said. 'An orientation meeting,' I replied, 'considering that in Libya…' The *Duce* cut the conversation short. 'You will leave tomorrow.' 'I would like to leave the day after tomorrow, there aren't any planes ready at Centocelle airport for…' I clarified, until I realized that there was no one on the other end. In typical fashion, Mussolini had hung up, leaving the interlocutor talking to himself like an idiot.

Graziani, dutiful to the orders he received, flew from Centocelle airport on the following day, 30 June. He was met by Gen. Tellera—Balbo's former chief of staff—at Tripoli's Castel Benito Airport with the operational orders. After a general preamble ('you have two armies at your disposal, the 5th in Tripolitania and the 10th in Cyrenaica. With France's surrender we don't have to worry about any threats from the west, from Tunisia…'), the instructions stated: 'It's of the upmost importance to attack the British forces in Egypt by, and not after, 15 July'. According to those present, when he read this message, he started fuming. Later in the evening, he became even more furious when he received two reports sent by Balbo to Badoglio prior to his death. The first, from 11 May, read:

> … I have two armies with a few old artillery pieces, almost entirely devoid of anti-tank and anti-aircraft weapons. As for our fortifications, they lack weapons

and are therefore useless. We need to urgently reinforce our antiaircraft defences. Sending me thousands more men is totally pointless if I can't equip them with the necessary tools to move and fight...

The second, dated 20 June, sounded more like a cry for help. It stated:

Our assault tanks, already old and armoured only with machine guns, are long out of date: as we saw in the first clashes, the machine guns of the British armoured vehicles effortlessly tear up and cut through our armour.... Furthermore, our anti-tank weapons are just simple makeshift expedients, and the more modern ones lack the right ammunition.... Every encounter in these conditions is like a fight between meat and iron.

The marshal, who already suspected something was afoot, did not need any further confirmation that he had been set up. They had refused him a meeting in order to confront him with a *fait accompli* and left him to face the music on his own. Mussolini had chosen him because he was the 'hero of Neghelli', 'the African General *par excellence*', and Badoglio sent him to the slaughter without giving it a second thought.

Further accounts of the disdain and bitterness that pervaded are referenced within the pages of his personal diary. After various recriminations, Graziani—who, at the end of the day, was a practical man—rolled up his sleeves and got down to work. He immediately dismissed an offensive against Egypt 'by the 15th of July' as absurd and informed Badoglio; then, he installed himself in the

The front page of *Il Piccolo*. On 11 June 1940. The headline reads: '"Victory" is the rallying cry of the *Duce* to his people'. The day before, Italy declared war on Britain and France. In the weeks that followed, the Italian army would launch a clumsy offensive in the French Alps, and there would be skirmishes on the Libyan–Egyptian border.

Command Headquarters at Cyrene and tried to put together a plan of attack that he thought might have some degree of success. He began bombarding Rome with secret reports and ultimatums. In Rome, Badoglio was biding his time, and an impatient Mussolini, who had learnt about the delay of the offensive, was greatly irritated. At the end of July, the marshal, along with a briefcase full of various documents, finally obtained permission to return to Rome for a meeting at Palazzo Venezia. The plan he intended to illustrate was linear—an advance directly on Alexandria and onto the fertile Nile delta—but on two conditions: firstly, to wait until mid-October when temperatures started to drop, because in the desert heat it was difficult to move and sustain great masses of soldiers; secondly, the 10th Army needed to be reinforced with more divisions, plus further naval squadrons and 1,000 lorries and aircraft. He might as well have asked for the moon. Mussolini coldly pointed out: 'Graziani, I'm not demanding the conquest of Alexandria, which is 600 km from the Libyan border, I have never imposed a territorial objective. All I want you to do is to attack'. As for Badoglio, he seemed distracted, almost as though he were just passing through the meeting room. Col. Emilio Canevari, who would befriend Graziani after the war, wrote: 'The Marshal left that meeting rather disturbed. He said, "Had they misunderstood me or was it something far more serious?"'[16] Strong words, questions that with the benefit of hindsight seemed influenced more by anger rather than real conviction. The reality was that Badoglio, caught between the anvil Graziani and the hammer Mussolini, did not know which way to turn. Mussolini only wanted an advance, in his own words, 'so that we won't be left with nothing in the upcoming peace talks'. In short, political logic and military necessity did not coincide.

For the marshal, who was preparing to return to Libya empty-handed, the short trip to Rome only brought further disappointment. He also learnt from his informers that the higher echelons of the Fascist Party were vexed by him. According to Ciano's diary, party officials and ministers accused him of being 'a finished man', 'the shadow of the Graziani of Neghelli', and 'a soldier used to riding camels'. Fanning the flames were journalists, with whom Graziani had always entertained a bitter-sweet relationship and with whom he often refused to meet. According to them, the marshal suffered from 'anxiety neurosis', and he spent most of his time, 'shut inside the air raid shelter of Cyrene without ever visiting the troops'. The last of the naysayers was Pietro Badoglio, marquis of the Sabotino and duke of Addis Ababa, who, while talking with Gen. Roatta, had made this ridiculing remark, 'Let's see how our "warrior of instinct" will get himself out of this one.' 'Warrior of instinct' was the phrase used by the king in the citation for bestowing on Graziani the Grand Cordon of the Military Order of Savoy, after the Ethiopian War. Was it an explicit remark? Whether these jibes were real or not, Graziani, as irritable as he was, would write everything down and added venomous comments such as 'Two-faced Ciano!' and 'conniving Badoglio'. He must have been exasperated, to the point of forcing himself to do something he had never done before in his life. In the middle of August, Graziani summoned Gen. Mario Berti, head of the 10th Army, and Gen. Italo Gariboldi, head of the 5th Army, requesting their written opinion on the coming offensive. For Graziani, who had a high opinion of himself, this was more than just delegating his duties to others, it was an abdication. This is demonstrated by a letter he sent to Mussolini on 18 August, which included a note containing the generals' own negative comments. One of the notes in the margins read: 'It is obvious that it is my duty in these circumstances to put myself at the complete disposal of the higher authorities whenever this is considered to be of use'. If this was an act of resignation, it never came to anything, as the marshal's letter coincided with the arrival of one from Mussolini on 19 August:

> ... the invasion of England has been decided, it is in the completion phase and is going to happen. As for the date, it could be within three weeks or a month. So, on the day when the first platoon of German soldiers touches English soil, you will simultaneously attack. I repeat, I am not setting any territorial objectives. This is not about capturing Alexandria or even Sollum. I ask you only to attack the British forces in front of you. I assume full responsibility for this decision which I have taken. You have an undoubted superiority of troops, vehicles and morale. Five battleships are ready. We can send further aircraft.

Receiving the *Duce*'s telegram provoked Graziani to fall back in line and immediately abandon any thoughts of resignation. The marshal responded with a blunt: 'Orders will be executed'. Whether this was due to submissiveness or unconscious admiration, we do not know. He then arranged for the 5th Army to cede most of its weapons to the 10th and formed an armoured battalion with the few tanks available. He also gathered up all 2,700 lorries and transport vehicles in Libya, and even though he knew that most of the soldiers would march on foot, he gave the order for an attack with Sidi Barrani as its objective. Years later, he would tell Canevari:

> Sidi Barrani didn't mean anything, it was a dot in the desert, its only use was lengthening our supply lines and shortening the enemies. I was led there like a dog on a leash, like a cow brought to the slaughter. It was not for me to know the important political reasons behind what I had been ordered to carry out.

And so he set out and Sidi Barrani was taken on 13 September 1940 with few casualties. Mussolini was overjoyed ('It doesn't matter if Britain has not been invaded, now we have a victorious battle which we can throw onto the peace table...'), and thus the newspapers changed tack and became pro-Graziani. Even Badoglio sent his congratulations and continued to promise the long-awaited reinforcements, which ultimately never arrived. Within this celebratory moment, the only one unsatisfied was the marshal himself. The conquest of Sidi Barrani had worsened the situation. During their retreat, the British had filled up the water wells with sand, emptied the stores, and destroyed all lines of communications. The Italian soldiers were in dire need of supplies and most importantly, they needed water. In Graziani's opinion, what was required was an aqueduct and a proper cement road. This meant lengthening the via Balbia, a 1,822-km-long highway that ran the length of the coast from the Tunisian border to Egypt. The marshal claimed that, in this way, he was 'waging war, as in the times of Antony and Cleopatra'. Without tanks, ships, and transport planes, he could not see any other solution. The construction of the aqueduct and the 120-km road between the Capuzzo redoubt and Sidi Barrani was an impressive feat, one of the many accomplishments that gives credit and world recognition to Italian civil engineering. For more than two months, tens of thousands of men alongside military engineers toiled like slaves under the desert sun and in scorching temperatures, overcoming an array of obstacles. They were forced to demolish the abandoned aqueducts in the Gebel and recuperate the tubes, which were often of different diameters and shoddily welded together, then send them to workshops for repairs. Along with explosives and pickaxes, they also had to excavate rocky ridges, pick up the rocks, and transport them to the construction sites.

In Rome, all this flurry of activity was viewed with irritation. 'Graziani is leading us up the garden path, either he takes his time or he wastes it'; 'This is a dilatory tactic'; 'He should think about waging war'. These were the recurring

North Africa, 13 September 1940. The Italians had driven the British out of Sidi Barrani. On the cover of the weekly *Tempo Illustrato*, Scipio Africanus leads the victorious march of Rodolfo Graziani's troops. The emphatic caption reads: 'Marshal, I will accompany you: I know the way'.

criticisms of the dictator's entourage. It was the same old story. Mussolini now demanded that 'the victorious march of our troops must continue as far as Marsah Matruh.' In contrast, Badoglio was evasive, and Graziani once again reminded him of the 'much promised armoured divisions, ships and aeroplanes'. By the end of September, after being pressured by streams of irate telegrams from the *Duce* ('No one is irreplaceable, Graziani', 'Graziani, what are you waiting for, for the enemy to strengthen their position?'), the marshal was once again asked to report to Rome. He expected a mild rebuke, but he found an impatient and angry Mussolini: 'It is imperative to attack,' said Mussolini, 'August gave us British Somaliland, September Sidi Barrani, October will give us Marsa Matruh.' Graziani seemed stunned. He was unresponsive and did not dig in his heels. On the contrary, he promised to 're-examine the situation'. It seemed like a comedy, yet sadly it was the prologue to a tragedy.

The month of October was uneventful in Libya. There was very little to 're-examine'. However, there were great events taking place elsewhere. On 28 October, Italy declared war on Greece. The marshal only heard of this via the radio, which made him burst into an uncontrollable rage. Although, one cannot blame him, as he was, after all, chief of staff of the army. Badoglio had kept him in the dark. In the days that followed, Graziani found out from his own sources that armoured divisions were being amassed in Albania. That was why nothing had arrived in Tripoli. Those were his armoured divisions, which had been 'deceitfully taken' from him. While the marshal went into angry diatribes (Embaie: 'He started blaspheming, he, who was so religious'), Mussolini defended his position: 'We needed to make this decision. The Italian people could accept being beaten by the British, but not by the Greeks'. There was definitely some truth in this cynical observation, but even if he had heard it, it would hardly have consoled him. He felt ridiculed, abandoned, and forced to rectify this situation all by himself. Oddly enough, Graziani never shifted blame for his troubles on to the *Duce*. In his defensive statement written after the defeat in Cyrenaica and in his autobiography published in 1947, almost nothing was blamed on Mussolini. In the eyes of Graziani, the culprit was Badoglio. The one behind all these machinations was the 'conniving Badoglio'. Their relations, based on suspicion and mistrust, quickly degenerated into open hatred. Even Badoglio's controversial resignation on 4 December (in Greece, things were not going well and Farinacci accused the General Staff of recklessness) would be interpreted disapprovingly by Graziani, commenting: 'He showed his true colours', 'the ship sank and the rat fled'.[17] In short, for Graziani, whatever Badoglio did or said was proof of his lying and two-faced nature. Continuing in his diary entry of 7 November 1940: 'Badoglio addressed me with the formal "*voi*" even on the telephone. And yet, it's a custom between Marshals to address each other with "*tu*" [informal]'. On 9 November, the diary continued: 'An unbridgeable chasm has been dug between Mr. Pietro Badoglio, Duke of Addis Ababa, Marquis of the Sabotino and my own stainless conscience as a soldier'. It was truly a huge chasm, a sort of burning resentment that Graziani would carry with him for the rest of his life.

In mid-November, the marshal sent a final report to Rome. It seemed like he was yet again presenting the facts as they were, reiterating his request for 'weapons, tanks and spare parts'. In truth, he was safeguarding himself, underlining his own and the others' responsibility—bracing everyone for the prospect that there would be no offensive from the Italian side. The letter drew to a close in the following manner:

> With this, I have said everything. My efforts cannot go beyond the limits of what is possible, of human capability and of the firmest will. I do not want to find myself in the tragic position of having done my utmost to build roads and aqueducts, and still having to procrastinate everything else. And so before the Nation, for only it is immortal, the responsibility for what happens next cannot fall on me.[18]

Rhetorical language aside, Graziani's words would prove prophetic. December was drawing near, and with it, the moment of truth.

It was raining on 11 December, a Wednesday, when Wavell decided to leave the Supreme Headquarters in Cairo. He put Gen. Henry Maitland Wilson, his second-in-command, in charge, then proceeded to get into his car and drive to the frontline in order to inspect the ongoing military operations. Although he was comforted by this visit, doubts began to emerge. Wherever he went, the soldiers celebrated him, cheering 'Hurrah!' Morale was high, and they were indeed singing the song from *The Wizard of Oz*, which was so popular at the time. However, many were hungry and fatigued, their eyes burned from the sandstorms, and they were short of water. Wavell admitted to his fellow officers that perhaps they had pushed themselves too far.[19] The state of the tanks was also a cause for concern. The motors and treads were showing wear and tear, and it would have been foolish to drive them on further into the desert with the risk of breaking down or running out of fuel. As the inspection progressed, Wavell became more and more convinced that the entire Army of the Nile had dangerously advanced too far forward. Hypothetically, an Italian counterattack would catch his troops off guard with serious consequences. It was all well and good for Churchill to say that it was necessary to pursue the enemy and give him no quarter, he was in London, not in the desert. It was time to stop this mad chase, slow down the marching troops, and reorganise the units and the network of logistical supplies. This all needed to happen without delay, as Wavell had heard worrying rumours from Britain that they were considering a partial transfer of his troops from North Africa to the south, on the Ethiopian Front, and of diverting large quantities of supplies to help troubled Greece.

Wavell's fears were confirmed when he returned to Cairo on Friday. Churchill had given a second triumphant speech in the House of Commons: '… the whole coastal region around Buq Buq and Sidi Barrani is in the hands of British and

Imperial troops ... 7,000 Italian prisoners have already reached Marsah Matruh ... it would not be surprising if at least the best part of three Italian divisions, including numerous Blackshirt formations, have either been destroyed or captured'. The prime minister had, in the meantime, ordered the 4th Indian Brigade to be immediately called back from the frontline and sent to the Sudan to strengthen the border with Italian East Africa. In addition, various mobile infantry regiments had to be dispatched to Greece. Like Graziani, even Wavell had to pay heed to 'higher political decisions'. Wavell now reassessed his strength: he had a higher number of armoured vehicles but was lacking in infantry, he had 50,000 men at his disposal, which was less than half of what the Italians had. However, he could count on the support of the RAF and the ships of the Royal Navy, backed up by the arrival of the aircraft carrier *Illustrious*, which carried Hurricane fighters. 'The situation did not appear to be in jeopardy, and yet, I did not feel at ease,' he would write in a small sixty-three-page booklet called *Destruction of an Army* in 1943. His reasons for feeling uneasy were not unfounded. After the first hammering, the Italian army was showing signs of recovery. There was fighting in the Capuzzo redoubt and between the Halfaya pass and Sollum, which had been surrounded. Aerial reconnaissance had sighted further troop movements and new Italian tanks were appearing on the battlefield. 'The medium M11s and the heavy M13s,' observed Wavell, 'even though they were bravely driven, could not compete with our tanks. The medium ones had good cannons but weak armour, the heavy ones had good cannons and good armour, but speed-wise they left much to be desired. In any case, compared to the earlier, lighter tanks we had encountered, the latest Italian models were a significant improvement.'

More from Wavell's recollections:

> Apart from the new tanks, we also had to deal with the Italian Air Force, largely absent in the skies on the 10th and the 11th, but heavily present in the following days: the torpedo-bombers failed to hit any of our ships, but the fighters and fighter bombers gave our armoured columns a run for their money, bombing them twenty times during a time span of twenty-four hours. If we added to this the fact that Bardia and Tobruk, two very well fortified ports, were garrisoned by four Italian divisions with a fifth arriving from Tripolitania, it was evident that I needed to modify my plans and pause for thought.

The result of this 'pause for thought' was the temporary halt in the offensive plan. The plan consisted in driving straight through the desert of Marmarica and cutting off the enemy entirely. Taking Bardia and Tobruk was necessary in order to resume the offensive, as only these ports allowed for the docking of ships, thus permitting a regular stream of supplies.

As for the rest, the orders generically talked about advancing 'with caution and without leaving large enemy pockets at our rear'. The tactics of the operation remained unchanged: the light tanks of the Hussars were ordered to scout the perimeters, encircle and isolate Italian units; the onerous job of finishing off the enemy fell to the heavy tanks of the 7th British Division and the 6th Australian, while the mobile infantry and the 16th Brigade were left to eliminate remaining pockets of resistance. 'With these arrangements in hand,' concluded Wavell in his book, 'I believed I had, without a doubt, done all I could. However, I still didn't feel at ease. I remember conversing with my friend Gen. Wilson, saying: "I would give everything to know what Graziani is doing, and if he has something up his sleeve."'

Graziani admittedly suffered from insomnia.[20] 'At the start of December I started sleeping little and poorly. I was worried. On the night of 9 December, around three o'clock, I had a strong feeling that something was about to happen, so I picked up the phone and...'

When these words became known, Graziani became a laughingstock. Even though he had at his disposal aerial reconnaissance and an espionage and counterespionage service, the marshal resorted to apprehensive feelings or a hunch to discover his enemies' plans? Why not premonitions, spiritual sessions, and fortune telling? Jokes about 'Graziani the diviner' and 'Graziani the clairvoyant' were all the rage in official Fascist Rome. Years later, in official anti-fascist Rome, the marshal's 'feelings' were used to support a real indictment. In November 1944, the Action Party edited a slim volume, which contained these passages:[21,22] 'They [premonitions] constitute the definitive proof that Mussolini put the fate of hundreds and thousands of men in the hands of a madman, who would condemn them to die in the desert'. Almost fifty years have passed, and the time for being polemical is over. What Graziani meant by that recollection was likely a literal account of what he thought at the time, not that the British attack took him by surprise while he was lying in bed—as in this case, not even the Italian frontline troops were caught off guard. News of the incoming offensive was well known. There was only uncertainty surrounding the actual date.

In the marshal's case, it should be noted that if 'on the night of 9 December he had a strong feeling that' it was not the first time he had had similar premonitions. The journalist Sandro Sandri, in a favourable biography on the marshal, recounted how on 16 February 1928, during a march in the desert, Graziani gave his column the order to halt. A short while later, a sandstorm blew in. 'I asked him,' wrote Sandri, 'how he knew that was going to happen, he replied: "I don't know, I felt that a storm was brewing."' Again, from the *Berliner Illustrierte Nachtausgabe* of 13 September 1932: 'Whilst Graziani waited for his train to Paris, he envisioned his men capturing Omar al-Mukhtar. Then, suddenly, it was confirmed. Omar had been captured just as the General had imagined'. Another comment by the same German journalist recalled: 'Evidently, Graziani has a mysterious sensibility, a sort of sixth sense'. When one is in a position of such high authority, it is generally ill-advised to admit having paranormal capabilities.

As his recollection continued, the marshal therefore 'picked up the phone'. He essentially spent the whole day on the phone and the radio-transmitter. Messages from the battlefield began arriving in quick succession, each more alarming than the last. As we know, these were crucial hours for the Italian army. At Cyrene, those were moments of extreme anxiety and emotion, but also of paradoxical misunderstandings and setbacks. Here are some examples: In the early hours of the morning, two sergeants who were returning from a night on the town were arrested by a patrol of *Carabinieri* who believed them to be spies;[22] later, a switchboard operator who had been overcome by a sort of derangement, blew a raspberry to Gen. Berti who was trying to get in touch with Graziani. Towards midday, a coach of special correspondents arrived at the Command Headquarters in Cyrene, all of whom were unaware of what was happening on the battlefield. A few days prior, the marshal had summoned them to attend one of his rare press conferences. However, upon their arrival, they were told to leave. As they began to protest, a young officer tried to get rid of them with these words 'Things are happening at the front, His Excellency has many things to do, the sandstorm is not blowing in our favour'. Angered, the unfortunate guests left convinced that Cyrene was a madhouse.

The sandstorm that blew across the battlefield effectively hit the soldiers head on, and directly in the face. In the morning, the adverse weather conditions (made worse by the heavy rain, which was flooding the makeshift airstrips) caused heated discussions within the General Staff. With the airstrips flooded, the Italian air force could not participate in the ongoing battle, unlike the RAF whose fighters took off from aircraft carriers and the airport at Marsah Matruh—which had a cement runway. Other problems included the fact that the Italian 5th Air Squadron, the only one operational in Cyrenaica, had 131 aircraft at its disposal, unlike the RAF, which had 700. In actual fact, the young officer who spoke to the journalists mentioning the sandstorm was not making a ludicrous or nonsensical remark. The officer had been sworn to military secrecy and therefore made his ambiguous remark purposely. Cyrene was not a madhouse and the marshal, at least until that moment, seemed lucid. Lt-Col. Heinz Heggenreiner even described him as 'calm and admirably present'. In fact, in the afternoon, Graziani ordered the frontline divisions to fall back and sent all the tanks he could assemble to Buq Buq. In the evening, he proceeded to Tobruk to inspect the defences of the port. At Bardia, he alerted the Blackshirt divisions *Ventitre Marzo* and *Ventotto Ottobre* and ordered the *Sirte* Division, stationed at Ajdabiya, and the *Sabratha* Division, stationed at Tripoli, to be immediately sent to the front. Like Wavell, he did all he could.

On 10 and 11 December, great adjustment and great confusion occurred. The EIAR news station, supervised by the Ministry of Popular Culture (Minculpop), modestly reported the retreat as a 'disengagement manoeuvre'.[24] At Sollum, small units of the *Catanzaro* Division, which had been battered and driven out of Buq Buq, were battling the enemy with the support of heavy tanks, while in the desert of Halfaya there was dogged fighting. Gen. Annibale Bergonzoli, incredibly popular with the troops and nicknamed 'electric whiskers', went to aid the stragglers of the *Cirene* and *Marmarica* Divisions in order to reorganise them. According to the historical archive

Christmas Eve, 1940. The British advance, while things are going badly for the Italians. However, on the regime's newspapers there is no mention of this. All that is mentioned is the sinking of a British cruiser and the shooting down of three Blenheim bombers.

of the Ministry of Defence: 'Bergonzoli would get out of his car, personally lead a counter-attack, get back into his car, ride off and start again'. Despite this, the British continued to advance, although they had to fight hard for every inch.

It is relevant to mention the experience of the Italian High Command and how the first seventy-two hours of the battle on 12 December 1940 transpired, as what happened was quite extraordinary and complex in its unravelling. Initially nothing noteworthy occurred on the battlefield. As the weather improved, the air force took to the skies, Sollum continued to resist, Bergonzoli continued to risk his life, and Wavell was faced with a series of problems that made him believe that a lightning offensive was no longer possible. He asked himself, what could the marshal's intentions be? Graziani was planning something big indeed, he was thinking of throwing in the towel. In fact, at 10 a.m. on the 12th, the marshal sent a telegram to *Stamage* (abbreviation of *Stato Maggiore Generale* [chief of the general staff]. After accepting Badoglio's resignation, Mussolini had appointed Gen. Ugo Cavallero to that position, and as his vice, Gen. Alfredo Guzzoni), who was destined to go down in history. After a catastrophic exposé of the situation, the telegram in question read:

> Danger of complete collapse of the Cyrenaican front is inevitable. I have ordered the 5th Army in Tripoli to immediately start digging trench defences. Engineers are preparing roadblocks on the route to Benghazi. I believe it is my duty to

proceed to Tripoli and at least try to keep the Italian flag flying on that castle, rather than sacrificing myself here. I await to be put in a position to operate by the mother country. Everyone, from the last soldier to myself knows that we have done everything in our power to resist and to make Rome comprehend what the real conditions of this theatre of operations were and which tools were required to face them. Putting a man with his rifle, without sufficient anti-tank weapons on the battlefield is like putting a flea against an elephant. Let this be written down for the record.[25]

In Italy, Graziani's incendiary telegram appeared like a thunderbolt. On the *Duce*'s orders, the message was destroyed, but by that time, everyone in the major offices of state had read it. The reactions went from incredulity to consternation. Roberto Farinacci maintained: 'Graziani wants to "proceed" to Tripoli, 1,300 km away from Cyrene. This is shameful, it's like "proceeding" to Milan after being attacked at Reggio Calabria'. Badoglio, who was a guest at the villa of the Milanese industrialist Vittorio Necchi, added: 'Graziani must have lost his nerve'. In Ciano's opinion, 'Graziani, apart from everything else, is an example of bad reading. A mixture of exaltation and rhetoric'. From Mussolini, 'Graziani talks about the fight of the flea against the elephant: what a peculiar flea we have with a thousand cannons at its disposal from Sidi Barrani to Tobruk'. In the evening, Mussolini had cooled down and prepared a conciliatory response to the marshal: 'As always, and more than ever, I am counting on you. From Bardia to Tobruk there are sufficient cannons to stop an enemy advance. Even the enemy is worn down. Make my unwavering decision known to your men and the generals'. If Mussolini had decided to diffuse matters ('Graziani is nothing but a common soldier, he always loses his temper…'), the hardliners of the Fascist Party did not want to let this pass. Some proposed teaching Graziani a lesson by ransacking his villa at Arcinazzo and his Roman apartment at via Paganini 7. This *squadristi*-like action was eventually shelved, but the bad blood between the Fascists and the marshal would continue and would only dissipate with the birth of the Italian Social Republic.

Years later, in his autobiography, Rodolfo Graziani would assert that he wrote that telegram with a cold and calculating frame of mind. He was the commander-in-chief, and he had a panoramic, not two-dimensional view of the situation in Libya. He knew that in the desert a battle 'is like a game of chess', if the opponent makes certain moves with certain pieces, the final result is inevitably 'checkmate'. All true. However, Graziani's remark—'not sacrificing himself' when there were still tens of thousands of Italian soldiers in Cyrenaica—did him little credit, especially considering that he had made being honourable his main virtue in life. What conclusions can be drawn from this? That, as his friends would claim, Graziani had had a mental breakdown? Heinz Heggenreiner denied it and persisted in describing Graziani as 'serene and an example to the officers of the General Staff, who actually appeared to be becoming nervous and starting to panic'. One can either refuse or accept the marshal's version of events, which are as follows: with the fall of Sidi Barrani and the collapse of the front, North Africa, on a strategic level, was already lost. Defending Bardia, Tobruk, Derna, and Benghazi served only to gain time and without armoured vehicles nothing could have modified the course of events. Perhaps, this is a sound assessment. It is only unclear when Graziani found himself in this particular state of mind. In the beginning, the marshal had demonstrated efficiency and manoeuvrability, so when did he convince himself that any form of resistance was futile? It is certain that starting from 13 December he directed the military operations with neither conviction nor aggressiveness.

The British attacked slowly, and the Italians retreated slowly and orderly. Everything went as it should have and he could have done no more. The divisional commanders updated him on the situation:

'The artillerymen are short of ammunition,'
 'we calculate that, for the infantry, there is an average of 135 rounds per man,'
 'many of the men are forced to march long distances, they complain about fatigue and low morale.'

Graziani passively took note, he was resigned to his fate. Nothing seemed to matter to him. He now thought of his enemies in Rome—the Roman clique—on whom he blamed his humiliation, his disappointments, and the frustration that he had had to suffer in the past months. On the 14th, the marshal replied to Mussolini's conciliatory telegram with another resentful recrimination, this time, directed personally at the dictator:

Duce, your affirmation of complete trust in me may be moving, but it will not make me forget that you should have trusted me beforehand, when I tried in every way possible to make you comprehend the truth. You did not listen to me. You did not allow me to talk to you directly. You continued to listen to those who deliberately deceived and misled you. I have been painted as a fool, as someone who is incapable, preoccupied only with saving my own face. I know everything. Facts and names. In this moment of supreme responsibility before History and the Nation, it is now essential that I speak with you man to man. You have misunderstood me ever since I returned from the Empire. You appointed me Chief of Staff of the Army without giving me the chance to exercise my duties freely and whilst being undermined by those who surrounded you. I was the only one who had the courage not to deceive you. Then, you sent me here without even giving me the chance to talk to you. You have forgotten that for twenty years I have served you with faithfulness and dedication beyond compare. You have forgotten that the Ethiopian victory was possible thanks to the fact that you allowed me to speak with you openly, bypassing all the scoundrels who would have prevented me from doing so. Now *Duce*, there is only one judge left, and that is destiny, which I cannot face alone. I am paying a debt created not by my blindness or my own will but by those who have miserably betrayed you, and Italy along with you.

In the capital, Graziani's new telegram provoked an earthquake. Firstly, the way he had addressed Mussolini. A furious Farinacci exclaimed: 'not even I would dare speak like that to the *Duce* of Fascism'. To declare that its contents were out of order was also being generous. The higher echelons of the party, who had often accused the marshal of treachery, now called for his head. 'He needs to be removed this instant!' At the general staff in Rome, Guzzoni and Cavallero, although dismayed by this recent turn of events, remained quiet. Meanwhile, Badoglio, who had initially deplored Graziani, now had a change of heart and sent letters of solidarity to his former colleague (Graziani's entry of an unknown date read: 'I received a letter, given to me by a certain Maj. Malcovati written with a shaky hand by Badoglio. What a joke, Badoglio expresses his solidarity. Solidarity in what? In the defeat which he helped bring about?'). And Mussolini? According to Ciano's diary, he simply stated: 'I cannot get angry with this man because I have only contempt for him'. Mussolini knew how to take things in his stride, and so he opted to gloss over the telegram and proceeded to amend the situation: 'Marshal Graziani, let bygones be bygones. What matters now is the future and the salvation of Cyrenaica'. The 'Graziani case', as it appeared, had been closed, but only for the time being. From that moment until February 1941, Mussolini was cold towards the marshal and never asked for anything further. He was content with tormenting him with diatribes, exhortations, suggestions, and Napoleonic ideas, which, in his opinion, 'could change the course of the war in Cyrenaica'.

Meanwhile, the war in Libya went inexorably on. On 15 December, the British were 25 km from Tobruk, and at Christmas, they were still 25 km away. Although Wavell was not in a hurry, he was anxious about supplies, replacements, and reinforcements. The grip was tightened only in the New Year, when the light tanks of the Hussars managed to cut off the coastal road and isolate Bardia. Bardia constituted the hard core of the Italian defence. Within its 17-mile-long defence perimeter there were a series of ditches, interrupted by minefields, barbed-wire entanglements, and cement bunkers. Behind the defences there were 45,000 men and 462 cannons waiting. In order to conquer it, Wavell had to mobilise the entire 7th Division, all his field artillery, then all the infantry, engineers, and machine gunners. The bulk of the work, obviously, had to be done by the fleet anchored off the coast and the RAF bombers. The attack commenced in the early hours of 3 January 1941 and the battle that ensued lasted for two days. On the 5th, the white flag fluttered over the ruins of Bardia.

At the HQ in Cyrene, Graziani seemed to be behaving more and more like a clerk, jotting down facts, underlining orders he had been given, which had not been followed due to 'material impossibility'. He was writing reports more for posterity than anything else. He had even thought about taking his own life. According to Ciano's diary: 'A long meeting with Melchiori, Graziani's liaison officer, veteran of Cyrenaica. He says that Graziani openly accuses Badoglio of betrayal, and that the only thing preventing him from killing himself is the thought of one day dragging Badoglio to the dock'. Another entry reads: 'Meeting with Marchioness Graziani. She is beside herself. She has received a letter from her husband containing his last will and testament'. With *Stamage*, the marshal had kept contact to a minimum. This is demonstrated by his laconic telegrams on 4, 6, 9, and 10 January:

> Cyrene, 4 January 1941. Our Air Force is in difficulty, many of our aircraft have been shot down, many more damaged on the airfields and cannot be re-utilized.

> Cyrene, 6 January. After the fall of Bardia, The British are headed towards Tobruk. The first tanks have already been sighted outside the defensive perimeter. I have given orders accordingly.

> Cyrene, 9 January. Transport vehicles are missing. I have ordered the commandeering of all civil vehicles in Libya.

> Cyrene, 10 January. Today, the 33rd day since the beginning of the British offensive in which the first signs of our inferiority were immediately evident, the following reinforcements have arrived from the mother country: a regiment of *Bersaglieri*, a battalion of M13 tanks as expected. Second: twenty batteries of various calibres as expected for the reconstruction of the 5th Army. Third: two Flamethrower companies and fifteen armoured vehicles, which are still in Tripoli. Fourth: about 125 aircraft for air fighting and bombardment.

In Rome, *Stamage* replied in bureaucratic language that was equally cold in tone. Guzzoni continued to remain silent and Cavallero pretended to be extremely busy with following the events in Greece. Only Mussolini, as first marshal of the empire, was frenetic and extremely agitated. The fascists considered Graziani as nothing more than 'an annoying pest'. Others did much worse; they started spreading rumours that Graziani had abandoned his post to flee, secretly, to Tripoli. Lies, of course, but the marshal's unpopularity was such that it grew to a half truth, then soon afterwards a full truth, which was years later exaggerated and spread by the anti-fascists. In the already cited volume from 1944, edited by the publishing house Sagittarius on behalf of the Action Party, Rodolfo Graziani's 'escape' was described in disparaging terms: 'Faced with disaster, the "great leader" took flight, not even dismayed by shame, not even saddened for the plight of his soldiers, no torment, no remorse.... He didn't rest until he was safe in his refuge in Tripoli'.[26]

Tobruk was the new objective of Gen. Wavell. It had the same defensive structure as the port of Bardia: a double anti-tank ditch that ran across its

 An Italian broadcaster explains that the Blackshirt Generals in Libya did not run away. Apparently it was just a coincidence that when Bardia fell they started on their journey to Rome to resign.

A joke from the British newspaper *Punch*, 22 January 1941.

27-mile-long external perimeter, along with minefields and bunkers. Inside the garrison there were 28,000 men with 300 cannons. The British, once again, did not seem to be in a hurry. On 6 January, they were in sight of the city, however, only on the 21st did they finally advance for what ultimately was a fast and bloody assault. Supported by the artillery and the guns of the Royal Navy, the 3rd Australian Brigade managed to build a bridgehead on the very evening of the 21st. The engineers filled parts of the anti-tank ditches, then armoured vehicles drove into the breach and began firing at point-blank range. On 22 January, the Italians surrendered. Churchill declared to the House of Commons: '... with the conquest of Tobruk, we have at our disposal a port where we can unload 13,000 tons of supplies a day. Now, in Marmarica, our glorious Army of the Nile has captured a total of 113,000 enemies and 700 cannons'.

For the Italian 10th Army, collapse was now a reality. However, according to the *Duce*, a new line of defence could be formed between Mechili, in the desert and the Derna embankment on the coast. Derna, which was garrisoned by 20,000 men, did not have adequate defences. Against enemy aircraft, they had only old Skoda cannons, given to Italy by Austria-Hungary as war reparations. In order for these cannons to be pointed towards the sky, they had to be placed on a carriage. This carriage was supported by an unstable wooden frame that would collapse with every shot, battering the poor fellow manning the gun. Graziani concluded that Derna should not be defended but urgently evacuated. Everything had to return to Benghazi and beyond, away from Cyrenaica, which had become a death trap. At 12:30 p.m. on 31 January, the marshal ordered a general retreat. He then transmitted a message to Maj. Castagna, promoting him on the spot to colonel for his heroic resistance at Jaghbub. He then gave Gen. Tellera command of what remained of the army and departed for Benghazi, where he then flew to Sirte in Tripolitania. On the via Balbia, the retreating Italian troops formed a continuous column. There were regiments at full strength, albeit scattered and without weapons and units in full combat gear, which had somehow come from Bardia and Tobruk. Soldiers with both clean and tattered uniforms attempted to board the few working lorries (850 in total). Otherwise, most went on foot, while some others had created makeshift vehicles: cars pulled by horses or military lorries and tractors hauled by mules and bulls. At the head of the column, there were cars transporting high-ranking officers (including Bergonzoli) and about sixty of the remaining armoured vehicles. As they headed west, the column grew larger in size, picking up the garrisons of Barce and Tocra, some coastal detachments and men of various support branches along the way. From afar, the column resembled a giant snake moving slowly along the desert landscape, which ultimately grew to be several kilometres long. This giant snake was immediately spotted and photographed by British aerial reconnaissance. Up until then, many thought Wavell seemed to be resting on his laurels, but now, he acted with lightning speed. He regrouped all heavy tanks of the 7th Armoured Division, the medium tanks of the 6th Australian, the light tanks of the Hussars and sent them south across the desert with Mechili as their objective. His plan was simple, yet brilliant: to repeat the manoeuvre he had carried out after the taking of Sidi Barrani and perfect it. A race into the desert towards Ajdabiya, a location beyond Benghazi that would enclose the enemy's entire army into one giant pocket. The manoeuvre was successful and went better than expected, mainly because, while the Italians walked, the British ran.

On 5 February, after marching beyond Benghazi and subsequently abandoning it, the vanguard of the 10th Army reached the Beda Fomm pass, near Ajdabiya, where they were welcomed by enemy fire. During the night, the Hussars blocked off the via Balbia and guarded it with squadrons aligned in three rows on either side of the carriageway. O'Connor's report reads:

This time our surprise had worked perfectly. The Italians couldn't believe what they were seeing. They thought the British army was behind them, but then they saw it was right in front of them. They were so disorientated that they simply started engaging us. This was fortunate, as it allowed our heavy tanks and motorized infantry, which had been left behind, to get to the scene of the battle. I must concede that the Italians fought tenaciously, almost out of desperation as they knew that their salvation lay beyond the British lines and they wanted to break through at all costs. They threw everything they had at us and continued to arrive in dribs and drabs along the road. Towards the evening, they attacked us with heavy tanks, but they were pushed back. On the morning of the 6th, they re-organized their forces and deployed about eighty M11 and M13 tanks. This was the first tank battle in the desert. The Italian tank drivers drove bravely and well, however, our tank crews were clearly superior. In any case, the Italians put us to the test and at one point, they even managed to push themselves all the way through to the officers' mess of the Royal Fusiliers, where we suffered many casualties trying to repulse them. I learnt from Gen. Desmond Young that his brigade had to face almost nine consecutive attacks by tanks. Leading the Italians was their Commander-in-Chief, General Torrelli [Tellera], who was gravely wounded and then died later in the afternoon. Many Italian tank drivers suffered the same fate, we found them dead in their own vehicles. Subsequently, the Italian infantry came forward. The RAF intervened immediately, and the Italians went back to where they came from. Only a few scattered platoons of infantrymen, which had gone towards the coast, managed to breach our defences and get to safety. The rest surrendered, and late in the afternoon the battle was over. I can still see the battlefield now, it was incredible. On the via Balbia, as far as the eye could see, there were shattered lorries and tanks that were upside down and burning. Cannons and vehicles piled up one on top of the other. And prisoners everywhere. We captured 25,000 troops and a large number of high-ranking officers, including generals Bergonzoli and Babini. We messaged Wavell telling him that we were victorious, and that Mussolini's army had been annihilated.

On 7 February, the Hussars carried out a reconnaissance mission in Tripolitania and occupied El Agheila in the Sirte region, only to encounter terrified civilians, not a single soldier. Although the road was clear all the way to Tripoli, Wavell did not feel like continuing with an advance of thousands of miles, racing across the desert at breakneck speed. The soldiers of the Army of the Nile were worn out and as their commander observed, 'they looked like boxers who had gone nineteen rounds'. In London, Churchill insisted that the ships of the Royal Navy be sent to the Aegean as soon as possible, and with them 'a good deal of fighters'. In the prime minister's mind, Libya was becoming a secondary front, and it was now Greece that became a priority. Wavell's war game, as it were, had run out of steam, and thus, he ordered his troops to halt. Let the Italians keep their sand box if they so wished.

At about the same time in Tripoli, there was an overwhelming feeling of desperation and panic. At night, the city was deserted due to the curfew, but during the day, it was swarming with men and women, party officials and their families, civil servants, merchants, and landowners all looking for a ship or a plane that could take them back to Italy. News of Wavell's halt was not yet known, what was apparent, however, was the overwhelming weakness of the 5th Army. As defending the city did not seem possible, there was nothing left to do but leave.

Rodolfo Graziani had come to the same conclusion. On 8 February, from his HQ in the castle of Tripoli, he telegraphed Guzzoni:

> Please forward the following message to the *Duce*.... Recent events have deeply weakened my nerves and strength so much so as to prevent me from keeping this command any further. If I were to continue out of pride to say nothing, then I would be guilty. Therefore, I ask to be recalled and replaced. I am sure that new energy could accomplish much more than I can in this final phase of the operation which is being prepared.

It was a pathetic and cunning declaration. Pathetic because the marshal, who never revealed his true feelings or showed signs of weakness, was forced to admit his impotence, shielding himself behind true or hypothetical claims of ill-health. It was cunning because he knew very well there was no 'new energy' that could rectify the situation. He simply wanted to pass on the hot potato, so to speak. Mussolini, however, authorised the marshal's departure from Tripoli. On 10 February, Graziani landed at Centocelle airport in Rome, to find only a car and a driver awaiting him. What could he have expected? He was a defeated general, the destruction of an army and the loss of Cyrenaica would not be forgiven so easily. At home, he was greeted by his wife, Ines, and in order to console her and himself, he said: 'I don't care about anything, all that matters is having a clean conscience, and I know I have done nothing wrong'.

If Graziani believed that there was no 'new energy' that could replace him, then he was very much mistaken. It was an evening spectacle during the first days of March. The lights of Tripoli glowed in defiance of the curfew, crowds of people gathered at the port and transport ships had dropped anchor. From these vessels soldiers dressed in splendid khaki uniforms could be seen emerging along with massive tanks, and mountains of material and equipment. On the bridge of the flagship, a military band played a medley of marches, Viennese waltzes, and the famous *Alte Kameraden*, inspiring and dispersing a jubilant and cheerful mood among the crowd. When the gangplank descended, an elegant Erwin Rommel marched off the ship, and along with him the *Afrika Korps*.[27]

Present among the crowd was a young medical officer named Mario Tobino, who ten years later would become a famous writer. Of that day, he would recall:

> We Italian soldiers, who had wraps on our feet instead of socks, looked at the Germans in silence. They were all smiling and sure of themselves, clean shaven with white gloves on their hands. They made us feel like poor relatives. Around them, the crowd clapped enthusiastically. Italians always feel titillated during military parades. Those who cheered the loudest were the same who, a few days before, were saying that the British were deep down good generous people and our friends. That's just how the world works, and that's how the second phase of the war in Libya started.[28]

But that is another story.

2
A Home in the Mountains

Today, Piani di Arcinazzo is a holiday resort in the mountains near the border between Ciociaria and the Abruzzo.[1] To get there, one must drive on twisting roads, coming from the towns of Fiuggi or nearby Piglio and Guarcino. After driving up steep hairpin bends, you come out on to a plain 900 metres above sea level surrounded by fir trees and valleys dotted with villas, holiday homes, hotels, and rustic restaurants, which serve up rich but authentic cuisine. In the summer, Piani di Arcinazzo hosts a large number of tourists who go there seeking peace, quiet, and fresh air. The best time to visit is winter. At the weekends, the place is crowded with 20,000 or 30,000 visitors: they are for the most part skiers who drive past the villages of Trevi and Filettino in Lazio in order to get to Campo Staffi, the top skiing resort in the region.

Fifty years ago, Piani di Arcinazzo was unknown to tourists. It was according to books of the time 'A karstic plateau' with a few shepherds, some poultry farms, and herds of sheep, cows, and wild horses. As a child, Rodolfo Graziani would often climb the cliffs of the plateau. These were the final years of the nineteenth century. His father was a local doctor in Affile and he would accompany him on his rounds. Dr Filippo Graziani earned a pittance, 166 lira a month. In order to maintain his family, he had to take on patients from the surrounding areas like Panza, which would later become Arcinazzo Romano, and other nearby villages. Back then, there were no roads leading to Piani di Arcinazzo, the only way to get there was along rough mountain paths. Little Rodolfo walked ahead, with his father following steadily but surely behind on his donkey, which, following the defeat of Adwa, he named Menelik. Although those were arduous walks, at times they offered inspiring moments: one day, Dr Filippo found the boundary stone of the Papal State and the Kingdom of Naples hidden in the grass. 'He stopped,' remembered the son, 'and used it as an opportunity to give me a lengthy history lesson.' Time passed and Graziani was now an adult, but the mountains would always remain in his heart. He loved it there: clean air, wild nature, the silence broken only by the bells of the cowherds. So, in 1938, he took a momentous decision and bought a house in Piani di Arcinazzo. He paid in cash, for the first time in his life. He could never have afforded it before, as a child he had lived in poverty. At forty years of age in 1922, he was still paying off debts run up in his youth. But in 1938, Graziani considered himself rich and with good reason: he was marshal of Italy, he had been viceroy of Ethiopia, and his majesty had bestowed on him the title of the marquis of Neghelli. During his year and a half as viceroy, on top of his salary as army general, Graziani was earning 100,000 lira a month (the average salary back then was between 400 to 600 lira a month), an astronomical sum—considering that in those days, many Italians were singing 'If I could only have 1,000 lira a month!' On Graziani's return from Ethiopia, Mussolini had awarded him with a special 'salary of recognition from the Nation' of 20,000 lira a month. So, there was enough money to lead a good life. The marshal gave up his frugal ways and started spending. Apart from the land in Piani di Arcinazzo 'which included a mountain range between 900 and 1,100 m', he bought 2½ hectares of an olive grove in the province of Piglio, the Villa of Casal Sant'Anna, and 90 hectares of individual lots of land in the Sacco valley, near Anagni. In the past, Graziani had also played at being a landowner. He had 'paid for it upfront' as he himself would say, which meant he used funds from the Bank of Rome's agricultural credit. Similarly, in 1929, he came into possession of a 100-hectare farm in Bu Maad in the Cyrenaican desert. Again, in 1935, he was granted a 500-hectare piece near the port of Kismayo in Somalia, and in 1938, when his period as viceroy had come to an end, he was given 465 hectares of arable land in the Arsi region of Ethiopia.

The marshal loved the land. Wherever he went, he wanted to pitch his tent. In one place, he wanted a vineyard, and in another, a model plantation. But above all, he loved his native land: Affile, Arcinazzo, il Piglio, and Anagni. During his trial in 1948, he would talk of this love for the mountains in moving terms, his face red with emotion, shaking with anger:

> That land, your Honour, I paid for with my own savings, thirty years of savings to be precise, and I spent every last penny on it. It was uncultivated, abandoned, full of weeds and rocks. But I wasn't a man of leisure, I did not sit back and watch. No! I removed the rocks with my bare hands, I tilled the land, hoed it, fertilized and sowed it. I created gardens which looked like those of Villa Borghese. Together with the state, I built up a breeding farm of horses and livestock of all kinds which were the envy of everyone. I had sixty horses, your Honour, 1,000 sheep and thirty dairy cows…

It was an honest and sincere confession. In the hall of the extraordinary court of assizes, everyone listened in silence. No one uttered a word, even when Graziani defiantly concluded his statement with these words 'Some fascist I was! At work, I was an ultra-leftist...'

But let us not get ahead of ourselves, we were describing the land of Piani di Arcinazzo, because it was here, on 20 February 1941, that Graziani sought refuge after the debacle in North Africa. He arrived by car, late in the evening with his wife, and he was fuming. He told his secretary, Dr Magno Bocca, who had accompanied him: 'I do not want to be disturbed, I've had too much dirt thrown at me'. It was Mussolini who had been throwing dirt at him. On 13 February, forty-eight hours after his return to Italy, Graziani had gone to Palazzo dei Marescialli in Rome, which today houses the High Council of the Judiciary. The telephone was silent, his desk was uncluttered, apart from a few anonymous letters containing insults. No one had been looking for him. On the 14th, Graziani tried to get in contact with the duke of Acquarone, asking for a 'dutiful visit of homage' to the emperor king. He was kindly told that would not be possible. Then, finally, on 15 February, the phone rang; it was the *Duce*, who wanted to see him the following morning. We only have the marshal's version of this meeting, which he described in his memoirs:[2]

> I entered the Map Room. Mussolini did not look up to greet me 'Sit down. Graziani,' he said. I reminded him of my resignation. He replied 'No resignation, it would be like admitting defeat. You will go back to Libya and have your comeback.' 'Go back? When?' I asked. 'When the German forces land in Libya,' replied the *Duce*. 'But this will complicate the functions of command,' I said. Mussolini: 'I intend Rommel to have the command of the operational forces.' To which I replied, 'I expect our dignity and my authority as superior Commander-in-Chief to be safeguarded.' He glanced at me from the corner of his eye and said 'Of course.' He then changed the subject, 'Is there any enthusiasm for the war?' 'Not much,' I replied. I explained that not everyone understood what the final goal was. What's more, this war was devoid of the sentiment which had galvanized the people in 1915. He interrupted me, 'this comparison is used too often.' He said that 'even then, there were interventionists and non-interventionists.' I pointed out that, back then, his generation and mine had been inculcated with irredentism. Mussolini said nothing. To finish up, he asked me, 'How are the officers fighting?' 'The old ones well,' I replied, 'the younger ones not so, that is, the ones that were brought up during Fascism. I believe that these young men are too used to the finer things in life: camping in the mountains and by the sea, pools, ladies, free meals and a lot of other things. They have been told little of the hard life, of sacrifice, and of work, unlike us in our day; but above all, the concept of *dulce et decorum est pro patria mori* has not been instilled in them, which for us was the most important rule of love and sacrifice.' Here Mussolini ended the conversation and told me not to mention a word of it to anyone, 'especially the senators' and he dismissed me.

Graziani's memoirs continue:

> I said nothing, I was making an effort keep quiet. However, in the days that followed I learnt some very interesting news from my friends in the Ministry of War. The man who couldn't stop talking about me was Mussolini himself. He ill-advisedly went around saying and allowing others to say that 'Graziani has more ambitions than brains,' or, 'one should not give important jobs to people who aren't looking for at least one promotion. Graziani has too much to lose,' or even, 'Graziani has dealt the country three blows: he has damaged our military prestige, brought the Germans into Italy and lost us the Empire' I refused to hear anything more, all I wanted was to go to my self-imposed exile in my home at Piani di Arcinazzo.

Having left Rome, the marshal did not know that his self-imposed exile would last two years, until 8 September 1943. Neither did he know what else Mussolini still had in store for him. On 21 March 1941, without warning, he accepted Graziani's resignation. However, before this, on 23 February, he dealt him an even crueller blow. That day, Mussolini gave a speech at the Adriano theatre in which he gave his analysis of the latest events in North Africa. He started off by saying: 'From October 1937 until last January, I sent 14,000 officers and 396,000 soldiers, 1,924 cannons, 15,386 machine guns, 779 tanks and 9,584 various other vehicles. Weren't they enough?' The crowd started clapping. The *Duce* went on:

> We are not afraid of the truth; we worship the truth. For this very reason, I tell you that the British had fifteen divisions recruited from three continents and armed by the fourth. I tell you that it was a mistake to send our Libyan divisions to the front line. Yes, they were valiant and faithful, but they were not ready to sustain the onslaught of enemy tanks…

According to Embaie Tekle-Haymanot, at that moment, Graziani—who was listening to this speech on the radio from Arcinazzo—went into a fit of rage: 'He started shouting, saying that it was all lies, slander, nonsense and defended the Libyan soldiers'. He would continue to defend them on other occasions. On 30 January 1942, while talking to the journalist Mr Balloti, director of the *Oltremare* magazine, he stated that 'the Libyans are excellent soldiers, the desert is their natural habitat, they were born there and they know how to fight in it'. In this regard, credit was certainly due to the marshal: he had many defects and a bad temper, but he was not petty. He never blamed the soldiers for his or the general staff's faults, he fought with almost everyone, but never with those weaker than him or below him in rank.

In March, snow fell on the mountains, heavy wet spring-like snow. In the fields, work had stopped. Graziani now started to think about projects for stables, poultry pens, and fences for the horses. He shut himself away in his home. The house had been built in his absence, but according to his precise instructions. It was a solid and austere grey stone building. Half farm, half fortress. However, the name of the house was in complete contrast to its nature, Casal Biancaneve—Snow White house. There was a long story behind this name. Graziani was not an intellectual man: he did not read much ('only the classics'), he did not go to the theatre very often ('only to the opera'), and to the cinema either ('only to watch documentaries, I have to'). But one afternoon, in November 1938, his wife, Ines, dragged him off to see *Snow White and the Seven Dwarfs*, Walt Disney's masterpiece. He left the screening room enthusiastic, so much so that he wanted to call his countryside home 'Snow White'. He even had an artist paint the fairy-tale princess on the majolica tiles near the entrance, however, without the dwarfs. The builders of pretentious villas with little garden gnomes on the front lawn now know who to thank.

The marshal's *art pompier* tastes were also manifest inside the house. Its interior design, to use the words of the interior decorators, was 'tragic'. Black renaissance Florentine furniture, willow couches, nineteenth-century chests of drawers, chairs with ornate cushions, Littorio-style furniture in white maple or wood veneer. On the floor: Persian, Italian, or Tripolitan carpets. On the walls: old oil paintings, panoplies of weapons, photographs, various certificates, and framed poems. As if this was not enough, Graziani was restless when it came to furniture. Now and then, he rearranged all of it. He would do the same when he was in prison at Forte Boccea, and there, he only had a bed, a desk, and a slop bucket. Embaie recounted: 'One morning, as I walked into the dining room, I suddenly found myself in the living room. The owner had switched the rooms during the night'. This changing around of rooms in 1941 was looked on kindly by the marshal's wife. It meant that her husband was slowly going back to his old habits and that psychologically the worst was over. The old Graziani was coming back. For example, when reading about a new medical discovery, he demanded it be purchased immediately, a sort of conditioned reflex. He was a hypochondriac, and so he filled his cabinets with all sorts of pills. Also, he always wanted four pillows on his bed. The first one had to be hard, the second one a little softer, the third one soft, and the fourth one a feathered pillow. He explained that this reminded him of Africa where he would sleep almost sitting up against the *rakla*, the camel's saddle. When he went to bed, he punched a hole in the last pillow, lay his head on it and went off to sleep instantly like a child. 'No alarm clock,' he said, 'I wake up on command, I have an alarm clock in my head.' He was convinced he had green fingers and he always told people to give him seeds or a plant as presents. He would then plant these in the garden, in pots in the house, or on the balcony. He would spend hours digging, watering, and fertilising them. Years later, at Forte Boccea, he would pride himself on having been able to grow a lemon plant on the windowsill of his cell. He gave it to his wife as a gift. He wrote an accompanying card saying 'Sorry. I have nothing else'.[3]

In April, Graziani had a meticulous daily routine, which consisted mostly of farm work and other duties. In the morning, he worked in the fields. The marshal was a hard worker and he expected Giustino, his farmhand, to work even harder. He was also full of ideas, projects, and initiatives. He read about a type of sheep from Karakorum, very resistant to illness and the cold, which he wanted to crossbreed with his sheep from the Abruzzo. He was extremely interested in horses (horse riding and fencing were the only sports he practised), and before any purchase, he would seek out the advice of Capt. Albertazzi of the equine breeding facility in Passo Corese. At midday, he consumed a frugal meal and then took a nap, the famous Roman siesta. Around this time of day, a sentry on a motorbike used to arrive regularly from Rome to deliver the mail and the secret post parcels from the offices of the general staff and the Minculpop. Despite not holding any office, Graziani had many friends in the various ministries. From his friends in the Ministry of War, he would receive the 'red bulletins', the uncensored ones, and from his friends in the Ministry of Popular Culture, he obtained prohibited foreign press cuttings. The marshal would sit down at the dining table, put on his monocle, and with a red and blue pencil, underline the phrases that had the greatest impact on him, adding indignant comments and exclamation marks as he went. Some 'red bulletins' and newspaper clippings with Graziani's comments on have survived, here follow the most significant:

North Africa, February 1941. Jaghbub resists. Col. Castagna is in great difficulty. Kufra attacked by 3,000 Senegalese soldiers led by Sef en Nasser. Lt-Col. Di Leo reports that they've run out of fuel. Yet, he resists. (Graziani's comment: 'My heart cries out, here are two men of valour!').

The Times, 31 January 1941, article relayed by the Royal Legation in Lisbon. In truth, the Italians did not have the means to fight a rapid war in the desert. If they advanced, they had to entrench themselves. Also, the Italian vehicles were not equipped with tyres suited for uneven terrain, and the officers were given toy compasses. Meanwhile, the officers and NCOs of the British army used prismatic compasses, essential for orienteering in the desert where there are no reference points. (Graziani's comment: 'Good, that's right, this is the truth!!!').

London, 8 February, '41. From Churchill's speech to the House of Commons, source: Ministry of Popular Culture. '... Special praise goes to the Australian cavalry, who charged with sabres drawn...' (Graziani's comment: 'Scoundrel, what he means to say is armoured cavalry. If only I had had half of the tanks he had, I would be in Alexandria by now'.).

Military Information Service, 6 March 1941. Secret. Composition of the 15th Panzer Corps. Troops: 16,000, motorcycles: 1,600, vehicles: 923, lorries: 1,874, tanks: 360, armoured cars: 319, individual weapons: anti-tank carbines and machine guns. (Graziani's comment: 'so basically, no one walks with their rifle anymore!').

La Suisse, Geneva, 18 March 1941. Graziani awaits his turn and is trusted by all. (Graziani's comment: 'That may well be, but you've got your facts wrong').

The Times, March 20, 1941. Article by Maj. Henry J. Jayme, veteran of Cyrenaica and now British Military Attaché to Portugal. Relayed by the Royal Legation in Lisbon '... I have to say that the Italians fought better than most people think.... Our losses were negligible because our advance was always preceded by heavy aerial and naval bombardments...' (Graziani's comment: 'Straight from the horses' mouth, just look who I have to be defended by'.).

We need not continue. In the evening, having got tired of reading, Graziani had dinner with his wife and, occasionally, with visiting relatives, such as Uncles Peppino and Augusto. The time after dinner was spent in a homely *petit bourgeois* manner. If Graziani was alone, he listened to the radio, even tuning into Radio London. He liked listening to Col. Stevens, after all, he had met him in Libya during the '30s and even had a picture of him with Ines.[4] He liked to call him '*fijo de 'na mignotta*', meaning 'that son of a bitch', without any offence, because intimately Graziani did not shy away from speaking in dialect. In April 1945, Cardinal Ildefonso Schuster said that 'he spoke Neapolitan'. Not quite, Graziani spoke in the Romanesco dialect depending on the circumstances. The cardinal, however, being from Milan, could not understand this, given the common northern misconception that everyone south of Florence must speak Neapolitan. Lady Ines often invited a few selected guests over to take her husband's mind off things: the mayor of Filettino or Fiuggi, Dr Bocca, Lt-Col. Mario Zingoni, and Affile's notary Mr Zardi. The evening would always end up with a card game. Graziani was a terrible player; he only knew how to play Scopa and Briscola.[5] Nevertheless, he was an expert at doing magic card tricks and if you did not find these funny, you were in trouble. You had to laugh even when he told his jokes, of which he was an avid collector. And so from card games to funny stories the night went on. These evenings cannot have been very entertaining.

May marked the end of this peaceful familiar routine. From the capital, calumnious, offensive, and insulting voices were reaching Piani di Arcinazzo. In Rome, 'The scum of the earth Fascist officials and that pig Farinacci' (these are the marshal's exact words) were going around saying that 'we lost Cyrenaica for the simple reason that Graziani was shitting himself with fear, so much so that he hid in a tomb 30 m deep, which he transformed into his own personal hideout at the cost of millions of lira.' In Frosinone, Federal Rocchi, primed by Party Secretary Adelchi Serena, swore that 'his boys couldn't teach Graziani a lesson, because he had put himself under the protection of eighteen Carabinieri who were on guard at his farm day and night.'[6] Embaie stated: 'His Excellency was furious. He would pace up and down the house like a lion in a cage, saying to me: "let them come, I'll be waiting for them with my machine gun." Lady Ines was very scared'. Graziani, however, did not stay in his house pacing up and down for long; he drove off to Rome and did the rounds of the various offices and ministries of the city: the HQ of the Carabinieri, Gen. Gambara's office, the Ministry of War, and the office of the new Chief of Staff of the Army Gen. Roatta. He begged them for a written declaration telling the truth and 'making them retract their shameful slander'. He obtained nothing. No one wanted to interfere with party business. Regarding the eighteen *Carabinieri* who were 'guarding his farm' only in 1946—when Fascism was over and the war had finished—did Graziani obtain his long-awaited declaration:

> I, Lieutenant-Colonel of the *Carabinieri* group of Frosinone, before and after the tenure of Major Geronazzo, declare the claim that eighteen *Carabinieri* were guarding the villa of Arcinazzo where the Marshal resided, to be false. I should also like to add that no special vigilance service was ever predisposed by the Command of Frosinone to protect the Marshal of Italy Rodolfo Graziani. Yours faithfully, Lieutenant Colonel Giacinto Molinari, Terracina 1946.

Apropos the famous tomb in Cyrene—being unable to track down Lt-Col. Granata who directed the work of transforming it into an anti-air raid shelter—we only have the marshal's word on the matter, or rather, his letters. He wrote many, copied them, and sent them in all directions. They were very prolix and long-winded, full of minute details and distinctions, and would later turn into the first drafts of his defence case. The core of the marshal's argument was that Cyrene had been chosen as the operational HQ by Balbo; that every commander in a war zone must have a shelter in order to ensure the continuity of orders; that the tomb-shelter had not cost a dime; and also that it was a makeshift shelter and that he had never gone into hiding there, he had only used it during air-raids. What Graziani said may have been right, yet he certainly found no one to corroborate what he said. However, it is also true that in May 1941, everyone considered him to be a nuisance and someone who was best avoided.

At a certain point, Graziani realised this and decided to let his anger simmer down by going to Fiuggi to take the waters and to be around friendly people. In 1938, Fiuggi had welcomed him as a triumphant hero. In the Fonte di Bonifacio, there was a sign dedicated to him which said: 'To the undefeated warrior and the great Ciociarian'. But the years had passed, and things had changed. Now the people of Fiuggi greeted him with deference but showed no cordiality. And so, Graziani packed his bags and went straight to Filettino, a stone's throw away from Fiuggi. There he really felt at home. The village bore his name, as back then it was called Filettino Graziani; even the main boulevard and the communal park were named after him. For the people of Filettino, the marshal was a *paesano* who had made it in life, 'His Excellency' who you could slap on the back and address with the informal '*tu*'. There, nothing seemed to have changed. As in the past, everyone strove to be as polite as possible, they offered him lamb, fresh ricotta, seasoned meat, and fresh eggs. His birthplace, 100 metres beyond Piazza Tavani Arqueti, had been restored and furnished by the municipal town hall. Old people stopped to talk to him in the street and asked, 'do you remember Your Excellency?' and there were those who talked about his father, and those who wanted to tell him stories about his grandfather, Benedetto, or his great-grandfather, Giuseppe. Graziani was truly moved and for a moment, he thought that he had gone back in time.

Giuseppe De Caesaris, the marshal's great-grandfather, was a great shepherd who possessed 15,000 sheep, in those days a sign of great wealth. Every year, at the beginning of winter, the De Caesarises left Filettino—the highest village in the Lazio region—and herded their flock onto the Cisterna plain to get through the cold season. Along the way, Don Giuseppe stopped at Frascati to invoke the protection of the Holy Virgin in front of a small statue, which still exists to this day at the crossroads of the Frascati–Montecompatri motorway. 'I know it's there,' said Graziani in his autobiography, 'because when I was little, I too used to kneel down in front of that small statue.' In 1838, Giuseppe's oldest daughter, Domenica, married Benedetto Graziani, a peasant originally from Affile. They lived in poverty but happily, they had fourteen children including Filippo, the third born, who wanted to study. He obtained his degree in medicine and then got married in Rome to a woman from a good family, Adelia Clementi. The Clementis were socially a rung above the Grazianis. Among their ancestors they boasted the famous musician Muzio Clementi who in the 1700s wrote the book *Gradus ad Parnassum*, a collection of piano studies well known to conservatoire students. The marriage between Filippo and Adelia was, despite these social differences, a happy one, made difficult only by economic restraints and hardened by the daily task of bringing up nine children born in rapid succession. Rodolfo was the fourth, and he nurtured feelings of true adoration towards his parents. He would describe them as follows:

> Mother was a woman of high virtues, very religious and devoted to doing good: she gave me a strict patriarchal upbringing. Father was an excellent doctor, a good, righteous, honest man. He did his specialization in the first Baccelli clinic, together with Marchiafava, Durante, Pensuti and other future medical luminaries. He had wanted to work in Rome, however, there was never enough money and so he had to resign himself to doing his rounds first in Filettino, and afterwards in Affile and its surroundings. I owe it to my parents, if I grew up with sound moral principles.

Graziani was always proud of his humble background. In relation to this, there is some amusing correspondence in the State Archive from 1934–1936. Although he was not yet a marshal, in those days, the general was already an important icon of the regime: he had 'pacified' Cyrenaica and he was about to become governor of Somalia. The newspapers showered him with praise defining him as 'the Napoleon of the desert' (*Il giornale d'Italia*), 'the White Lion' (*Berlingske Aften*), 'the Scipionic warrior' (*La Domenica del Corriere*). His crowd of fans also included heraldists, real and amateur ones. Mr Paolo Contini of Bergamo discovered that he was 'a descendent of Colleoni', Professor Bartolomeo Fani of La Spezia insisted that he descended from none other than the Emperor Graziano.[7] And then, a letter from the ubiquitous man of family trees himself, the aristocratic Dr Rodolfo Emiliani of the Heraldic College of Rome, who—in a letter of 24 July 1936—told him: 'You are recognized as belonging to the house of Pierleoni-Graziani'. Graziani's reply on 13 September 1936: 'Dear Doctor, I am sorry to disappoint you. I do not descend from noble stock. My surname is incredibly common and it's evidently Latin. There are thousands of Grazianis in Italy. Many of them write to me claiming to have family ties with me. They are peasants and workers. None of them are noblemen. I am the son of poor folk and I feel like a man of the people'.

But let us get back to Graziani as a child, in the words of the man himself:

> I was born on the 11th of August 1882 and I was baptized on the 14th. Those were festive times with bells ringing because the 14th was the holiday of the Assumption of the Holy Virgin, patron of Filettino. During the banquet which accompanied my birth, a jug broke, and wine spilled all over the floor. This, and the fact that on the civil registrar my name appeared written in blue ink rather than black was, with hindsight, interpreted as a sign of destiny. I had an unremarkable childhood: I was tall and frail, from the window of my room I could see Monte Viglio, part of the Ernici mountain chain, and the Serra of Sant'Antonio which marks the watershed between the Liri and the Aniene rivers. During the winter evenings, I was always enthralled with my father's stories about Hannibal and how in 211 BC, he crossed the mountain chain in order to march his troops to Rome, reaching the Mammolo bridge where the legions were waiting for him. I daydreamed about those fascinating adventure stories. Besides, dreaming was the only thing I could do, my village offered nothing, and I was extremely poor. When it snowed, only the elderly remained in the village: the young went down into the valley taking their flocks to the Pontine marshes, which hadn't been drained yet, fighting malaria and the unclean air as they went. I attended primary school in Affile where we moved to in 1888, and then I went to middle school at the seminary in Subiaco. My father enrolled me there because it was a good institute, and also because it was free. He always had to count his pennies as he had inherited very little from his father Benedetto: just a three and a half-hectare plot of land. I remained in Subiaco until the fifth gymnasium, and I obtained my school leaving certificate in Rome at the Royal Ennio Quirino Visconti Institute. For the occasion, a friend of my father wrote

a *raccomandazione* for me. I had to deliver it personally to a professor at the Visconti institute. But the envelope was not sealed properly, and so I opened it and read: 'Just so I can get rid of him, here is...' It was a tough lesson. From then on, I learnt to rely only on myself, not to trust others and to never ask for letters of introduction.[8]

Graziani's phobia regarding *raccomandazioni* became with time almost pathological. Among his personal documents, we have found dozens of letters asking for *raccomandazioni*, always with a note attached saying: 'Say no, he should take part in the regular competitive examination'. In Cyrenaica, Graziani's circulars about the 'Fight against *raccomandazioni*' were of a bimestrial frequency. When he was viceroy of Ethiopia, he would bin the *raccomandazioni* letters of political ministers, including one from the *Duce*'s cousin Professor Temistocle Castelli, who asked for a licence in the 'export-import branch of leather and coffee'. But at the end of the day, Graziani was an Italian with a family to look after, and so to counterbalance, in December 1937, he too found himself writing a *raccomandazione*. He wrote one in favour of his son-in-law, Dr Count Gualandi, and it was addressed personally to the *Duce*. It makes quite strange reading in today's Italy of chronic unemployment, written as it is on headed paper from 'Viceroy of Ethiopia', with phrases such as:

> ... my son-in-law, who has a degree in law and works for the Luce institute, would like to be given a role of responsibility in the Ministry of Popular Culture. He speaks French, English and Spanish, however, he is not rich and doesn't know how to show his worth.... As for me, I am already obliged to look after my spinster sisters and my only brother, who is a petty officer in the Navy...

However, Mussolini refused, as 'Doctor Gualandi is not directly employed by the Ministry and therefore can only be employed as a member of the temporary staff with adequate pay and responsibilities'. To which Graziani responded: 'I thank you all the same, it being understood that my son-in-law will prepare for the regular competitive examination'.

Graziani's high school days from 1899 to 1902 would be spent in Rome, as a guest of his aunt who lived in the Prati district. He had enrolled at the Liceo Torquato Tasso, one of the best schools in the capital. To save money on the tram journey, he went on foot as far as the Ludovisi quarter. The lessons took place in the morning and the afternoon, his daily walks then amounted to four. But the young Graziani did not shirk from walking. He had become strong and tall (6 feet 3 inches), and he had also become vaguely socialist. From his autobiography: 'On my daily walk to Tasso, apart from admiring the monuments of ancient Rome, I observed some construction workers intent on building the new Palace of Justice: so much hard work, I thought that there should be a greater collaboration between work and capital'. An entry in his diary from 1904: 'Today, during my entrance examination for admission to the Military Academy, a cavalry captain with a long moustache caught me reading *Avanti!*. Naturally, during the oral exam, the selection board saw it fit to ask me about the social question. Thankfully, I handled it well'. From his autobiography: 'In 1905 I participated, in civilian clothes, in a protest in front of the Russian embassy. In Russia, after the disaster at Tsushima, there had been a revolution which the Tsar had brutally repressed'. Graziani's socialist leanings ended there. He would never talk about them again; he would always remain a defender of the established order. He would remember that youthful folly only during the Italian Social Republic, adjusting it as best he could to justify the socialisation program of the final days of Fascism.

After high school, Graziani recounted:

> I would have liked to enter the Military Academy of Modena. My father, on the other hand, hoped that I would become a doctor or a solicitor. I had to disappoint him. In any case, there was not enough money to be able to send me to the Military Academy and to pay for the uniforms. I cried; I told my father I would become a solicitor. It was October 1902. I enrolled in the jurisprudence faculty of the University of Rome, attending the two-year notary course, which cost less, and which would have allowed me to work immediately as a young student in a solicitor's office. At university, my professors were distinguished men of law: Orlando, Salandra, and Filomusi-Guelfi; with their teachings, maybe, I would have become a competent lawyer. But then, the call up papers arrived. As a student, I could have postponed my service, but I preferred to enter the platoon of reserve officer cadets which was being formed in Rome as a part of the 94th Infantry Regiment. In the barracks, I was given board and lodgings, and nothing stopped me from continuing my studies. Then, in May 1904, I was commissioned as a second lieutenant and sent to the 92nd Infantry Regiment stationed at Viterbo. My father, who died that month, was at least given the solace of seeing me become an officer. In the meantime, my studies were going badly, not because I wasn't applying myself, but because I needed more money and I had to find a way of earning some. I thought of taking part in a competitive exam for the position of public safety delegate and I took lessons under the guidance of Commissar Grippo. I decided not to go along to the exams held in Rome's prefecture: that job wasn't for me, and so I returned to Viterbo downhearted. At the end of 1904 I was discharged. What could I do now? I found out about another competitive examination, this time, announced by the Ministry of War with fifty places for reserve officer cadets to be made into regular officers. However, to take part, one needed to have already served six months. I had only done four, so I asked and was re-enlisted without pay. I was thin and emaciated, and so, ignoring my hunger pangs, I prepared for the entrance examination for the Military Academy. The Commandant of

the Academy, Col. Sagramoso, was known for his strictness and he used to say 'Reserve officers becoming regular? What is the world coming to coming to!' The title for the topic of the written exam was 'Demonstrate how Nations, even though they have fallen into ruin, can resurrect themselves as long as they maintain their honour and love for liberty and independence intact.' I remember it well because I have based every single action of my work on the principles set out in that question. Having passed the written exam, I went on to the oral exam, and here, when I was caught reading *Avanti!*, I risked being expelled. But in the end, everything went well. Out of the 350 who participated, only nine passed and I came third. I was finally a regular officer, and because of my height, I was sent to the 1st Grenadiers Regiment in Rome.

Between 1905 and 1915, the life of second lieutenant, lieutenant, and then Captain Graziani was spent in an unremarkably grey anonymous manner: barracks, marches, manoeuvres, battle school, summer and winter camps, infantry school, and lots of yelling and being told off. The only way in which Graziani differed from his fellow officers was money: he had none. From his autobiography: 'When on leave you had to be elegant, socialise, go to the Salone Margherita, to the horse races, to restaurants. For me this was impossible. I always had to refuse the invitations of my comrades to avoid looking more curmudgeon than I already was'. Entry from his diary on 8 February 1908: 'Troubles because of my clothes. I need uniforms for the summer and the winter, for the field and for ceremonies. I am now indebted to the tailor'. In April 1908, tired of all this economic hardship, Lieutenant Graziani asked to be sent to the colonies. They sent him to Eritrea on an old tramp freighter. He would remain in the colony for four years, and not in the port of Massawa or the capital Asmara, but in a village in the interior, Adi Ugri, where he would command the colonial *Turitto* Battalion. To his mother, he would write:

> I am studying Arabic and Tigrinya, Africa fascinates me. Here everything is so big, there are an infinite variety of animals and birds with beautiful feathers. By the way, I have learnt how to stuff birds and now I have a small collection. You know how much I liked studying science at school. At the seminary, I knew Buffon's *Histoire Naturelle* off by heart. Don't worry about me, I am doing fine. I have always had an impetuous character, but I am now starting to see the importance of discipline.

The war in Libya began in 1911, the only war which Graziani did not take part in. On 11 November 1911, while he was lying in a tent, he was bitten on the hand by a poisonous snake. It seemed like nothing, actually, he risked losing his life. There were no doctors or antidotes at Adi Ugri, the battalion medic could only wrap his arm up and give him permanganate injections. There was no alternative but to transport him to the hospital in Asmara. Months later, when he was discharged, he was incredibly weak and caught malaria. In 1912, the authorities repatriated him. He returned to Italy on a stretcher.

With his military career well underway, Lt Graziani's sentimental life was in full bloom. He had fallen madly in love with Ines Chionetti, a minute, good-looking brunette, with large expressive eyes. He had decided to marry her. The Chionettis, a Piedmontese family that had moved to Subiaco, had always known the Grazianis as Filippo had been their doctor. However, no one in the family had ever thought of Rodolfo as a possible suitor. So, when he presented himself in the full-dress uniform of a grenadier officer at the Chionettis and asked to speak to Ines's parents—the father, a landowner, and the mother, Countess Nobili Fanzi Bentivegna—they were truly surprised. Even Ines was disconcerted. Many years later, when everyone called her ma'am and marchioness, Lady Ines would recount this moment: 'It was the 13th of May 1913 when Rodolfo, without any preamble, made his brave proposal. I burst out laughing in his face. I would never have thought, I said, that you felt any feelings other than friendship towards me. "Because before you were a little girl," Rodolfo replied, all red in the face'. They married on 9 August 1913 at Belvedere Langhe, in the countryside of Cuneo. The reception was a never-ending wedding dinner of the old Piedmontese aristocracy. Not many guests were invited, only close relatives. In those days, Graziani was in mourning as he had just lost his mother, Adelia. A whirlwind trip by train to Rome, and a short honeymoon, forty-eight hours in all. The 1st Grenadiers had their summer camp at Monopoli, and Lt Graziani had to reach his unit immediately. For the newly-weds, there was only enough time to settle into the rooms of their house at Affile and bid each other goodbye. The moment they were about to take leave of each other, Graziani told his wife: 'Our marriage was brought about by love and passion, not by calculation, and so, I promise you, it will last forever'. And it did last forever, in sickness and in health, and it was a union of rare beauty. Ines had a calm and gentle temperament, she would be an exemplary spouse, a caring mother, and a loving grandmother. She would never be the object of gossip. It would be said of her that she was a woman both at ease with humble people and the powerful. During the days of the Italian Social Republic, many would call on Marchioness Graziani to beg for mercy or justice in favour of this or that family member who had been jailed, deported, or sentenced. They would all receive help or at least concern. The marshal, whom she would intimately call '*Pucci*', showed the same amount of loving affection towards his wife. He would say that only his wife deserved 'unconditional trust', only to his wife could he not 'refuse anything'. While being a bad-tempered and difficult man, Graziani would turn out to be a loving husband, one of those whom other wives would quote as an example, much to their husband's chagrin.

The correspondence between Rodolfo and Ines occupies an entire drawer in the Central State Archive. He would write to her on average two letters a week and he never forgot her birthday, saint's day, and other anniversaries. On these occasions, he would shower her with flowers and telegrams. He even telegraphed her from the oasis of Kufra, just after it had been occupied, and from Neghelli, right after it had been conquered. From his diary, 20–21 January 1936: 'At sunrise we start marching towards Neghelli which is occupied at 12:00.... It's Ines' feast day, this day always brings me victories ... I telegraph her from Neghelli'. She gave a moving reply: 'My love, I'm thinking about you', 'My dear Pucci, the living room is full of flowers, for your victory and for my celebration'. Until the day they were both old and grey, Graziani was incredibly jealous of her: he did not want her to wear too much make-up, he chose clothes for her, and he did not want her to dress in black as 'it brings bad luck'. Once, Dr Salvatore Janni, the head of the government commission in Benghazi, became a victim of the marshal's jealousy. The poor man, who was simply trying to be courteous, sent a great bouquet of roses to 'the very kind Lady Ines'. It was the '30s, and Gen. Graziani was vice-governor of Cyrenaica. He summoned Dr Janni and gave him quite an earful. He ended his admonishment by saying 'and from now on, if you really do need to send flowers, address them to "the home of his Excellency the Vice Governor." Have I made myself clear?' He had definitely made himself clear. Ines belonged to him and he belonged to Ines. He never betrayed her, even with a glance.

If on one hand all this fidelity gave credit to the regime that supported stable nuclear families, on the other, it fuelled malicious rumours. Graziani was a notoriously good-looking man, the newspapers described him as 'virile, manly, gigantic, imposing', and so on. Can it be possible, that even as a bachelor, he never had a fling, a romance, a relationship? The aforementioned Titta Madia tried to grapple with the topic 'Graziani and women' in 1937, in a small gold booklet called *Umanità di Graziani*.[9] Madia, not knowing what to say, filled the blank pages with his Neapolitan eloquence: 'and what about his passions? Of course. A young man of such rich sanguine stock certainly couldn't live like a priest. He loved, he loved women, gambling, merrymaking. He was young and in the prime of his life...' In reality, looking at Graziani's account book from 1906, we can deduce that, in his youth, Graziani did not have any serious or steady female relationships. He had a healthy appetite and was content with women of 'dubious profession'. Sex, in his mind was, 'that sin!' To Archimede Mischi, whom he met in Ethiopia and whom he would meet again in the Italian Social Republic, he would say that that Neapolitan expression reminded him of his days at the seminary, when his confessor Don Lorenzo Jella would enquire by asking: 'and that sin, do you confess it or not?' On the one hand, if he was personally chaste, he did believe that his soldiers had the right to have fun. He wanted the marching troops to always be followed by 'wagons of pleasure'. In Cyrenaica, he looked after the proper functioning of the brothel, and in Addis Ababa, he took an interest in the tariffs of the *maison* of Madame Brunette, a French woman. From *Diario segreto in A.O.I.* (Secret diary in Italian East Africa) of journalist Ciro Poggiali, entry of 3 July 1937:[10]

On the orders of the Viceroy, Gen. Mischi has organized public prostitution for his Blackshirts in quite an interesting way. He rigorously considers copulation as a service. The militiaman asks his direct superior for permission to copulate. The superior grants permission and sends the militiaman to the doctor who examines the postulate and after deeming him healthy, affixes a go-ahead on his permission paper. At the entrance of the brothel, there is a sergeant of the *Carabinieri* who looks at the document, and after finding the militiaman's papers in order from a military and medical standpoint, allows him to enter. If something's wrong, he is denied entry. Officers are severely prohibited from entering this house, on pain of repatriation. The Viceroy takes these things seriously.

For Graziani, this was not a very dignified occupation. But it did contribute to increasing his popularity. Soldiers and veterans of the nation's battles were always grateful for this even in Filettino and its surroundings.

The summer of 1941 in Piani di Arcinazzo went by calmly without any noteworthy events. The marshal worked the fields, fed the cattle, and sheared the sheep. He was concerned about whether the barn roof was strong enough to withstand the snow during the long winter months. He had bought a broodmare called Fanny and he hoped it could produce good colts. He started receiving post again, and this time, not only the usual anonymous letters, but also letters of solidarity and greeting cards from officers imprisoned in India and in other Commonwealth countries. From Benghazi, which had been reconquered by the *Afrika Korps*, he received a letter from the Prefect Ercoli Villani who 'remembered him with fondness'; from Bombay, the POW Gen. Armando Pescatori sent greetings from himself 'and your Libyan soldiers'. Every Sunday, Graziani and his inseparable wife went by car on a trip to Terracina, not to go for a swim in the sea as he was easily prone to catching colds and flus, but to eat spaghetti with clams, the only dish he truly appreciated. On their way back, he asked the driver if he could take the wheel. Driving relaxed him, he drove calmly but fast like a racing driver, so it was a good thing there was no traffic back then.

Around mid-August, his daughter, Vanda, her husband and grandchildren, Rodolfo and Alberto, came to visit him to get some fresh air. The marshal was happy about this, they celebrated his fifty-ninth birthday all together at the dinner table. Vanda was born on the eve of the First World War and was Graziani and Lady Ines's only child. It had been a difficult birth, which excluded the possibility of having other children. She was baptised in Affile with the names Ethel (Graziani liked it) and Vanda (Ines liked it) Adelia (in memory of the paternal grandmother). She would always be called Vanda. Graziani could command the armies, but at home, it was his wife who was in charge. Looking at the family album, we can see that when she was a baby, Vanda was a beautiful, smiling blonde girl. But at twelve years of age, she was the victim of an accident that

Flowers given to Graziani by his nephew Rodolfo, Jnr.

would change her life forever. She fell and fractured the elbow of her left arm, and despite various operations, her limb was permanently affected. From then on, feeling as though she had been cheated of a normal life, Vanda's personality changed: she became withdrawn, insecure, shy, and moody. The diagnosis of the doctors was 'a clear case of psychological trauma'. The parents overprotected and mollycoddled their unhappy and difficult girl. Among the marshal's personal letters, there is one from his now twenty-one-year-old daughter who asks for her father's permission to get engaged to Sergio Gualandi from Bologna. The letter is from 27 September 1936, written in shaky handwriting, it said:

> ... See, Mamma swears that she's already talked to you about Gualandi and I want to tell you openly that I am even thinking of marrying him. Even Mamma isn't against this, but I am a little kitten and I need to be guided by you two. We could all come down to Africa so you can get to know him and judge him for yourself. It's okay to become a mother and give you lots of grandchildren as you say, but there has to be some fun in it as well, doesn't there? I may not be thoroughly modern but I am not that old-fashioned!!!

The official announcement of their engagement was given the following year, with a reception in the Imperial Ghebbi of Addis Ababa, which used to be the former residence of the Negus. From the diary of journalist Ciro Poggiali, 20 July 1937: 'Lovely bash, courtesy of Lady Ines, sumptuous buffet with sparkling wine and roasted suckling pigs. I am able to win over the reluctant Viceroy Graziani by presenting him with my telegraphic report of the event, which in the end, he and his wife liked a lot'. In October 1937, the wedding. Sergio and Vanda got married in Addis Ababa (Graziani's note: 'They received thousands of presents, one from His Majesty the King was a set of precious coffee cups and saucers in heavy silver. I take note of all this in order to send my thank you notes later'), and they soon made Graziani very happy by making him a grandfather. Rodolfo, Jnr, was born in October 1938 and Alberto in September 1939. Grandfather Rodolfo would call them 'my pupis' and had feelings of tenderness and affection towards them beyond compare. Preserved in the Central State Archive are documents and letters that attest to this love. There is an envelope full of pressed flowers bearing the words: 'March 1940. The first flowers given to me by Rodolfo the second'. And there is another one containing a child's drawings which says: 'August 1942: Here are Alberto's first drawings. What a dear child! He gave them to me for my birthday'. Graziani even obtained the passing of an exceptional royal decree by King Victor Emanuel III in which the aristocratic title of marquis of Neghelli, which before could only be inherited by male heirs, was now bestowed on his daughter Ethel Vanda and on 'her first-born Gualandi Rodolfo'. Count Sergio Gualandi (he was given this title a few days before the wedding) also had to consent to little Rodolfo having the surname Graziani added to that of Gualandi. We do not know what his reaction to this was.

Despite all this, Graziani, even as a grandfather, would be possessive and controlling. He loved his grandchildren, he would help his son-in-law find a job, he would financially aid his daughter, but always with the tacit understanding that he, and only he, had the final say in everything. Towards Sergio Gualandi—who despite calling him 'father,' addressed him with the formal '*Lei*' in contrast with the regime's directives (Graziani: '"*Lei*" has been abolished, use "*voi*!"')—he would often act indiscreetly and with little tact.[11] He would constantly involve himself in Sergio and Vanda's private affairs, always having something to say about their marriage.

In October 1941, new guests arrived at Casal Biancaneve. They were ten grey-haired noisy former comrades from the *Lazio* Brigade, on their way back from a gathering of veterans of the First World War held in Naples. The marshal gave them a warm welcome, he had served as an officer in the *Lazio* Brigade in 1915. As usual, the reunion ended in a large meal with singing, drinking, and stories from the war. This is the odd thing about human memory, it turns the horrors of war into happy and comical tales. Lady Ines took great care to put enough food on the table: fettucine, chicken, lamb, vegetables from the garden, and a chocolate chip ricotta tart prepared especially for the occasion. 'Eat up, this is all home produce, from my chicken pen, from my garden,' Graziani kept repeating happily. Surrounded by his ex-comrades, whom he knew personally, the marshal became a chatterbox, talking almost non-stop. He had many stories from the Great War, which he remembered and wanted to tell.

He had left a captain; he had come back a colonel. Such a thing had never happened before, it was unheard of, a colonel at thirty-six years of age, the

A royal patent from the king making the title of marquis of Neghelli also transmissible to Graziani's daughter, Vanda.

youngest in the Italian army. In 1915, he was an officer in the 131st Infantry Regiment of the *Lazio* Brigade, sent to the San Michele sector of the Isonzo, summit one and summit two. It was the frontline of the army of Duke Emanuele Filiberto of Aosta, the bloodiest part, the one where Gen. Cadorna experimented his frontal assaults and brutal 'shoulder pushes'. In December, the 131st had already been decimated and Capt. Graziani was now the only remaining officer. He took command of the regiment. On the night between 6 and 7 December 1915, Graziani became the protagonist of a daring and extraordinary exploit, mentioned in dispatches, referred to in the historical diary of the *Lazio* Brigade, and recounted in the book *L'esercito italiano nella grande guerra*.[12] Graziani's men had to break through the enemy lines with a fixed bayonet assault preceded by a heavy artillery barrage. Graziani asked that the shelling not take place as it would put the enemy on guard: they were Hungarians of the 1st *Honved* Regiment. He waited until the fog descended and sent five soldiers with wire cutters forward, he followed them crawling along the ground with fifty of his men—all armed with daggers and hand grenades. The enemy was caught completely off guard, the Hungarians were either massacred in their sleep or captured.

From *L'esercito italiano nella grande guerra* (second volume, page 608):

> With this action, nine officers, including the Commander of the 1st *Honved* Regiment, several NCOs, 148 soldiers and a large amount of military equipment

fell into our hands. The day after, the enemy counter-attacked in greater numbers, forcing the Italian units to abandon parts of the trench which they had conquered. In the harsh fighting that followed, which involved the entire 29th Division, we received heavy casualties: fourteen officers and 502 men put out of action. Even the enemy suffered heavy losses, the 1st *Honved* alone lost 438 men, including dead, wounded or captured.

We have described this episode in full in order to illustrate how Graziani was always a master of the *coup de main*, a technique that he would later perfect in Libya, and then in Ethiopia. If it is difficult to judge how well he performed as the general of an army—in North Africa, as we have seen, everything went awry—it is only right to say that, as a subaltern officer, he had few equals. Even Pietro Badoglio recognised this. Paying back Graziani's hatred for him, he would one day say, tongue in cheek: 'What a shame, he was a magnificent battalion commander'. In 1916, after being promoted to major for his actions on the field and having been conferred with the Knight's Cross of the Order of the Crown of Italy, Graziani was intoxicated by poison gas during an attack at the battle of Gorizia and was thus sent to a troop deposit to train the reserves. He had been on the frontline uninterruptedly for fifteen months. The deposit was based at Alatri, a few kilometres from Affile. The echo of his heroic exploits had reached his hometown thanks to the newspapers and the weekly letters delivered by the courier of Subiaco. His wife waited anxiously with their little daughter, and the townsfolk were preparing to celebrate him. He was their local hero, word got around that they were about to decorate him with a medal (they would give him one, but only in 1928, and it was a bronze one): banquets were prepared for him along with wine and fireworks. Schoolgirls quoting Cicero declaimed, 'our land is harsh and mountainous/but loyal and true and a champion of its sons.' The grand finale 'Long live the Ciociarians, *viva* Ciociaria!' In 1917, after Caporetto, Maj. Graziani asked to be sent back to the front. He fought on Mount Grappa, where a bullet grazed his left shoulder during the assault on Col Berretta. He fought on the Asiago plateau, where he suffered another superficial injury. In 1918, when the Armistice occurred, he was in Salerno, fresh from his promotion to colonel and busy training the latest recruits.

Although this curriculum merits respect, there was, however, one miniscule flaw to be found in it, which was due, as always, to his litigious and distrustful character. A dossier kept in Palazzo Baracchini, the seat of the Ministry of Defence, attests to this. The dossier begins with a simple reprimand, issued by the general staff to Lt-Col. Graziani, who—after 11 December 1917—in relation to his actions on the Col Berretta of Mount Grappa 'has behaved in a manner unbecoming an officer of his rank by personally petitioning those under his command so that he could receive a decoration'. Graziani's rebuke of 19 May 1919: 'It's true, but what is also true is that my work was exploited and distorted by other less deserving officers'. Here follows the reply of the general staff: 'The simple reprimand remains. In the action of Col Berretta the claimant did not hold any command and did nothing of note'. Graziani continued to protest: 'I was wounded yet I exposed myself to enemy fire courageously!' To cut a long story short, the quarrel between Graziani and the general staff would last for almost twenty years and ended in 1937. It would be the stubborn Graziani that would come out on top. He obtained a silver medal for the 'valour demonstrated in the fighting at Col Berretta'. A marshal of Italy and viceroy of Ethiopia could no longer be refused his long-awaited medal.

But let us return to the lunch of October 1941 with the former comrades of the *Lazio* Brigade. For Graziani, that meal among friends was the last moment of calm before the storm. The storm was announced, in a casual way, on 18 November. The marshal learned from a friend, who had learnt it from a federal who in his turn was a close friend of party secretary Adelchi Serena, that Mussolini had formed a military Investigative Commission charged with 'ascertaining the validity of Marshal Rodolfo Graziani's command in North Africa'. He was shocked and incredulous. So this is what they wanted to do, to disgrace and degrade him, and even to put him on trial. He raced off to Rome, in order to pull strings and find out what was really going on. He learnt of the truth from an officer at the general staff, Maj. Giuseppe Perrot, who told him that what he had heard was no joke. The Investigative Commission had already got down to work and it was chaired by Grand Admiral Thaon di Revel, the other investigators were reserve Gen. Ago,

In 1916, after fifteen months on the frontline, Maj. Graziani returned to Affile and was celebrated as a hero. Here is a postcard signed by the village postman.

Air Sqn Cdr Marmi, and National Councillor Mannaresi. Graziani remained in the capital for about a fortnight, waiting to be summoned, heard, or invited to justify his actions. He was and never would be summoned. On 9 December, a gloomy and sullen Graziani returned to Piani di Arcinazzo. He told his wife: 'I understand now, this isn't a trial, it's an execution, a stab in the back'.

Every day, for months afterwards, the marshal phoned Dr Magno Bocca, his personal secretary, to find out about any updates on the situation. He thought they were listening in on his phone calls, so he invented a few secret phrases in code, when he called, he would ask: 'Any news on the *notorious question*?' He mostly occupied himself with reading. He read Tacitus, and *The Prince* (Graziani's heirs found a copy of Machiavelli's famous treatise with many written notes and underlined phrases in it). No one visited him during this period, he was not in the right mood. He made an exception on 15 December for Mrs Ungari. From his personal diary: 'Mrs Ungari visited for lunch. She read my hand. I will live a long life beyond seventy-four years of age. I will have to fight, but in the end, I will triumph. I have the sign of victory on my palm'. This escapism from reality, this seeking refuge in magic and chiromancy was a constant habit of the marshal, who, as we have seen previously, was incredibly superstitious. In Libya, Graziani became an intimate friend of Shekib al-Aftan, expert in mind reading and interpreting the dregs in coffee cups. In Ethiopia—because he thought it brought 'bad luck'—he ordered not to execute the witch Uorkemariam and the wizards Aden Arerù and Menghestu Teghegn, who incited the local population against the Italians with their predictions. In 1938, in Italy, he entertained a long epistolary exchange with Mrs Eyat Loss from Genoa, who claimed to be Graziani's medium. The letters between Graziani and Mrs Loss are quite amusing. One day, the imprudent medium wrote to Graziani telling him that he would 'die of cancer'. Graziani replied post-haste while trying to ward off bad luck with all the means at his disposal. He wrote: 'Please do not bother me anymore'.

Magic aside, in those sad days of 1941, the marshal's other great consolation were his dogs and his horses. Graziani seemed to have a privileged relationship with animals, more as a friend than master. He stroked them, he talked to them tenderly, and he rewarded them with biscuits and lumps of sugar. In old age, this man who was always quick to resort to the firing squad would boast that he had never killed an animal—that he never went hunting, and once when he did go, he went without a rifle 'only to take a breath of fresh air'. In 1941, the marshal owned two dogs, a Dachshund called Topolino and a female Pomeranian called Concitella. Concitella, daughter of Quoncit, which means gracious in Amharic, was the family favourite. There would always be a Concitella by Graziani's side, even at Salò, and even on 25 April 1945 during the escape from the prefecture of Milan to Como. The first, Quancit, was given to him as a gift in July 1936 by Haile Selassie's butler. Graziani was lodging in the Imperial Ghebbi of the just recently conquered Addis Ababa, when the butler arrived carrying a little

The Gualandi-Graziani coat of arms.

dog in his arms and said: 'This is Quoncit, it belongs to the Negus. Today, you are the Negus, it belongs to you'. Quoncit and Graziani became best friends immediately, they were inseparable. The little dog, a rare breed which originated from Karakorum, was always just a step behind the marshal, huddled up in his office, curled up on the seat of his car, or on guard in front of his bedroom door. It was Lady Ines who started calling her Quoncitella, and then more simply, Concitella. When she died in the days of the conquest of Sidi Barrani, the marshal was almost taken ill. Luckily, Quoncit had puppies, and waiting for him at Piani di Arcinazzo was a new Concitella. Topolino and Concitella the second who grew up together in the mountains helped alleviate the pain of the defeated Graziani. Together, they formed a strange trio—he, a giant, and they, two tiny little dogs. The amount of attention he paid to their daily activities will be judged as moving by animal lovers and ridiculous by those who are not. From Graziani's personal diary:

> 'Arcinazzo, 27 September 1942. Wedding of Concitella the second.'
> 'Arcinazzo, 26 November 1942. Happy occasion for Concitella during the night.'
> 'Rome, 25 June 1943. *Sunt lacrimae rerum*. Last night, at 1.50, our dear and faithful Topolino died. I called the veterinary surgeon Doctor Gospodinoff for the prescribed formalin injection.'
> '26 June 1943.... we are at Casal Biancaneve to bury Topolino who will be placed next to Quoncitte, under the fir tree which covers them both and where a tombstone will be placed.'

The days of the Italian Social Republic would be those of Concitella the third who would not abandon her master for one second, barking at everyone, including Mussolini. In order to speak with Graziani, the civil servants of the Ministry of National Defence would have to learn to ingratiate themselves with the little dog, famous for biting people on the shins. Once, Concitella the third even tried to protect her master with her own body. When an enemy fighter plane machine gunned the marshal's car, Graziani jumped out and fell into a ditch; at the end of the attack, his armed escort found him with his dog amusingly perched on his head, growling and ready to attack any approaching foe.

Christmas was getting closer. Dr Bocca in Rome had no news on the *notorious question*. The commission's work went on, shadowed in secrecy. Graziani decided not to waste any more time, he would counter any accusations by preparing his defence with documents and witnesses who would exonerate him. The 'Roman clique' could not possibly think that they could drag him in front of a court martial without expecting him to fight back. He would react, and how! Reassured by this defensive strategy, the marshal spent a seemingly peaceful Christmas with his wife, his daughter, his son-in-law, and his beloved 'pupis'. It snowed in the mountains at Christmas, the home fire was burning bright, the nativity scene glowed, presents were being opened, and others were ready to be opened. It was a Christmas in the family like many others. In the following days, while the marshal was looking through his papers for any documents that could be useful for his defence, he found an old photograph of himself. He wrote about it in his diary: 'I found a snap-shot from 1922. Then, no one had yet accused me of being mean and cruel. And, come on, I was already forty years old. Where was my ferocious nature back then, where was my cruelty?' An interesting question, worthy of the attention of a psychologist.[13] In simpler terms, Graziani wanted to say that either you are cruel or you are not. You cannot become cruel after a certain age, when you have lived an all-round normal life. However, the facts will show that this is possible. After forty years of age, in Libya, Graziani would become the man of the concentration camps and the flying tribunals. In Ethiopia, the man of the bloody reprisals and poison gas. He was not cruel by nature. He became so out of necessity, through cold and calculating thinking, as he would often say, war is war, and it does not allow for weakness.

3
Postcards from Libya

One of Graziani's many fixations was ink, it always had to be green. He wrote with a big Waterman fountain pen, his handwriting was sharp, neat, and well-spaced. On 1 January 1942, the marshal inaugurated his new diary, writing in large green letters: '*Ense et aratro*, I will dedicate the entire year to the plough'.

Ense et aratro, the sword and the plough, that was his motto. He had copied it from Marshal Bugeaud, the 'pacifier' of French Algeria, and he had it engraved on the façade of his colonial house in Bu Maad in the Cyrenaican desert. He submitted it for King Victor Emmanuel III's approval when the sovereign had conferred the aristocratic title of marquis of Neghelli on him. The small king was delighted by Graziani's choice. Finally, an emblem and motto that were not pretentious, but peaceful and simple, befitting a freshly nominated nobleman. To comprehend the king's relief better, it must be remembered that Marshal Badoglio, the new duke of Addis Ababa, had just asked if he could use Caesar's *Veni Vidi Vici* as his motto. Only after an animated discussion in Piedmontese dialect was he forced to fall back on the humbler *Come Falco Giunsi*, (like a falcon, I descended). After expressing his wish to 'dedicate the entire year to the plough', still in January 1942, Graziani added:

> Today I went to mass, I prayed, and whilst I was walking back home, I took out my bible and opened it. It was the Book of Kings, chapter eighteen, and this is what was written: 'And it came to pass after many days, that the word of the Lord came to Elijah, in the third-year, saying, Go, and shew thyself unto Ahab; and I will send rain upon the earth'. I think it's an omen, I believe in these things. The third year which the bible talks about was a year of drought and hunger. Maybe the Lord will make the rain pour down for me as well. At least I can hope.

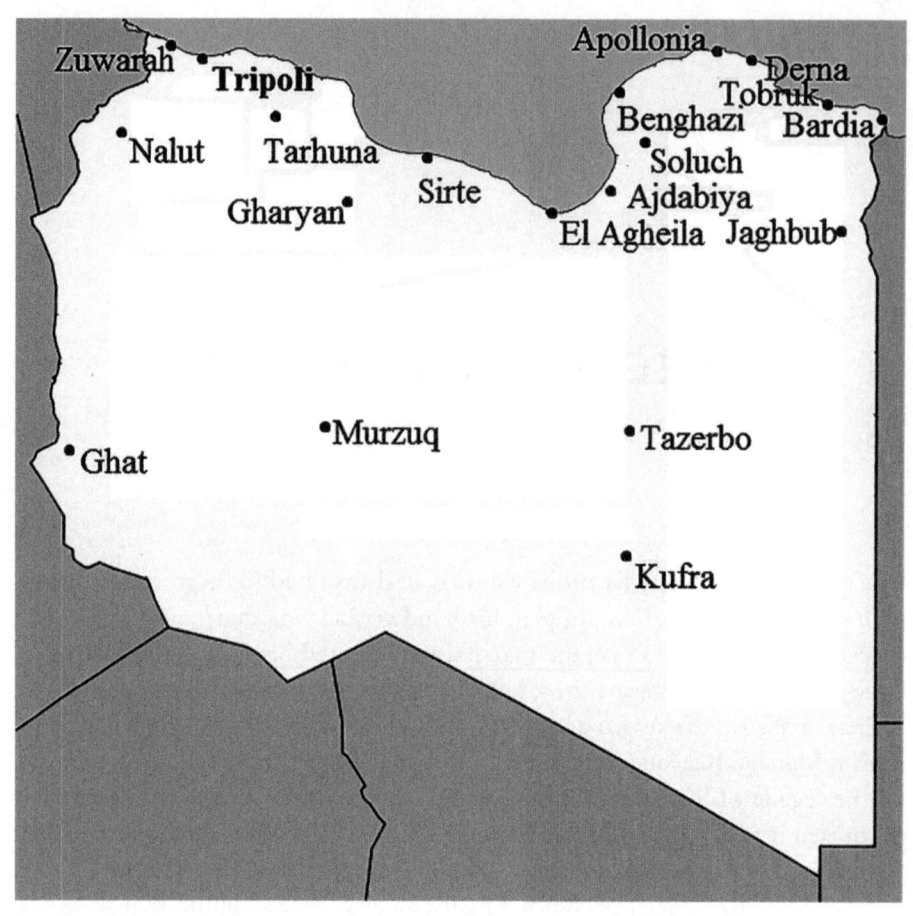

A map of Libya with locations mentioned in the book. (*Wikimedia Commons*)

His prayers were not answered; 1942 would be a year of misfortune for the marshal. The Investigative Commission would blacken his name, Rodolfo, Jnr, would fall ill, there would be problems in Vanda's marriage. Graziani would occupy himself with the completion of his defence statement and other mundane tasks. He would be consumed with past regrets, kept busy with laughable disputes, recriminations, and petty squabbling. Looking through his diary and the attached farmer's ledger, we can find bills that need paying, blank receipts, shopping lists for 'chick-peas, beans, corn, hay', unremarkable entries such as: 'I am planting a poplar'; 'The bull's restless'; 'The hay harvest is proceeding slowly'; 'We're nearly ready to plant the potatoes'.

Even the other notes which have nothing do with farm work are of little interest. Here are some examples: '15 January. No news on the *notorious question*. What are the judges doing? It's a mystery'; '21 January. Lunch at home for Ines' feast day'; '2 February. End of my role as President of the Caproni group. Bonus of 100 thousand lira'; '11 February. Snow. It's the first anniversary of my return from North Africa.

Sadness'; '16 February. Trip to Assisi with Ines. Very cold. At Foligno, the crowd recognizes me and starts applauding. A good sign, they haven't forgotten me'; '22 February. Lunch at Count Volpi's. We avoid talking about politics'; '5 March. The King doesn't ask to see me'; '29 March. I start editing my defence. I have been authorized by the *Duce*'; '5 April. Easter. I give out lamb and ricotta to my friends. From Rome, news of underhand manoeuvres against me by Farinacci. It seems I am to be watched'; '24 April. The Duce considers me to be someone who conspires against people. Of course, I live in isolation!!'; '3 May. At the Colonial Museum, I meet Attilio Teruzzi and I go out of my way not to say hello to him'.

It goes on like this for hundreds of pages, in a daily nothingness characterised by anniversaries, family reunions, walks with the 'pupis', visits to the priest of Filettino, and appointments with the chiropodist. Until 2 June 1942 when we have a heartfelt confession:

> 2 June. I feel crucified like Christ. Eight years ago, I was in Benghazi as Vice Governor. I was about to leave that colony which I had loved so much. Those were my glory years, when destiny smiled upon me. My departure caused great sadness: my Libyan *askari* shouted 'Goodbye, Baba Graziani.' I remember the speech I gave: 'Cyrenaica, land of legend and greatness, you will not play Cinderella again. Men and history wanted to make you Levantine, but Fascism redeemed you...' I can still hear the words of Mohammed Ben Amey, doctor of Sharia law, as he bid me farewell: 'Even the rocks are crying.' I admired the sabre given to me by the Arab notables with *Te teneo Cirenaica* written on the hilt. I can still see the proud and emotional face of the faithful Kalifa Kaled. So much nostalgia. Those were my golden years. And now it's all over, *sic transit*.... It can't be true, it's not right, it's not possible.

Rodolfo Graziani landed at Tripoli on the morning of March 1922. He had volunteered for service in that colony in 1919, but the Ministry of War had refused to grant him permission, and instead sent him to Thessaloniki to command the 61st Infantry Regiment stationed in the Balkans with the Allied expeditionary force. It was a nice trip, the Orient-Express to Constantinople, the discovery of the Eastern world, of different people with unknown habits and customs. To Col. Graziani, who was provincial through and through, it all seemed very fun and exciting. However, Graziani would remain in Thessaloniki only a few months: he was repatriated with his regiment in August, having been given the order to return to Parma, the city from which he had departed. Parma's mood and its flags were, in the summer of 1919, red. There were Frisian horses on the Oltretorrente bridge, soldiers were consigned to their barracks, the real power in the city was held by a revolutionary committee. The divisional command of Piacenza told officers not to show themselves in town too often and not to wear ribbons and medals on their uniform.

Graziani soon got into trouble. Word got around that he was the son of Gen. Andrea Graziani. After Caporetto, Andrea Graziani 'had distinguished himself for his untiring energy with which he brought order to the rear ranks'. In other words: he had had deserters shot. Graziani's disclaimers were of no use, neither was a letter he wrote to the *Corriere della Sera* on 6 August 1919, saying: 'I have been mistaken for another person'. The revolutionary committee of Parma decreed that the 'son of such a murderer' ought to be eliminated.

Private communication of the divisional command of Piacenza to Col. Rodolfo Graziani, 23 August 1919: 'From now on you will remain in the barracks and you will travel to your home only under armed escort. We suggest you avoid evening outings. We also suggest verifying whether your home might possess alternative exit routes through the roof or the basement'.

Lady Ines, skilful as always, tried to placate her fuming husband by organising dinners with friends, card games with fellow officers, and even concerts, in which Graziani was imprudently invited to play the drums. Sadly, this was not enough. From Graziani's autobiography: 'In the end, I couldn't take it anymore. In July 1920, I asked for a two years' leave of absence and, ignoring the flattery of the early fascists—because a soldier is of the Nation and not of a faction—I packed my bags and departed once again for the Balkans'.

Graziani stayed in the Balkans for more than a year, until the autumn of 1921. But doing what? No one knows exactly. On this subject, his autobiography is incredibly vague: 'I went to Macedonia and then beyond to the Caucasus region,' the marshal explained evasively, 'in search of a lucrative job which would alleviate the financial difficulties in which I continued to find myself.' It would seem that he turned his hand to selling Persian carpets. We only know two things for certain. The first was that, apart from a postcard from Constantinople saying 'I am fine, but this medicine is quite bitter', Graziani did not keep in touch with anyone, not even his wife, for quite a long time. Secondly, when he came back to Italy (the Ministry of War, with Luigi Facta as prime minister, had finally accepted his request to be transferred to Libya), Graziani was, unsurprisingly, penniless. Throughout his entire life, Graziani would be extremely naive regarding business matters, a sort of King Midas in reverse. He would become marshal, he would become rich, and he would let other people swindle him. They would tell him 'You give us the money and we will give you our experience,' he would gain experience and others would make money.

And so, in 1922, Col. Graziani landed in Tripoli. In the colony, the situation was disastrous. The Italians only controlled the cities on the coast, the rest of the territory was held by the rebels whose spiritual guide was El Sayyid Muhammad Idris al-Mahdi as-Senussi, the future King Idris of Libya, and they were led militarily by Omar al-Mukhtar, General Representative of Senusiyya. The ratio of troops on the ground: 1,000 or 2,000 rebels to 20,000 Italians and their Libyan collaborators was, in theory, in the government's favour. In practice, the Italians' numerical

King Victor Emanuel III conferred the aristocratic title of Marquis of Neghelli on Rodolfo Graziani, 6 December 1937.

superiority was a handicap. Omar al-Mukhtar's men did not need to learn about guerrilla warfare from instruction manuals—it was in their blood. Once they killed a sentinel, another time a messenger, in one place they lured a platoon into an ambush, in another they overwhelmed an isolated detachment. Then, they disappeared.

Report by Divisional Gen. Alfredo Taranto, commander of Italian troops in Libya, Homs, 1921:

> The rebels refuse to give battle and during our searches, they disperse. They are not tied to anything or anyone. They have nothing to defend, nothing to protect. They appear in one place and the following day in another, they disappear one week and reappear after a month without any apparently logical explanation. Militarily, we can occupy the villages of the interior and as much territory as we like. But as soon as we walk away, it all starts up again.

Col. Graziani was received favourably by the governor of Tripolitania, Count Giovanni Volpi of Misurata, probably on account of the fact that his arrival had been announced by the prime minister, Giovanni Giolitti. 'Well, if Giolitti's telling me about him,' Volpi wrote to the Ministry of the Colonies, 'then he can't be that stupid.' Sent to Zuwarah to command the local garrison, Graziani demonstrated he was anything but stupid. He did two things that most Italian officers made sure they did not do. He studied the motivations and the end-goal of the rebellion, he beat the rebels at their own game with ambushes, incursions, surprise raids by commandos, and swift mobile columns. This was counterinsurgency, a tactic that came easily to him.

The origins of the rebel movement were to be found in the Senussi order, a brotherhood of orthodox Sunni Muslims. In the centuries following the *Hijrah*, the Senussi preached asceticism, hermit life, and meditation.[1] Only after the collapse of the Arab systems of government did the Senussi become a religious and political organisation. At the top of the pyramid was the supreme leader of the Senussi, surrounded by twenty sheiks and by 1,000 *ikhwan* or brothers, whom the *muntasabin*, the adherents of the fraternity obeyed. Almost all the Arabs of Cyrenaica and the Bedouins of the desert were *muntasabin*. Against the infidel Italians, the Senussi waged a Jihad for Allah and their independence. Resistance to the invaders was carried out by any means possible. The *zabet*, the armed combatants, were supported by the *mtalyanin*, Arabs who had officially submitted to the Italians but who, in reality, were spies and informants. As a result of this, Graziani understood that he could not trust anyone, and that fomenting tribal rivalries by funding the village elders had to stop. There was only one enemy, and that was Senusiyya, better known as the 'government of the night', and they could certainly not be bought.

Graziani's new way of waging war started with a sign in Arabic which said: 'There is no safe at this headquarters'. A pennant hung alongside it which read '*Audacia vincit*', yet another reminiscence from his time at the seminary. The sign quickly became his motto. He would bravely plant it wherever he went. As his guide, he had chosen a Tuareg, Muhammed Soliman, and as his interpreter, the Berber Capt. Kalifa Kaled, both of whom were hostile to the Arabs. He had formed a mobile column of 480 men. He pretended to leave Zuwarah at sunset but returned soon afterwards. He left in earnest late in the morning when long marches in the searingly hot sun were ill-advised. The rebels were bewildered. During the evening of 2 June 1922, at Sidi es-Saiah, the Graziani column appeared out of nowhere and massacred seventy *zabet*. The Senussi were making tea, they could never have imagined that against all the rules of war, the colonel and his men would march for twenty-two hours in 50-degree heat for 70 km. On 6 June, Graziani occupied Giosc, one of the centres of the rebellion. Same tactics, same battle formation. At the head, there was a company of *Spahis*, followed by a group of *mehari* camel artillery, a *Mehalla* or an armed band of *Berbers* and then a squadron of *Zaptié* on horseback. Along the way, many horses died of thirst or from heat exhaustion, and nearly 300 soldiers suffered from sunstroke. Only 150 arrived at Giosc. The town was levelled by mortar shots and the rebels were mowed down by machine-gun fire. From Graziani's diary: 'We hoisted the Italian flag on the ruins, the Eritrean soldiers improvised a *fantasia*'.[2]

In nine years, this is how long the guerrilla war lasted, there would be thousands of fights, encounters, and skirmishes of this kind. There is no need to recount all of them in detail, they were all the same, of equal audacity and ferociousness. Instead, let us focus on Graziani. A few photos of him are kept in the Central State Archive. He was forty years old but looked younger, his face was tanned and his physique lean. He wore a light-coloured safari jacket, his socks were rolled over his boots, his *kepi* worn at a slant on his head. The straps of his binoculars were slung across his chest, he carried a long-barrelled pistol and an Arab *qirbah*, the leather flask of the desert nomads. At times, he wore a *burnous*, holding the reins of the camel in one hand and a whip in the other. In another photo, he can be seen relaxing, lying against a saddle in front of a bivouac fire, his body covered by a black and white-striped Tuareg cape. In these snapshots, Graziani looked as if he was enjoying himself. Compared to the trenches of the Carso mountains, the guerrilla war was a joke: rarely did fights with the rebels end in slaughter as they usually ended in long-distanced shootouts or in fast-paced pursuits on horseback. Everything, especially the scenery, smacked of adventure. Those fascinating exotic landscapes, the surreal experience of a life like that of Lawrence of Arabia. Col. Graziani discovered the desert and he fell in love with it: that sea of dunes interrupted by oases, dotted with Bedouin camps, and the trails of moving caravans, it all fascinated him. 'Greetings, O desert!' he wrote in a dreadful poem, 'greetings, O wonders of immenseness!' When talking of himself, he would smugly cite a passage of the Arab writer Al-Mutanabbi, which went: 'Only the desert, the night and the enemy know me'. When roaming in the desert, Graziani either rode an Arabian horse or a racing camel. He had found the horse while on his way to Tarhuna: it was white and restless, he called it *Uaar*, 'the difficult one'. The racing camel was one of many at the garrison at Zuwarah, his first encounter with it was quite dramatic. From the Comte de Buffon's book *Histoire Naturelle*: 'The *mehari* is one of the marvels of the desert, made for the central Sahara with an organism in perfect harmony with its environment. It is shrewd and loyal like a dog, and much faster than a horse'. Faster, of course, but a lot more irksome to ride. It took Graziani a fortnight of tumbles and headlong falls before finally being able to stay firmly in the saddle of his *mehari*. When he finally managed to feel stable on the *rakla*, the *mehari*'s special saddle, he asked the garrison's officers to repeat exactly what he had done. He observed the spectacle with amusement.

Count Giovanni Volpi was quite pleased with Col. Graziani's dynamism. Finally, an officer who took the initiative and did not do things the easy way. In his report he described him as a 'born colonial'. He telegraphed Giovanni Amendola, Minister of the Colonies, saying: 'Rodolfo Graziani is methodical in his preparation and rapid in action. His behaviour is exemplary'. Amendola took heed of this and rewarded Graziani with two civil decorations, the Knight's Grand Cross of the Order of Saints Maurice and Lazarus and the Commander of the Colonial Order of the Star of Italy.

Meanwhile, Italy's young democracy was nearing its end. The Fascists were about to march on Rome. On 28 October 1922, while Mussolini was boarding a sleeping car in Milan bound for the capital, Col. Graziani was in the Gharyan region, ready to receive the surrender of the Kamaikan Al-Hadi Coobar. Coobar was a respected chief, a pious and learned man. His act of submission, the first in many years, was recounted by the local press (*Il giornale di Tripoli*, *La gazzetta di Bengazi*) in epic proportions. The 'rebel' was presented as utterly evil, and

Graziani was defined hyperbolically as 'our Colonel Storm'. In reality, during the pacification of Libya as a whole, the Coobar episode was of little importance. It would become important after the war, when an unknown columnist by the name of 'Colonel X' dug up the story in order to accuse Graziani of being a thief and a braggart. In 1946, Colonel X wrote that 'Al-Hadi Coobar was hanged after Graziani had promised to spare his life in exchange for the family jewels and a gold bracelet. He then kept his ill-gotten gains'. Pandemonium broke out. They had called his honesty into question. Despite being in prison, he obtained a series of reliable testimonies in his favour. The archaeologist Professor Biagio Pace declared that Coobar's widow was still in possession of the jewels and the bracelet; Gen. Riccardo Brunei, president of the military tribunal of Tripolitania, swore that during the trial, Al-Hadi had denied ever being given an assurance that his life would be saved and had gone to his execution happy to die 'for Islam and the Nation'. From then onwards, no one accused Graziani of being dishonest. In fact, on a personal level, the marshal was well mannered and always behaved correctly. He gained no profit from the regime and never funnelled public funds or anything of the sort. He had other faults, however.

With the advent of Fascism, Rodolfo Graziani grew in prestige and popularity. Mussolini needed heroes and that 'darned soldier' was just what he was looking for. He promoted him to brigadier-general and made him commander of the Order of the Crown of Italy. For the conquest of Bani Walid, in which two cohorts of the Blackshirt Militia took part, he gave him the honorary badge of the Fascist Party. On top of this, he made sure that Gen. Graziani's exploits were documented by film operators and immortalised by the best journalists of the time. Mussolini had previews of the films projected at Villa Torlonia, his Roman residence—charging horses, fluttering banners, sabres drawn. Commenting on the more salient moments, he exclaimed 'Bravo, very good, this is a good one to show in schools'. And as for the journalists, after 'Colonel Storm', they came up with all sorts of nicknames. He was called 'the Scipionic general', 'the smasher', 'the sphynx', 'the terror of the Bedouins', a sort of precursor of Rambo. The years went by, Volpi was substituted by the *quadrumviro* De Bono, but Graziani remained the main protagonist in Libya. He kept being showered with decorations (1926, Officer of the Order of Saints Maurice and Lazarus; 1928, Grand Officer of the Colonial Order of the Star of Italy), praise (De Bono: 'to me, he is indispensable, precious, extremely useful'), promotion (1928, divisional general), and medals for military valour (1928, Bir Tagrift, silver medal with a special allowance of 250 lira a year). If grandiose operations were being planned (the conquest of the castle of Murzuq, the occupation of Zella, the taking of the wells at Tagrift, nine hours of fighting and 500 rebels killed in all), the Italian High Command always chose Graziani; if newly appointed officers had to be trained, then the governor chose Graziani.

In these lectures to the young officers, Graziani sometimes said things that were quite evident, such as 'The desert is the desert, it's not a stroll down Corso

Umberto', but for the most part, his ideas were very interesting, and for the 1920s they were completely accurate.

> In the desert, the real enemies are the sun, sandstorms, long distances and the sand. One fights for water. Where there is a well, a ditch, a *wadi*, there are rebels. Apart from being physically fit, marching in extreme temperatures requires moral strength and mental concentration. Whilst fighting on the dunes it is essential to maintain compact formations. A scattered column is a finished column. Apart from aeroplanes which are helpful for reconnaissance and machine gunning, vehicles are of little use. A lorry only transports the fuel it needs to move, so basically, it's not transporting anything. Only the camel is self-sufficient. In the desert, anyone who thinks they can do without a camel is an amateur.

We have illustrated the simple way in which Graziani set out his arguments because, in his daily life, he really did speak in a clear and simple manner. Mario Bassi, reporter for *La Stampa*: 'Rodolfo Graziani was well liked by his soldiers. They felt that he was one of them, he wasn't a haughty officer from the Military Academy. With his troops, Graziani used simple, direct language, often seasoned with swear words. He often said "bloody" to his Arab interpreter: "What the bloody hell are you translating?" To his guide he would say: "Where the bloody hell are you taking me?"' In 1920, Graziani thought about becoming a writer, but instead he would become an incorrigible whiner. He started jotting down notes for his forthcoming books, *Verso il Fezzan* (1929), *Cirenaica nuova* (1931), and many others. He wrote for *La gazzetta di Bengasi* and the monthly *Oltremare* magazine under the pseudonym *Gebelicus*. Intricate sentences, clichés, Latin phrases, exaggerated rhetoric: a disaster. In 1930, Roberto Cantalupo, head of the Italian Legation in Cairo and managing editor of *Oltremare*, committed the grave mistake of commissioning an autobiography. And so, Graziani gushed forth: 'I am so grateful to be able to write down my biography here in the desert, here, where everything is so similar to my nature. I was born ... [and here we go with the stories of his poor youth, his poor childhood], I grew up ... [and here we go with his sacrifices]':

> I walked alone in the world, trusting only my lucky star and my strength. *Vitae, sed non scholae discutir.* I have remained poor, I despise money, I despise all baseness and all the wretchedness which has been attributed to me. I am a monarchist, I have never been a freemason, I believe I have been a fascist since I was born, subconsciously. I have an iron will; I adore noble exploits. I have not written much because I have worked a lot. To make up for this I have studied a great deal: military matters, philosophy, economics, and politics. I know how to speak Arabic and Tigrinya. *Verso il Fezzan* is the book of my life. I have written it for this reason. In the world there are philosophers, merchants, and fighters: I am one of the latter, something of the former, and I have always had

an idiosyncratic relationship with the rest. Pythagoras said that in life, one must have a child, plant a tree, write a book and build a house. I have done all four of these things. The house I'm building in Bu Maad in the Gharyan, on the edge of the desert. I plan to live there in a simple manner. *Et de hoc satis.*

In 1929, Emilio De Bono was appointed Minister of the Colonies, taking the place of Luigi Federzoni. In Tripolitania, the newly arrived governor was Pietro Badoglio. Badoglio and Graziani did not know each other (from his autobiography: 'I had seen him once, he was an artillery captain and I, a young second lieutenant...'), but they immediately got on very well. Together, they examined the situation, and they concluded that it was necessary to start all over again. Badoglio had his own particular conception of war, considering it on a par with doing business, with losses and profits. In Tripolitania, things were not adding up—the oasis of Kufra was the last rebel stronghold. Even in Cyrenaica things were not going well, losses were exceeding profits. Of course, Graziani had done a great job, but the counter-insurgency operations were more importantly necessary for propaganda purposes. After seven years of 'victorious' fighting, all the Italians could boast of was miles of sand. Omar al-Mukhtar always managed to vanish into the wind. Idris was still leading the rebellion from his hideout in Egypt. the government of the night worked a lot better than that of the day. The *duars*, the villages of the interior, paid their tithes to Omar, they gave him food and shelter.[3] When asked, they replaced the fallen *zabet* with new 'martyrs of Islam'. Weapons were not a problem: they came as contraband from Egypt. Neither was ammunition: the collaborationist Libyan soldiers often gladly 'lost' their rounds on the roadside, so that the rebels could pick them up. To subdue the insurrection, it was time to change tack. Until then, things had been taken lightly; now, things would get serious. Mussolini did not want the word 'war' to be used, he preferred the term 'great policing operation'. But it was a war, and it had to be waged better. Badoglio and Graziani put together a plan called '*Delenda Senussia*'. The name said it all. Obviously, it was what Graziani did well.

The Italians possessed vague and inaccurate information on Omar al-Mukhtar. The identification cards of nine rebel chiefs can be found in the State Archive. Omar's document was the most generic, crammed with many phrases such as 'it has been said' and 'it would seem'.

Here follows a private report by Lt-Col. Raffaele Castriota of the Royal Carabinieri, Tripoli, 6 October 1926:

> The afore-mentioned Omar al-Mukhtar is notorious for being the leader of all leaders, the executive arm of the Emir Idris. It seems that he originates from the Defna region and that he is in his seventies. Taken individually, he is just an uncultured Bedouin. At best he can write his own name. Letters, announcements, and proclamations issued by him are really the work of the *ikhwan*, the Senussi scribes. Omar has been said to be a fanatic, more cunning than intelligent.

However, Omar al-Mukhtar exercises vast influence over the Arab population, in particular the nomads of the desert. Many consider him to be a saint or a holy man, or rather a marabout. Many believe he is protected by Allah. The truth is that al-Mukhtar rarely takes part in the fighting. He prefers to observe from afar, and if fate goes against him, he leaves, followed by his guards on horseback. There are no photos or portraits of him.

In this report by the *Carabinieri*, there are numerous inaccuracies. It is claimed that Omar al-Mukhtar could not write despite being a Sheik, and only if one had attended the Koranic school could they aspire to such a title.

Here is the real biography of the great rebel leader according to a document on the Senussi movement held in Cairo:

Date of birth: April 1862. Location: El Batuan in the Defna region, eastern Marmarica. Omar, together with his younger brother Mohammed, grew up in his parents' house with his mother Hargia Aisha and his father Mukhtar Ben Omar of the Mnifa tribe. In 1878, during a pilgrimage to Mecca, Mukhtar Ben Omar died. Before taking his last breath, he entrusted his two sons to his friend Hamedi al-Geriani al-Kemesi. When al-Geriani moved to Jaghbub, capital of Senusiyya, he enrolled the boys at the local Koranic school where Omar studied for eight years. Because of his lively intelligence, his knowledge of Islam and his proud and energetic character, when he finished his studies, Omar al-Mukhtar ingratiated himself into the family of the Grand Senussi, who wanted him by his side at Jaghbub and at Kufra. He had three wives: the first, a cousin, died a few months after the wedding; the second, the daughter of the famous Abdalla al-Gilani, head of the *zawiya* of Tocra, was repudiated as she was infertile;[4] the third, daughter of the head of the *zawiya* of Mirad Mesaud, was killed in the summer of 1927 during a foray by Italian troops. At forty years of age, being an eminent brother of Senusiyya, Ahmad al-Sharif nominated him Sheik of the monastery of El-Gsur, near the tribe of the Abid. He did not stay there long. In 1904 the Grand Senussi sent him as his delegate into the Wadai to fight the French; subsequently, Omar fought against the Turks, and at the same time, against the Italians who had waged war on the Turks. He never gave up, he never laid down his arms. After 1912 he tried to conquer Benghazi, but was pushed back with heavy casualties, and so he retreated into the Gebel to organize the guerrilla war and to create a *Mazbata*—a single block uniting all Muslims. In 1923, in recognition of his loyalty and his indomitable courage, the Grand Senussi elevated Omar al-Mukhtar to the post of Naib el'Am, General Representative of Senusiyya. He was then sixty, he was of medium height, sturdy, with white hair and a beard. He was always deeply religious and always extremely poor. Idris Senussi said of him: 'If we had ten men like Omar, we wouldn't need any more.'

The plan '*Delenda Senussia*' consisted precisely in capturing and eliminating Omar al-Mukhtar. This was logically what needed to be done according to Badoglio and Graziani: Idris was a philosopher and not a warrior (in fact, when he did become king, he was meek and tolerant), and the other rebel chiefs did not have sufficient authority. Following the death of Omar al-Mukhtar, the Senussi movement would disappear with him. And so, the main priority became capturing Omar in any way and by any means necessary. In order to isolate him, the nomads of Cyrenaica were enclosed in large concentration camps. The border with Egypt was sealed off by almost 300 km of barbed wire, many important citizens were incarcerated, put under house arrest, or banished. Many villagers were subject to lightning-fast trials conducted by special military tribunals where they were sentenced to death by firing squad. Rodolfo Graziani would be accused of atrocities, and even genocide. At Mecca, in the year 1349 of the *Hijrah* (1931 of the Christian era), the entire Muslim world proclaimed a jihad against the 'barbarous Italians'.

This lamentable page of our nation's history can be explained in a few ways. To the Italian people, the media of the regime explained the situation in this way. 'The concentration camps?' This expression was misleading. The nomads of Libya were used to moving and now they were being moved from one place to another. They were living as they had done before, in their encampments, in their tents, with their flocks. Actually, they were living better than before because in these protected areas the government offered the Bedouins hygienic living conditions, work, security, and education. The 'flying tribunals'? They guaranteed a rigorous application of the law. Honest citizens had nothing to fear from these tribunals but everything to gain. The frontier wire? A harsh but necessary measure. Added to the choir of minimising voices were, as there always are, the journalists and the overzealous writers. From Alessandro Sandri, author of *Il dramma intimo di Rodolfo Graziani*:

> In the most intense period of the pacification operation, the *kabila* of Abeidat was moved to an area around Derna and then transferred to the Barce area. The local commissioner arranged for tank-trucks filled with water to follow the mass of moving people, and that these vehicles be escorted by three battalions of Eritrean soldiers. The commissioner himself followed the great exodus by aeroplane: a multitude of people, some on camels, some on foot, and others on donkeys, followed by over 100,000 sheep. Graziani, accompanied by his wife, went to a pre-ordained spot and talked with the notables. He was struck by what they told him and by their sense of resignation. He was understanding and commiserated their state of tiredness, misery, and demoralization. Once, on a whim, he gave out all the money he had on him with his wife and his accompanying functionaries following suit. Graziani also gave an order to the commissioner to send all available funds to Barce and to enter these expenses under a column headed 'political expenses and subsidies'. He also arranged for medics, nurses and medicine to be sent to the camps. He had rice, fruit and other food stuffs brought over from Benghazi.

It was like something out of a fairy-tale.

The truth according to the Arabs was totally different. Every day, the Egyptian newspapers published stories and reports from refugees in Cyrenaica. They talked about burning villages, people robbed of all their possessions, and of mass executions. Graziani was portrayed as 'the cruel beast', 'bloodthirsty', 'the butcher'. Because of him, Cyrenaica was no longer green, but red. In the concentration camps, the *Carabinieri* seemed mostly busy with beating up prisoners whose fate was already sealed: having been deprived of their liberty, the Bedouins just gave up and died, and with them their cattle, which had been left without grazing land. One day, the weekly *Afrique française* printed a photograph on its front page—how it was taken no one knows—of six hanged Libyans from Barce: in Tunis, Fez, Cairo, and in distant Iraq, the crowds started pelting the Italian consulates and embassies with rocks. The Egyptian writer Mohammed al-Akhdar al-Isawi wrote an eye-opening account, explaining that for the Italians and the Europeans in general, the nomads of the desert were a burden because they could not integrate themselves into western society. Therefore, the concentration camps served two purposes: to drastically reduce the number of Bedouins and to replace them with colonists. 'Today,' al-Isawi concluded in an exaggerated manner, 'the population of Cyrenaica seems to have been halved.' Alongside the more or less truthful coverage of the events in Libya, the Arab press frequently fabricated stories. They claimed that Graziani had become ferocious 'because the patriots had castrated him'. Or that he was bloodthirsty 'because rather than having them be caught, he had had to kill his wife and daughter'. Or again that he had always been cruel, and he had demonstrated this during the Great War by executing retreating Italian soldiers. The old 'Andrea Graziani' mistake continued to cause problems.

There is a way of avoiding disinformation caused by using biased and partisan sources. In 1944, the American Military Intelligence Service confiscated four crates of Graziani's personal documents which were held in the Basilica of Saint Agnes in Rome. After the war, these crates were given back to the Italian government and the Joint Diplomatic Section entrusted them to Italy's Central State Archive.[5] Among the papers contained therein, many have to do with the 'pacification' of Libya. They are both interesting and comprehensive; therefore, we believe that the most honest thing to do is to narrate the events leading up to Omar al-Mukhtar's hanging according to the documents.

Tripoli, 8 May 1929. From Pietro Badoglio to Emilio De Bono, Ministry of the Colonies. Secret. Here, the rebellion hinges on one man. Omar al-Mukhtar is an incredibly able organizer and an inflexible commander. He executes cowards and traitors. Because of this, we have scant information about him. His *zabet* are loyal to him, they are rather like the *bravi* of the sixteen hundreds or the nineteenth century brigands of southern Italy. They fight for the love of their nation and hatred towards Christians. To corrupt them is impossible. I believe that a precise operation is in order, no more games. In any case, I will make a final attempt to come to some sort of agreement.

Rome, 12 May 1929. From Emilio De Bono to Pietro Badoglio, Governor of Tripolitania. Proceed, the outcome is all that matters.

Badoglio's attempt to parley with Omar al-Mukhtar actually did happen. A meeting was arranged through the intermediary Roberto Cantalupo in Cairo, who told Idris, who in turn informed Omar. The location would be the oasis of Sidi Rahumah, 6 km from Barce. Badoglio came on his own, as agreed. Omar al-Mukhtar came galloping up with 150 men on horseback and only at the last moment did he lower his Mauser in sign of peace. For the governor of Tripolitania, the meeting was humiliating. After giving him quite a scare, the rebel leader treated him like a servant. 'There will never be a truce between us *maqtub*, it is written,' said Omar. Then, he spat on the floor and trampled on the golden watch which Badoglio had just given to him. It was 19 June 1929. From that day onwards, there would be an all-out war between the Italians and the Senussi.

Tripoli, 9 July 1929. Here follows the governor's speech on the radio: 'Italy knows how to be generous. She promises peace, tranquillity and wellbeing to those who submit and death, destruction and ruin to those who try to resist...'

'Tripoli, 12 July 1929. From Badoglio to Graziani. Cyphered. Please inform me of the exact consistency of our armed forces and the spirit which rallies amongst the soldiers.'

'Benghazi, 13 July 1929. From Graziani to Badoglio. Cyphered. We have at our disposal 439 officers, 609 NCOs, 2,083 national soldiers and 8,475 natives. Morale is high. Only the Libyan troops cannot be fully trusted. I have therefore ordered the disbanding of two Libyan battalions. We've changed the rifles of the remaining ones, instead of the model 91, they are now using the Mannlicher rifle which is of a different calibre.'

'Tripoli, 15 July 1929. From Badoglio to Graziani. Cyphered. Begin clean up. Rebels captured with weapons are to be executed.'

The autumn and winter of 1929 saw the Italians engaged in large mopping-up operations. The rebels were hunted day and night in the Hamadah, in the desert, and in Shurayf. Being the highest-ranking officer, Graziani hardly ever personally took part in the fighting. He simply directed the operations by giving out draconian orders. For example: 'I do not want shootouts from afar as is the Arab custom. When the enemy has been discovered, it's better to resort to melee weapons, they are decisive. Give no quarter, pursue the enemy in a ferocious and relentless manner. We will go on for years if necessary. We are not here for a *fantasia*'. In the spring of 1930, despite a series of undeniable successes on the field, the situation remained unchanged, with Omar al-Mukhtar still free and on the run. However, the rebel ranks seemed to be thinning and, on 22 February 1930, Graziani wrote an optimistic report to Badoglio. 'We have learnt from a reliable source that, currently, Omar al-Mukhtar and his men are only 800 in total, 300 of whom on horseback. The *duars* still supporting him are few, those of the Braga, Dorsa, and Abeidat tribes. The noose is tightening, the holy man is gasping for air'. Satisfied by this report, Badoglio wrote to De Bono in reassuring terms and the latter proposed Graziani as vice-governor of Cyrenaica to Mussolini. On March 27, the new vice-governor debuted with a speech to the locals from the government palace in Benghazi: 'We have nothing against the Muslim world, we respect the Koran and your religion. We are fighting Senusiyya, a fanatical sect, a purulent plague...' He then went on to have a chat in the officers' club. To them, he said 'We must maintain our movements and intentions secret. My orders are to be cunning, find the rebels, take them by surprise, kill at least one a day. And move, move, move without mercy, without sentimentality'. The war once again took off in all its savagery. But there was still no trace of Omar al-Mukhtar. It was as if he had vanished into thin air.

> Tripoli, 20 June 1930. From Badoglio to Graziani. Private communication. Omar al-Mukhtar still refuses to give battle. It's the same old tactic, if attacked he disperses his troops. The plan must be implemented in full. We must gather the populations under our control in appropriate areas. Rome has been informed and approves. Of course, I am aware of the fact that such a measure will mean the ruin, economically and otherwise, of the populations in question.

> Benghazi, 21 June 1930, Graziani to Badoglio. Private. I agree. I also propose the formation of special mobile courts to administer justice more speedily.

Starting from 1 July 1930 until the end of the month, the frequency of telegrams and private messages between Tripoli–Benghazi–Rome increased tenfold. An almost biblical migration was taking place. Tens of thousands of nomads escorted by soldiers descended the Marmarican plateau towards concentration camps prepared for them in Sirte and Benghazi.

Badoglio to Graziani: 'I understand that the gathering up of the so-called subjugated populations is going as planned, and despite the great numbers involved, it's all in good order. I am pleased'.

Graziani to Badoglio: 'The Bedouins have understood that we are in charge here. They obey subserviently. There have been no hostile reactions worthy of any mention'.

Mussolini to Badoglio-Graziani: 'Urgent. Avoid, I repeat, avoid the term "concentration camps." Rather, call them collection camps or protected zones'.

Badoglio to Graziani: 'While we're at it, let's take advantage of this opportunity to carry out a census of the men and their cattle. At least we'll know how many of these Libyans there are. P.S. Ensure vigilance around collection camps'.

Graziani to Badoglio: 'I am proceeding in the desired direction. As for security, it's taken care of by the Eritrean soldiers, all extremely loyal'.

Badoglio to Graziani: 'I now await the surrender of the rebels. If this should not happen, we will proceed drastically in two directions: 1. Gather all the relatives of the rebels in a small well-guarded camp where the living conditions are rather uncomfortable; 2. Arrest the notables who are against us in the *kabilas* and in Benghazi. We shall see whether to exile them to Italy or to other distant colonies'.

Omar al-Mukhtar and his men did not surrender. But they were now no more than a band of ragged and poorly armed individuals. However, in August, on the Derna–Tobruk highway, two *Carabinieri* and five *zaptié* were killed. Badoglio arranged for an aerial reprisal and he telegraphed Graziani, telling him to 'Make restrictions in the camps harsher by forbidding the grazing of cattle'. Graziani went further: he ordered the requisitioning of all weapons in private possession; he issued a proclamation entitled: 'For the breaking of the rebellion' which included the death penalty for 'anyone supplying weapons to the rebels or paying a tithe to Senusiyya'.

The desert was getting a lot nastier. On the plateau emptied of its inhabitants, air squadrons from the airfield of Apollonia machine gunned and bombed down anything that moved. In the coastal cities and the villages of the interior, the mobile tribunals (better known as 'flying tribunals' because they flew on aeroplanes) worked around the clock, dishing out justice, going from a simple investigation to a sentence in less than three hours. In his desperate struggle, Omar al-Mukhtar could only receive supplies from Egypt with caravans that crossed the border at night. They would also cut off that last lifeline with a frontier wire entanglement laid down from Bardia to Jaghbub. In September 1930, aerial reconnaissance in Marmarica spotted a group of men on horseback coming through the undergrowth. Two columns of soldiers set off immediately from Derna. Graziani flew over to reach them and put himself at the head of the column. These were definitely rebels who had been surprised at dusk, they were attacked and routed. The chase lasted for days until the 9 October, when the Italians encountered a large rebel formation encamped in Wadi as Saniya. In the firefight that followed, Omar al-Mukhtar's horse was killed, causing him to fall to the ground and lose his glasses. He was about to be captured when his bodyguard shielded him and gave him a new horse to escape on.

Graziani to Badoglio, 10 October 1930: 'Yesterday we unequivocally confirmed the existence of Omar al-Mukhtar whose gold glasses in a silver case we now have in our possession. Gone are all the doubts regarding his existence and that he might have moved away from Cyrenaica. Thus, the rebel leader is beginning to understand what it means to wage a real war: isolated, without any immediate supplies, without the support of the local population allowing him to create the myth of his supposed invincibility. Now we have his glasses, next we will have his head'.

Badoglio to Graziani, 11 October: 'A heartfelt bravo! Do not give up! Let the Bedouin hunt continue, I've raised the bounty to 200,000 lira'.

In December, the hunt was suspended. Bounty or no bounty, Omar had gone missing again. On 6 December, Graziani was in Tripoli to confer with Badoglio. He told him: 'Things aren't going as they should. There's agitation in Benghazi, the population is tired. The notables complain because they are being slapped around by both us and the rebels. We need to hurry things up. I propose closing the border with Egypt with a frontier wire and going on an expedition to the oasis of Kufra. Kufra is the heart of Senusiyya. Perhaps al-Mukhtar is hiding there'. The march on Kufra— 820 km into the desert—was one of the largest operations of the pacification. In January 1931, 5,000 camels and 316 vehicles set off from Ajdabiya. The *mehari* squadrons had six days' worth of food and water, while the Saharan groups had thirty days of food and water and eight days of barley. They marched on at breakneck speed, two hours on the move and one hour's rest, uninterruptedly. Kufra was defended by 500 men. It was bombarded by twenty aeroplanes, surrounded, and then stormed in less than two hours; 100 rebels were left lying on the ground. Graziani, who had reached the expedition destination by plane, examined the dead one by one. Omar al-Mukhtar was not there, and he was not even among the prisoners. There was only one card left to play, barbed wire.

Graziani vented his anger to Roberto Cantalupo, Italy's man in Egypt:

Benghazi, 28 January 1931: From Rodolfo Graziani to Roberto Cantalupo, Italian Legation in Cairo. Through diplomatic courier. I can see you're having problems but try to understand mine. I'm not whining, this has to be done. The weapons supplied to Omar al-Mukhtar are coming from Egypt, and I cannot invade Egypt,

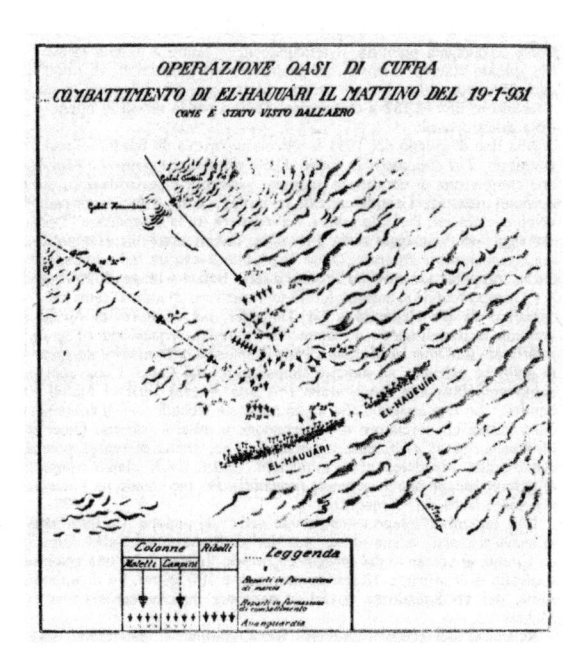

Libya, January 1931. The oasis of Kufra was the last stronghold of the Senussi 'rebels'. It was occupied by a large expeditionary force. Above, an aerial view of the operation.

a foreign country which is officially neutral. The Egyptians are protesting? Let them, they're all liars. I've had enough of Arab diplomacy and its tricky ways. If they think I'm an ass in lion's clothing, then they're mistaken. I'll strike the enemy at his heart, I'll strangle him with steely ferocity, a more western type of ferocity which, if I might say, is almost pagan. What I say is sincerely fascist.

The works for laying down the frontier wire began in March. Report from the military engineers' corps to His Excellency the vice-governor of Cyrenaica:

> As can be seen from the enclosed map, the entanglement is to be a double strip of zinc barbed wire. The cost, including the construction of small forts every 25 km and larger forts every 50 km, comes to an estimated 46,582 lira per km. Completion time: between three and four months.

At the end of June 1931, the entanglement ran from Bardia to the oasis of Jaghbub, 270 km in total. From the collection points, which could house about fifty men, the troops went out on patrols as far as the nearest small fort. Large signs in Italian and Arabic warned: 'Do not approach! Danger Mines!' The border between Cyrenaica and Egypt, which in the language of guerrilla warfare is called a 'sanctuary', was now sealed. Omar al-Mukhtar now had a hard time finding where to hide, he was trapped, and he could not stay on the loose for long. On 25 August, the 5th Saharan mobile group stopped a caravan of five camels coming from Bir Hemenin to Bir Tangeder in the Mechili territory. During the search the soldiers found forty letters written by Omar al-Mukhtar addressed to Emir Idris, Egyptian ministers, dignitaries, friends, and sympathisers in Cairo. The greetings were elaborate as is the Arab custom ('To His Highness Idris al-Mahdi es Senussi, may God aid him and may his seed be fertile…'), the content of the letters revealed his desperation and misery. Omar al-Mukhtar wrote: 'We urgently need everything, even shoes as we are now barefoot. Send us weapons, rounds, clothes, food: and for myself a pair of binoculars and the holy Koran…' On 11 September, the rebel leader fell into Italian hands. An informer had notified the authorities of his presence at the *dor* of Brahasa in the Gebel. A cavalry column made up of nine officers, thirty Italian soldiers, and 300 Eritreans led by Maj. Corrado Ragazzi raced from Cyrene immediately. It was Capt. Berté's VII Savari Squadron that captured Omar al-Mukhtar.

Report of Capt. Roberto Berté, Slonta, 11 September 1931:

> At six in the morning, I intercepted the enemy. When the rebels, who were about a hundred, saw us, they started fleeing in a compact formation. I put myself at the head of the squadron and started chasing them. We were getting closer and closer and at 300 m we started firing, and at this point, the rebels tried to confuse us by attempting a divertive manoeuvre and dispersing. I ordered my *savari* to keep on pursuing a group of about thirty horsemen who continued to flee in

a tight formation. Towards eight o'clock, at 6 km from the collection point at Slonta, a rifle shot brought down an enemy horse. The man who was riding it tumbled to the ground, he got back up with some difficulty, he tried to get away with a slow and heavy gait. Two *savari* who approached him were just about to cut him down with their sabres when they saw he was old and thought he might well be Omar al-Mukhtar. Therefore, I prudently stopped the chase. The man, wounded on his left arm, didn't resist. He was then loaded onto one of the squadron's horses and taken under armed escort to Slonta. A sanitation assistant provided him with medical care. Whilst awaiting further instructions we notified our casualties which were one horse and one wounded. Enemy casualties: eleven rebels and fourteen horses killed, eight horses captured, and five muskets taken.

Capt. Berté received his instructions at 10:40 p.m. There followed an urgent telegram from Pietro Badoglio, which said: 'Ascertain prisoner's identity and make sure he is completely isolated'. On 12 September, Omar al-Mukhtar, tired and refusing to answer any questions, was taken first to Apollonia and then on a torpedo ship to Benghazi. Meanwhile, Badoglio telegraphed Rome.

'Tripoli, 12 September 1931. From Governor of Tripolitania to Minister of the Colonies. '6318 top secret…. In the event of the prisoner really being Omar al-Mukhtar, I believe we have the chance to put him on trial with a subsequent sentence, which will no doubt be death. This should be carried out in an area with a high concentration of native people'.

Badoglio finally received confirmation from Benghazi commissioner Giuseppe Daodiace:

Today, 13 September, I talked with the prisoner who is a guest at the prison infirmary. In the end he admitted to effectively being Omar al-Mukhtar. I interrogated him. He said that we caught him because his men had run out of ammunition. He even tried to convince us that nothing would change on the guerrilla front. There would be a reunion of the *duar* where a new military commander would be chosen amongst four rebel leaders: the favourite seemed to be Yousaf Borahil. Omar al-Mukhtar then started blarting typical Arab lies. Such as: 'at Brahasa I had horsemen and 500 men on foot, the fighters of Allah are still in their thousands…' I tried ribbing him, I told him: 'Your capture was wanted by God.' He replied: 'Not by God, by the will of God. I did not fight for hatred but for religious faith. Now I'm in your hands, do what you will, God will plan my fate.' Regarding his wound he told me it was nothing, just a graze.

In those crucial days, Graziani was in Italy. He had observed the military manoeuvres, and on the morning of the 14th, he was with his wife at Termini train station in Rome. He was about to go on holiday to Paris, a chance to relax, and also to see the colonial exhibition. They called his name over the loudspeaker.

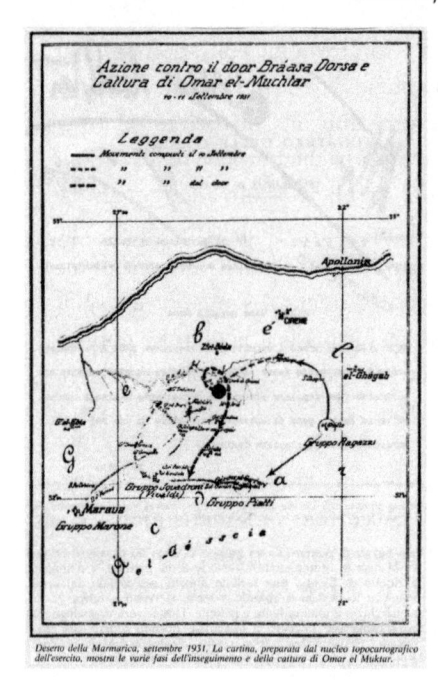

Desert of Marmarica, September 1931. The map shows each phase of Omar al-Mukhtar's capture.

He learnt of the news at the Ministry of War (the newspapers would claim that he had had a 'premonition' about it), and then he ran to Ostia where a seaplane was waiting to take off. Lady Ines said, 'And so it was, we didn't go to Paris, not then, not ever.' On 15 September at the government building in Benghazi, Graziani had a long interview with Omar al-Mukhtar. They talked for two hours; a secretary wrote down everything, word for word. Here is the conversation in its entirety:[6]

> *Graziani* (through his interpreter Capt. Kalifa Kaled): 'Because of you many thousands of Libyans are dead. Was it worth it?'
> *Prisoner*: 'They died serving a good cause. They are in paradise'.
> *Graziani*: 'This is religious fanaticism'.
> *Prisoner*: 'No, this is faith'.
> *Graziani*: 'Why did you fight so doggedly against the Italian Government?'
> *Prisoner*: 'Because of my religion'.
> *Graziani*: 'You had few men and even fewer means. Did you really think you could kick us out of Cyrenaica?'
> *Prisoner*: 'No, that was impossible'.
> *Graziani*: 'What were you proposing then?'
> *Prisoner*: 'Nothing. I just fought, that's all, the rest was in the hands of destiny'.
> *Graziani*: 'But the Koran says that waging a Jihad is only permissible when there is hope of victory, to avoid pointless suffering for the population. Does the Koran not say this?'

Prisoner: 'Yes'.

Graziani: 'I ask you again. Why did you fight?'

Prisoner: 'Because of my religion'.

Graziani: 'No, you fought for Senusiyya which is a crooked political gamble which you, Idris and all your gang have lived off, at the expense of the people of Cyrenaica for whom you've always shown little interest. This is why you fought, not because of your religion'.

Prisoner: does not respond, but grins.

Graziani: 'Why did you turn down all peace negotiations, why did you order the attack on Gars Benigden?'

Prisoner: 'Because for a month I had been waiting in vain for a reply to a letter I had sent to Marshal Badoglio'.

Graziani: That is false. Your refusal to collaborate in the pacification was a premeditated decision, and the proof is in this proclamation signed by you and published in Cairo'.

Prisoner: does not respond.

Graziani: 'Did you order the killings of the pilots Hueber and Beati?'

Prisoner: 'Yes. After all, it's always the leaders' fault, war is war'.

Graziani: 'When it's a real war, not a bandit assassination like yours'.

Prisoner: 'It depends on how you look at it'.

Graziani: 'With your crimes you've lost any right to the government's clemency'.

Prisoner: '*Maqtub*, it was written. When I was captured, I still had six rounds on me, I could have killed or been killed. And yet I did not defend myself'.

Graziani: 'And why didn't you defend yourself?'

Prisoner: '*Maqtub*, it was written. Listen general, I'm old, let me sit down'.

Graziani: 'Sit down and listen. Perhaps you may still be able to save your life. Are you able, with your authority, to make the rebels of the Gebel submit?'

Prisoner: 'As a prisoner I can do nothing. And I would never do it. We swore to die, all of us, one by one, but never to submit. I would never have given myself up of my own free will. This is certain'.

Graziani: 'If we had met each other before, perhaps we could have done something good for the pacification'.

Prisoner: 'And can't today be that day?'

Graziani: 'Too late. You just declared that, as a prisoner, you can do nothing'.

Prisoner: does not reply.

Graziani: 'Do you recognize these glasses?'

Prisoner: 'Yes, they're mine. I lost them whilst fighting at Wadi as Saniya'.

Graziani: 'From that day I was sure that you would fall into my hands'.

Prisoner: '*Maqtub*, it was written. Give me back my glasses, I can't see well. Actually, keep them: you have me and them in your hands'.

Graziani: 'Is it true that you considered yourself protected by God because you fought for a righteous cause?'

Prisoner: 'Yes'.

Graziani: 'Then listen. Before my troops, from Nalut to the Cyrenaican Gebel, all the rebel leaders have either fled or fallen in combat. But none have been captured alive. Why is it then that you are here? Were you not invincible, the uncatchable one, the one protected by God? Could it be that maybe I'm the one protected by God?'

Prisoner: 'God is great, and his designs are mysterious'.

Graziani: 'I have reason to believe that in your life you were a strong man. I hope you will continue to be one, no matter what may happen'.

Prisoner: '*Inshallah*'.

Rodolfo Graziani also published the text of his interview with Omar al-Mukhtar in his book *Cirenaica Pacificata*. Compared to the original document, there are few changes. What is more interesting are the minor observations. The rebel leader was shown into the office of the vice-governor in handcuffs and chains. He dragged his gouty feet, the impression he gave was that of a poor old man, humble and modest. When he was dismissed, he lifted his barracan, which covered his body and part of his face, bowed down, and stretched out his hand in sign of friendship. Graziani did not want to shake his hand.

Omar al-Mukhtar's trial started that very same day, 15 September, at 5 p.m. in the reception hall of the Palazzo del Littorio in Benghazi. The main square opposite the building was crammed with people. In front of the Military Tribunal (presiding judge, Lt-Col. Marinoni; the defence counsel, Capt. Lontano; the prosecutor, Col. Bedendo), Omar al-Mukhtar behaved with dignity: he insisted on being addressed by his titles, Sheik and General Representative of Senusiyya, he had no objections to being found guilty of all the crimes of which he had been charged, he only denied that he 'had ever directly ordered violence or torture against the Italian prisoners of the Senussite army'. He was sentenced to death by hanging. At 9 a.m. the following day, 16 September 1931, he stepped on to the gallows.[7] Soluch concentration camp had been chosen for the event. Here, Graziani assembled all the camps' prisoners and the Arab notables who had been exiled to Benina and other villages near Benghazi. While the hangman was putting the noose around his neck, Omar al-Mukhtar said: 'We come from God and to God we return'. His body was transported to Benghazi and buried in the Islamic cemetery of Sabri on 17 September. In the meantime, in Rome, the Stefani news agency reported the execution with but a few sentences, 'so as not to create any martyrs'.

As expected, the death of Omar al-Mukhtar meant the immediate end of the guerrilla war. '*Delenda Senusiyya*' had worked perfectly. It was time to look at the balance and Pietro Badoglio, who was a master with numbers, deemed everything to be satisfactory.

Sum of the counter-insurgency operations: From Army Headquarters: 'In the past twenty-one months there have been fifty firefights and 2,210 conflicts.

Rebels killed: 1,605. Rebels captured: 70. Cattle killed or confiscated: camels: 6,600; horses: 833; cows: 21,552. Our losses: 151 dead, no wounded'.

Balance of the activities of the special military Tribunal. Rodolfo Graziani to the Ministry of War. Report:

> The special military tribunals fulfilled five requirements: 1, immediate repression of crimes; 2, in the area where the crimes were perpetrated; 3, in front of the local populace; 4, by observing norms and laws in force; 5, sentences handed out with extremely clear and solemn judgement. All these necessities were carried out perfectly. Being able to utilize the most rapid vehicles, in particular the aeroplane, they have demonstrated to the people of Cyrenaica that Italian justice descends from the sky like a sword. The trials always took place in the main village squares, where the inhabitants were able to ascertain that justice is rapid but fair. The accused were granted the assistance of an interpreter and the sentences—given that it all took place on one day, investigation, debate, verdict—were swiftly executed. To debunk foreign propaganda, which has talked about summary justice and judges followed by firing squads, I should like to illustrate the following data. In the previous twelve months the special military tribunals, better known as the 'flying Tribunals', have carried out 520 trials against 899 people. There have been 133 death sentences, 177 varying other sentences, and 198 were absolved. A further 229 suspects were exiled: currently, 186 are located in Benina and forty-three in Ustica.

The balance of the situation regarding the native population in the 'gathering' camps. From the command of the Royal *Carabinieri*:

> There is no social unrest in the camps, and the living conditions of the nomads gathered therein are satisfactory. More specifically: The camp of Abiar presently holds 3,123 people and is equipped with drinking water, a medical tent, an entomological station to fight locusts and a primary school; the camp of Soluch holds 20,123 people and is equipped with drinking water, a hospital and a primary school with an annexed teachers' house; the camp of Sidi Ahmed el-Maghrun holds 13,050 people and is equipped with drinking water, a medical tent, and a school; the camp of Suani Terria holds 7,547 people and is equipped with the same services as the Sidi Ahmed el-Maghrun camp; the camp of El Agheila holds 10,900 people with the same abovementioned facilities; finally, the camp of Marsa Brega, holds 21,072 people who, given the camp's position next to the sea, benefit from fishing boats together with the usual medical and educational facilities. In total the number of prisoners is 76,815. Meanwhile, after the census, the population residing in the colony amounts to 156,000 inhabitants.

The balances which we have illustrated, being biased, are in all probability lower than what they really were, but they are also the only numbers we have. It would be unreasonable to consider as true the fantastical figures (21,123 Libyans fallen in combat, 15,131 crippled, 5,867 executed etc.) given by Col. Gaddafi to back up his request for war reparations. Moreover, the documents from the Italian side were secret and restricted to a few individuals who, presumably, wanted facts and not fancy. Precisely because of this, looking through other documents dating back to 1932 and 1933, it is possible to recreate a dossier of uncomfortable truths regarding the real living conditions of the nomads deported to the concentration camps. Let us look at the following examples.

Benghazi, 9 January 1932. Regional commissariat: 'We report a large murrain of cattle in the camp of Suani al-Terria. The prisoners complain that they have no winter clothing. Cases of illness such as trachoma and typhus are common. A steam room is needed to delouse the tents'.

Tripoli, 29 July 1932. Badoglio to Graziani: 'I believe it's premature to release the exiled Senussi sympathizers. Let's continue to keep the camps open. The Bedouins are fine where they are. What we do need are colonists from Italy'.

Benghazi, 6 March 1933. Regional commissariat 'Conditions in the Soluch camp are getting worse. There are seventy infected tents and 3,400 cases of petechial typhus. We have isolated the main camp in order to stop the virus spreading, the medical authorities have been informed'.

Benghazi, 12 March 1933. Medical directorate: 'Medics and medicine have been sent to Soluch. However, typhus has always been common amongst the Bedouins. We predict a regression of the disease with the start of the hot season'.

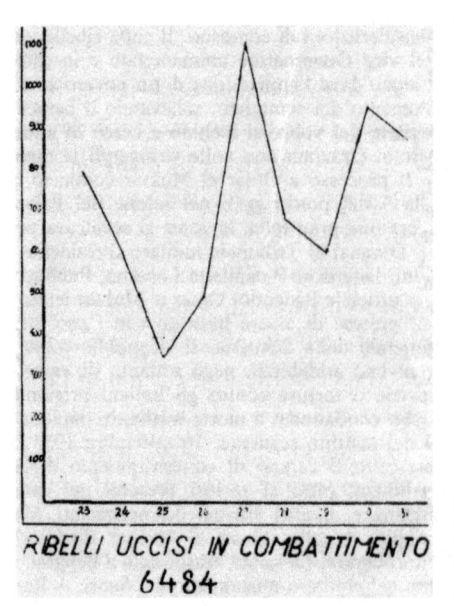

Libya, 1932. It was time to check the balance. This graph illustrates enemy losses between 1923 and 1931. In total, the rebels killed in combat amounted to 6,484.

Benghazi, 17 April 1933. Command Royal *Carabinieri*: 'we propose the evacuation of all children from Soluch, and, for everyone else, an increase in food rations. We have also arranged for a transferral plan with lorries for the sick and invalids. The only problem which remains unsolved is that of the dying cattle'.

Tripoli, 2 December 1933. Economic report: '... even the herds of cattle are being replenished. There were 270,000 cattle in 1930, dwindling to 67,000 in 1931. Today, they have increased to 220,000'.

Benghazi, 29 December 1933. Interview in the *Berliner Boersen Zeitung* with Rodolfo Graziani: 'I have destroyed one third of Libya's livestock. I had to take a decision and I took it. Italian honour first, then the sheep'.

Such was the reality of the concentration camps. They were not like Dachau, but they were not pleasant holiday resorts either. Anyhow, Mussolini said that it was time to stop talking about all of this. The guerrilla war, the flying tribunals, the camps, they belonged to the past, it was now time to think about the future.

If they had been busy as military officials, Badoglio and Graziani proved to be even more zealous as civil administrators. In a few short years, Tripolitania and Cyrenaica changed completely. Italian colonists arrived in droves (in 1938, there were already 120,000), building sites as far as the eye could see, houses, roads, and aqueducts were popping up everywhere. Where there used to be sand, there were now gardens and orchards, around the new model farms rows of date-palms and fruit trees were springing up. It was the '*Libia redenta*' and the 'New Cyrenaica' described in Graziani's new books of the same name. He had become a workaholic, spending twelve or fourteen hours a day at his desk. In his office in Benghazi, he put up another sign, which this time said: 'it is imperative to work with your head down'. His colleagues were at breaking point, but they dared not say anything as Graziani could have had them transferred immediately. He poked his nose into all matters, he wanted to know everything about everyone. The circulars that he sent out nonstop bore witness to this:

> The fight against bureaucracy, 20 February 1932. From Vice Governor to employees. Enough with coffee breaks. Business needs to be speeded up, you have the telephone, use it. Every letter which you receive needs answering. I demand a daily list of all written responses.

> The fight against gambling, 7 March 1932. From Vice Governor to officers. I have noticed a few officers busy playing poker in the Grand Hotel. I do not want to see this again. Those who wear the uniform shouldn't gamble, at least not in public.

> On bearing and discipline, 20 May 1932. From Vice Governor to officers, NCOs, and soldiers. Disregard for one's uniform, not saluting and incorrect behaviour towards ladies are traces of a non-military mentality. I will be implacable towards those who break these rules.

Relations with native women, 17 September 1932. From Vice Governor to officers. Today I have ordered the repatriation of Lt Gaetano Pizzi ['he shared his bed and his meals with a native prostitute from the local brothel'] and Capt. Giuseppe Alfonsi ['he held intimate relations with native women by sending sums of cash to their relatives']. Let those who intend to imitate them be warned. Relationships with native women are unbecoming of an officer.

Fight against laziness, 8 October 1932. From Vice Governor to officers. The end of the counter-insurgency operations is not an excuse for being idle. I would like to remind the gentlemen officers, and not only them, that here you are serving the Nation, and that if you're ambitious, you can further your career. I recommend reading specialist studies on colonial problems, attending conferences and the Benghazi library. I would like to highlight, amongst others, Lt-Col. Valletti Borghini's booklet *Guerra nelle zone desertiche*, the Italian Lambert manual and the French Piscer one, all about war in the desert. And also, the book *The Revolt in the Desert* by the Englishman Thomas Edward Lawrence.[8]

We could go on for many more pages, but it is unnecessary. Suffice to say, among other things, Graziani found time to establish the Arab Lictor Youth, to explain to the colonists how to cultivate the land (he claimed to be an expert.) and to tell the NCOs how to handle their money ('If you want, each one of you can save 200 lira a month'). For those under his command, he was a huge 'pain in the arse', but for the *Duce*, he was a collaborator of uncommon efficiency. In January 1932, on Badoglio's suggestion (who, while praising him, wrote of him: 'he is suspicious by character, he suffers from a persecution complex and because of this, thinks ill of his fellow man'), Mussolini promoted him to army general. A grateful Graziani responded with an overly obsequious telegram, which said: 'I can assure you I shall be devoted to you all my life until I die. My past actions bear witness to that'.

The past, which the Italians wanted to forget, had not been forgotten by the influential Egyptian societies in Cairo and the Muslims of the Arab world. Soon after Omar al-Mukhtar's hanging, a symbolic jihad was declared in Mecca against the 'barbarous and infidel' Italy. In Cairo, Baghdad, Yemen, and Saudi Arabia, there were protests and demonstrations, one after the other. Feelings were running high. Alongside commemorations of Omar al-Mukhtar, now called 'the Lion of the Desert', there were mass prayers where the crowds shouted: 'Arab brothers, let us pay homage to our great martyr'. In June 1932, the Cairo press proposed a boycott of all Italian goods. The boycott was formally adhered to by all of the Muslims in Africa and Asia: all things made in Italy had to be banned, Italian ships should not be allowed to unload, Italian schools and institutions abroad should be avoided as 'infected places'. King Victor Emanuel III, who until then had been watching from the side-lines, now summoned Marshal Badoglio to the Quirinale and declared himself 'annoyed and worried' by the violence of these reactions. The little king was not a sentimentalist, he thought along the same lines as Talleyrand, that mistakes were the worst crimes and that the execution of Omar al-Mukhtar had been a mistake. 'We could have exiled him, the French exiled Abd el-Krim,' he told the governor of Tripolitania. Badoglio took the scolding in silence; he then defended his and Graziani's work and assured the sovereign that 'the Arabs who are agitating are four nobodies, devoid of any real power. Therefore, their threats should not be taken seriously'. He was perfectly right.

If the Arabs protested, the nations of the west had nothing to reproach Italy with. As a matter of fact, in their own colonies, the British, French, and Belgians had behaved in more or less the same way as the Italians, and sometimes with harsher methods. This is how colonial politics were carried out in those days, and it would continue to be this way until the 1950s (see French Algeria, the paratroopers of Col. Massu, and the book on torture by Henri Alleg). It was inconceivable that guerrillas could actually win. Those that did win by hook or by crook were the regular army. To the western powers, the atrocities were just unpleasant but inevitable collateral damage. To confirm this, here are three hard facts that need to be evaluated. First, the history of the 'pacification' of Libya which we have just recounted according to official documents does not reveal anything new that, by and large, was not already common knowledge. The construction of the concentration camps and the frontier wire was no secret: on the contrary, it was allotted to a public contractor and given to the Italian construction and public works company based in Rome, via del Tritone, number 102. In his books, Graziani openly talks about this, and if few people are aware of this, it is due to the fact that—as Missiroli would say in his famous joke— 'there is nothing so unpublished as what is in print'.[9] Secondly, in relation to Libya and other renowned international organizations (the League of Nations, the international Red Cross, the Holy See), no charges or indictments were pressed against Italy. Graziani, in a speech on 11 February 1933 given at the Palazzo del Littorio in Benghazi, brought up the accusations against him made by the Arabs and rebuked them by saying: 'In the seminary I acquired the habit of examining my conscience. Often, in these months, I have examined my conscience in connection with these accusations of cruelty and violence brought against me. Well then, I can assure you that I have never slept so well. History teaches us that you cannot build the new without destroying all or part of the old'. On another occasion, Graziani invoked Machiavelli:

> I invite those who accuse me to read Machiavelli again, especially where he attests: 'A Prince should therefore disregard the reproach of being thought of as cruel where it enables him to keep his subjects united and obedient. For he who quells disorder by a very few signal examples will in the end be more merciful than he who from too great leniency permits things to take their course and so result in murder and bloodshed.'

After 1931 and until 1934, when he returned to Italy, Graziani received many foreign delegations (we have already mentioned those of Gen. Wavell and Col. Stevens), myriad decorations (1931, Commander of the Order of Saints Maurice and Lazarus, the sash of the Colonial Order of the Star of Italy; 1932, Grand Officer of the Order of the Crown of Italy; 1933, Knight's Grand Cross of the Order of the Crown of Italy; 1934, Grand Officer of the Order of Saints Maurice and Lazarus), and highly exaggerated praise and compliments. Marshal Hubert Lyautey of France, conqueror and 'pacifier' of Morocco, wrote to him in a letter of 6 May 1934: 'Regarding methods of occupation, of pacification and politics towards the locals, yourself and I have the same conceptions and I feel honoured'. Thirdly, the regrets and the reflections are only of these last thirty years, but the rejection of the past in every people is always accompanied by a collective removal of the past from people's minds. Only with the presidency of the socialist François Mitterand did democratic France allow the viewing of Gillo Pontecorvo's *The Battle of Algiers*. The democratic Italy of today, even though rejecting the colonial adventures of the past and condemning Graziani, has still not allowed the airing of the film *The Lion of the Desert*, a film about Omar al-Mukhtar directed by the Syrian American producer Mustafa Akkad. Perhaps it is not a great film, even though it is a British production made with American money and financed by Muammar Gaddafi. The cast, however, is certainly noteworthy (Rod Steiger as Mussolini, Oliver Reed as Graziani, and Anthony Quinn as Omar al-Mukhtar). That the film should be censored in Italy, considering what kind of other films are allowed in cinemas today, certainly gives food for thought.[10]

Let us get back to our story. We left Badoglio calculating the cost of the guerrilla war (his comment: 'a colony which costs a few thousand dead is a good deal') and Graziani was busy writing circulars to his underlings. However, it would be wrong to think that all he did was paperwork. As vice-governor of Cyrenaica, he was responsible for many other duties. He took part in military parades and reviewed the troops, healed the relations with the Arab notables, and hosted dinners, parties, and receptions in honour of important guests. In this latter task, his wife proved to be extremely helpful. Everyone now called her Lady Ines, and she proved to be the perfect hostess. She even forced the grumpy Graziani to dance, and on one evening, in the company of the duke of Bergamo and Marshal Caviglia, he managed a waltz. Soon, day-to-day life in the colony became very pleasant. Lady Ines dressed stylishly but not too extravagantly, and the wives of the officers and the high-ranking civil servants imitated her, they asked her for advice and shared their personal problems with her. 'We're doing well and we're having fun,' Graziani wrote to Uncle Peppino in 1933, 'my financial problems have also disappeared. On top of my salary, I have an annuity of 100 thousand lira a year for ceremonial expenses, which is a lot because down here ministers, high ranking officials and their spouses come and go all the time. Anyway, you know how things are here in Africa: as many servants as you wish, friends and clients who vie to give you gifts. In a word, I manage to put a few pennies by...' Graziani's new friends included the Libyans. Success creates friends, and the inhabitants of Cyrenaica, following the death of Omar al-Mukhtar, had abandoned the green flags of the Prophet and now embraced the green, white, and red. They sent gifts to Graziani, poems, and sickening adulation. In 1934, at the end of his mandate, the vice-governor found the soldiers of the newly formed 1st Libyan Division in tears, while Muhammed Ben Amey, head of the notables of Benghazi, would dedicate a homage to him ('Oh sincerely good man, you gave us back the freedom to walk and to graze, you gave us barley and seeds for planting...'). Words that were as gushing as they were insincere. Alongside the adulation of the natives came that of the great correspondents of the Italian and international press. Hitler's newspaper, the *Volkischer Beobachter*, wrote of Graziani: 'here is a man who delivers hammer blows like an ox'; the Swedish *Göteborg Handels*, which we thought would have taken a more detached standpoint, came out with the title 'Following in the footsteps of Napoleon' no less; the Corsican journalist Pierre Bonardi, writing for *Gringoire* in an article of 9 September 1933, surpassed the limits of decency by writing: 'his features should be chiselled in marble and he is adored by the population which he has subdued. The people are effeminate, and they love to be possessed...' For the Italian press, silence is golden. They limited themselves to publishing a few choice phrases: the Senussi hydra, the square legions, the tenacious colonists, and the soldiers whose valour is unmatched. Even Orio Vergani did not shy away from this orgy of rhetoric. Out of respect for the memory of this excellent journalist, we prefer not to reproduce what his pen dictated. Suffice to say, he was not reporting but playing a sycophantic serenade of celestial music on his violin. The only ones who behaved in a dignified manner were Emilio Cecchi and Amintore Fanfani. The former rambled on about the escapades of the young Graziani in a brilliant piece called *Cioce e Ciociaria*, where he dodged the pitfalls of ridiculousness. The latter, then just starting out as a university professor, analysed the economic aspects thus avoiding more delicate matters.[11]

To Graziani, who was completely devoid of a sense of humour, to be so widely acclaimed was a good thing. He was pleased with all of it, provided the articles were favourable. It could be that it all went to his head. The fact of the matter is that, if in private he talked as he did in his letters to Uncle Peppino, in public he would recite his speeches like a Shakespearean actor. While illustrating his project to the government of the colony, he launched into a speech of pompous and baroque oratory, peppered with Latin phrases and quotes from the great statesmen of history. Once he invoked Tacitus, 'With Tacitus in mind, I tell you that whoever is in power must be concerned with one thing above all else: leaving a favourable legacy of himself.' He had to bid farewell to Prince Amedeo of Aosta who, as commander of the Saharan *mehari* troops, had fought alongside him at the wells of Bir Tagrift. And so, he talked of the Saharan prince wrapped in a white cape, *tanto nomini nullun par elogium*. While he was giving these grand speeches, Graziani also wrote a few books in 1932 and 1933, published by Mondadori. The language was simple yet effective, readable from the first to the last page. But let us be frank, they were not masterpieces. No one ever considered them to be so, except for, naturally, the publicity office of Mondadori. The publishing house was forced to make encouraging noises: 'Rodolfo Graziani has released another of his works, it's like an adventure novel. The literary season looks to be very promising this year'. In truth, Graziani's books were simply the kind that generals write for other generals.

In January 1934, Mussolini decided to start moving the high colonial posts around. For Pietro Badoglio, he had prepared the post of chief of the general staff, and for Graziani the command of the army of Udine. In their stead arrived Italo Balbo, who had been nominated governor-general of unified Libya (Tripolitania plus Cyrenaica). Graziani was used to seeing plots everywhere, swallowed this bitter pill and complained about his sorrows to Count Volpi, who he could count on as a trusted friend. In a letter to Volpi from March 1934, he wrote:

> I thought I deserved the Governorship. Instead, I got nothing. I am only of use when there's fighting to be done, when it's time for merrymaking, then it's time for the *quadrumviri*. I hope my work here will not have been carried out in vain. I have started work on the new coastal road, I thought of naming it after myself, and calling it 'Gratiania.'

Unfortunately for Graziani, in the end it was called via Balbia. He was wrong, however, as to why he had been relieved of his duties. Italo Balbo had not been promoted in Libya; he had been banished there. In the eyes of Mussolini, the *quadrumviro* from Ferrara, who had just come back from leading the second triumphal crossing of the Atlantic with an air squadron, had gained excessive popularity. It was better to banish Balbo from Rome. Balbo arrived in May and Graziani put on a brave face and left. In his autobiography, the marshal wrote: 'I got on a public bus and I reached my residence in via Paganini'. This is not true, such an understated return was not in his nature. After arriving in Rome, he was received by Mussolini and applauded by the crowd, he went to the Quirinale and even though he received more decorations than a North Korean general, he asked the king to be given the Military Order of Savoy. He then subjected himself to a never-ending battery of welcome home dinners. During these dinners, the lawyer Giuseppe Bedendo, who had been the state prosecutor during Omar al-Mukhtar's trial, gave him a small booklet he had written of Romanesco poems as a gift.[12] This was made up of 180 pages of verses and rhymes about 'Grazziani the Affrican', which narrated his adventures in Libya in a popular vernacular.

The rebellion?

> *Old Graziani said I've known the Arab for some time*
> *And I treated him in Libya like dirt*
> *Let me get to work,*
> *and I'll have done with this rebellion! You mark my words!*

Omar al-Mukhtar's capture?

> *The Boss was taken while he fought*
> *He got just what he ought!*
> *A horse and rifle he had*
> *And this made Old Graziani glad.*
> *I heard him one morning say*
> *…I've known you for some time*
> *What made you get up to these crafty tricks?*
> *…He stood there thoughtfully and said*
> *It was Egypt that sent me out in the sticks.*

Marquis Bedendo was not on a par with Belli and was not made of the same ilk as Trilussa.[13] Nevertheless, Graziani liked his verses very much.[14]

4
Ethiopia and the Use of Poison Gas

In June 1942, Rodolfo Graziani bought some real estate. Since he had 700,000 lira in savings, they suggested he invest it 'in bricks and mortar'. The property was a block of flats on the via Tuscolana, number 178, which back then looked out on to open countryside. Four floors and twenty apartments with two rooms and a kitchen each. 'If rented you can make some good money out of them,' is what Graziani's financial consultant, Mr Guerra, said while accompanying him to the solicitor's office. Rome was growing by the day, and Mussolini wanted everything in the capital to be monumental and grand. Entire new neighbourhoods were popping up. The Parioli area of Piazzale delle Muse was popular among the party officials; at Primavalle, the regime had knocked down the old city centre and opened up via dell'Impero for traffic, forcefully moving the inhabitants of the Fori area; the military citadel of Cecchignola housed a never-ending assortment of barracks and headquarters. The onset of the war had stopped the completion of the universal exhibition area 'Roma 42', better known as EUR, where the *Duce* wanted to show off the glories of Fascism. From the unification of Italy onwards, building and investing in real estate in Rome has always been a lucrative business. Not for nothing being a *palazzinaro* (real estate developer) is synonymous with being wealthy. Graziani was the exception that proved the rule: he had little luck renting out his twenty apartments, and after 1945, not only had his property been confiscated but he also had to deal with the rents being frozen.

In that same month of June 1942, the marshal managed to cut a few other 'deals': he bought a 626 Fiat lorry intended for use at Arcinazzo for transporting hay, potatoes, and sheep. He then rented a luxurious villa on the via Nomentana. For the lorry, he had received financial aid from Senator Giovanni Agnelli and the grateful Graziani never ceased to be amazed by this, almost as if he had witnessed a miracle. In his diary entry on 9 June, he wrote: 'Thanks to the kindness of Mr Agnelli I managed to land quite a good price, what a nice person he is'. He was unaware of the

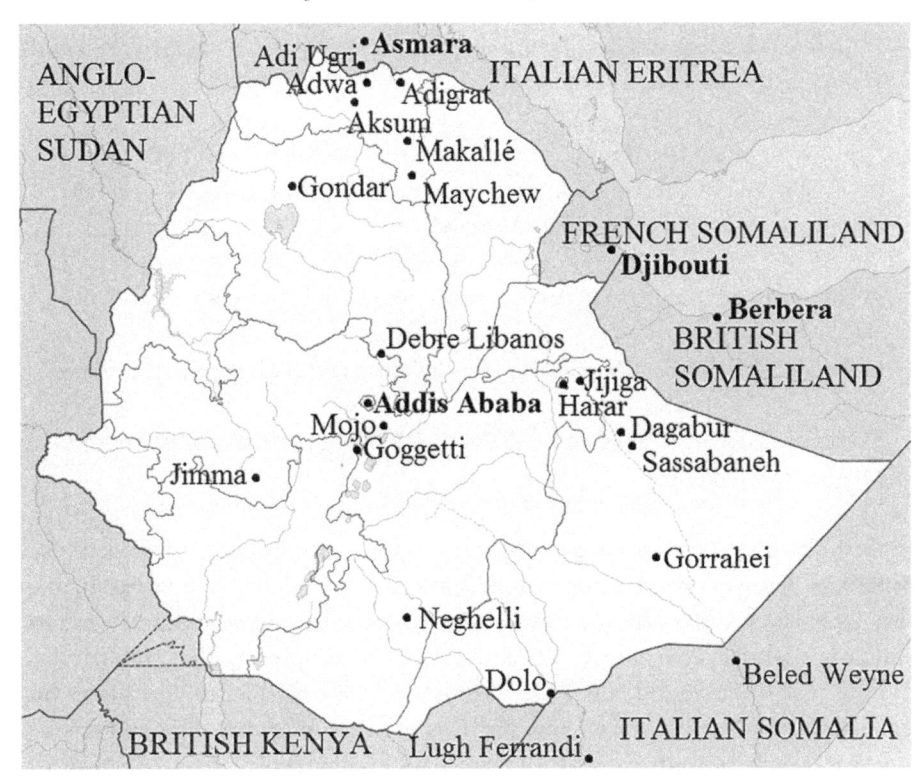

A map of Ethiopia with locations noted in the book. (*Wikimedia Commons*)

fact that the Agnellis always gave special offers to famous clients, it was a tradition. Regarding the villa, his family had encouraged him to move. They all agreed that a marshal of Italy who had been viceroy of Ethiopia should reside somewhere grander than an apartment. He had no problem with his abode in via Paganini and it took a while to persuade him, but how could he say no to his wife? He agreed, but on one condition, that he would keep his flat in via Paganini and one day give it to his grandchildren. The villa in question was Villa Liotta, a beautiful eighteenth-century residence surrounded by trees located in the second half of the via Nomentana. Today it houses the Iranian Embassy. It was another deal which went wrong. The Grazianis lived there for less than two years. In June 1944, when the Allies entered Rome, the villa was ransacked, the furniture destroyed, and the marshal's papers thrown to the wind. On the morning of 15 June 1942, while signing the contract, Graziani became ill. It was nothing serious, he just passed out. This often happened when he had to deal with things of which he understood nothing, such as money, which made him doubtful and uncertain. The doctor prescribed rest, and so, Graziani happily returned to his peaceful and quiet home at Piani di Arcinazzo.

Graziani's diary, which has survived fully intact, gives us an account of the everyday events that marked his life in that period. Here are a few entries:

26 June 1942. Alone at Casal Biancaneve. It's my feast day. My family are all at Viareggio, having a swim in the sea.

3 July. Went to see Gen. Puntoni, *aide-de-camp* to the King. I learnt that visiting the King would be a serious embarrassment. I objected 'I am, after all, a Marshal of Italy,' to which Puntoni replied: 'Exactly'.

31 July. Finished editing my defence statement. It's Friday, I hope it's not bad luck.

11 August. All of us at Sant'Anna for my birthday. I'm sixty!!! Uncle Peppino is also here.

13 August. I delivered my defence to the Duce's administrative office. I'm off to Pallanza to wind down.

In the subsequent pages, Graziani poured his heart out about a few personal problems that were tormenting him. His grandson, Rodolfo, had fallen ill, and serious problems had arisen in Vanda's marriage. These were intimate matters which are totally irrelevant to our story. We will simply say that the marshal did not just sit back and watch: he summoned the best doctors in Italy to his grandson's sick bed, he interfered in the marital issues of his daughter and son-in-law with a lack of prudence that was typical of his character. He initially insisted that Count Gualandi leave the flat in via Archimede where the couple lived; but then, he regretted this, perhaps after having a talk with his wife and so he asked for the support of priests and cardinals (specifically Cardinal Jorio who was a dear friend and a fellow Ciociarian) so that they might bring peace to his family.[1]

Let us return to the diary entries of September 1942:

1 September. Mussolini reads what I have written extremely carefully. Very good.

24 September. Montefoschi, the painter, is at my house. She's doing a portrait of me for the hall of the General Staff of the Army.

4 October. News about my defence. They tell me that the *Duce* finds it remarkably interesting. He read the typewritten document and put it inside a safe where I hope it won't lay dormant for long.

1 November. I'm being talked about. Perhaps they're going to send me to Croatia.

15 November. Rommel is retreating, the English radio said so this evening.

7 November. According to the English radio Rommel has even died. What is certain is the routing of his army. It could be that the Germans are behind my being investigated

since they blame me for not being able to dine out in Alexandria in a fortnight. However, I cannot be happy: many Italians are dying alongside the Germans.

13 November. Mussolini is bewildered, he has been annihilated. Sadly, the facts are proving me right. Bocca tells me that my name is on everyone's lips in Rome alongside that of Badoglio. Not too happy about this combination. I continue working as a shepherd.

21 November. Funeral of Duchess Badoglio which I didn't attend. I send a letter of condolence to her husband.

Even Countess Volpi has died. I have the flu; Ines will go to the funeral.

30 November. Macabre mixture of news from military and political spheres. As for my defence, Mussolini would have agreed with me.

On 1 December, there is an entry with only two words, 'MURDEROUS VERDICT', written in capital letters. On that day, Graziani learnt eight months late—from his usual sources—that the Investigative Commission presided by Thaon de Revel had found him guilty of gross negligence. The commission's verdict consisted of the six following points and a conclusion.

1. After the victory of Sidi Barrani time was wasted building roads and aqueducts. As a result of this, the enemy had time to strengthen their position. Instead, by attacking immediately there would have been greater chance of success. The Command Headquarters, being too far back, prevented a clear view of the situation.
2. The fighting on 19 November 1940 and the reports from our military intelligence indicated the enemy's intention to attack. The Commander should have adjusted the deployment of the front-line troops and fortified the defences of the Halfaya pass. Such negligence and the soldiers' relaxed attitude due to constant waiting contributed to the defeat.
3. The Commander-in-chief's statement to 'proceed to Tripoli' therefore moving the headquarters further back seems questionable.
4. Again, highly questionable were the unjust accusations made against the mother country. Had the rapid-fire artillery pieces been put to good use, they could have acted as anti-tank weapons and with the means available at the time, better results could have been obtained.
5. The request that an armoured division be sent was impractical, considering that it was possible to create one with the vehicles available on the ground. As for the requests made after 20 December 1940, they were futile as nothing could have arrived in time from the mother country.

6. The handling of the retreat from Cyrenaica was carried out quite poorly, considering the Commander's extensive knowledge of the field.

With these considerations in mind, the Investigative Commission concluded:

The Marshal of Italy Rodolfo Graziani exaggerated the success of Sidi Barrani purporting the enemy to be defeated. Then, when asked to exploit this success, he declined, citing logistical difficulties. During this lengthy wait he was informed that the enemy were strengthening their position, allowing them to attack in more favourable conditions. Despite this warning, Graziani remained far from the front and kept the front-line troops in neither an offensive nor defensive state. Even after the SIM had notified him of an imminent attack, Graziani did nothing to prepare and adequately face the incoming attack. In spite of the fighting on the 19th of November—a clear sign for an experienced Commander that something was wrong—he did nothing to amend the serious condition of our front-line troops. Because of this, the enemy's offensive on 9 December caught us completely off guard and resulted in the loss of four divisions and the collapse of the front. All trust in Graziani had disappeared and his leadership as a commander, essential in organizing and inspiring the men, was totally lacking. Instead of walking amongst the troops and raising morale, he only thought about moving his headquarters further back. Finally, during the retreat from Cyrenaica, Graziani ignored the various defensive capabilities offered by the land, despite having served in Libya for lengthy periods of time. Also, if he had not been stopped by the Supreme Command, he would have entrenched himself in Tripoli, seriously compromising the influx of supplies to that port.

The full text of the Investigative Commission's verdict was, at that time, a 'State secret'.[2] The marshal only knew of its contents from what his friends at the Ministry of War told him. He never knew that Mussolini had said: 'I can have him shot'. However, he knew that he could very well be court-martialled, and that what he had heard in the past few months were all lies: perhaps Mussolini had never read his defence, and if he had, he certainly did not agree with it. He was now a disgraced general, at best, someone who ought to be forgotten. After having got so angry before, he now did not have the strength to get worked up again. He became deeply prostrated, he came down with a fever and a stomach ache. He shut himself away in his farm at Piani di Arcinazzo 'to live like a monk'. He only left his house to hand out copies of his defence, which no one read.

Graziani's diary from December 1942 onwards is full of depressed and dejected comments:

They've killed the truth.

All I need now is for them to accuse me of being a weakling.

Bitter tears from my chalice.

And notes on the events of the day, public and private:

12 December. Enemy aerial incursion. Two bombs fell on Filettino.

14 December. I am in Affile with my grandchildren Rodolfo and Alberto. I wanted them here because there are rumours of an imminent bombing on Rome. They're ok.

19 December. I have a cold. I am taking the kids back to Rome for Christmas.

31 December. The year has come to a close and as promised I have faithfully dedicated it all to the plough. However, the rain still hasn't fallen on the earth for me.

1–15 January. 1943 started off quite badly, I'm in bed with flu.

21 January. Letter from the Bishop of Tripoli. He says he's given Bu Maad to Kalifa Kaled who will make sure that the farm is looked after. *Sic Transit* Bu Maad after fourteen years of work!

7 February. Snowing. Working at the Casale.

16 February. It's the fifth anniversary of my triumphal return from the Empire. Today I am forced to defend myself from a vile character assassination perpetrated against me. Back then I was at the apex of glory and there were no clouds on the horizon.

Apropos Ethiopia, Graziani's memory was faulty. Even then, there were clouds on the horizon. Many criticised and accused him. Had or had he not used poison gas on the Abyssinians?

Unlike many other badly kept secrets, the shameful use of poison gas on the Abyssinians was a real secret, the kind of secret one locks away in a drawer and throws away the key. Mussolini always denied it and the regime's press had a field day maintaining it was all 'disgraceful slander' as there was no evidence behind Ethiopia's accusations and the reports of foreign journalists in Addis Ababa were vague and contradictory. In 1936, no one in Italy believed that poison gas was being used. The newspaper *Il Popolo d'Italia* made short work of the Negus and his *rases*, 'So ignorant are they that they can't tell the difference between harmless smoke bombs and Yperite gas.' Other newspapers simply echoed these explanations. All in all, they seemed plausible. Abroad, public opinion was divided: the Germans, Spaniards, and South Americans supported the Italian version; the French and the Americans seemed divided and uncertain; those who believed Italy to be guilty were the Danish, the Swedes, and the British; the latter, after reading the reports of the journalist historian George L. Steer, who wrote: 'For the first time in world history, a nation considered to be civilized has used poison gas against another which is considered to be barbarous'.[3] Harsh words. But where was the proof? Many doubts remained. This is demonstrated by a document held in the National Archives in Washington, DC, a copy of which can be found in the Central State Archive in Rome. A three-volume report on the Italo-Abyssinian war penned by cavalry Maj. Norman E. Fiske, who had been sent as US military *attaché* to Rome in 1935. We will come back to this document later, given that it is the only one of its kind with sound judgements and accurate information. However, regarding poison gas, in May 1936, the well-informed Maj. Fiske wrote this:

> I was unable to obtain any information regarding the use of chemical weapons by the Italian army. I believe that a certain amount of mustard gas [Yperite, because of its particular mustard flour smell, was called 'mustard gas' in military slang] was used to cover the retreat of the troops from the Tacazzè area to the Adwa-Axum line, and that now and then the Air Force used mustard gas during bombing raids but not in the form of a sprinkling gas. I am of the opinion that if gas was used, it was not widespread and that its military effectiveness was negligible.

This time, Fiske was way off the mark. The reality was that the Italians did use poison gas against the Abyssinians and its use was widespread, and not only as a means of reprisal. But where is the evidence? After 1945, when Italy had been liberated and Fascism collapsed, all those who knew about this secret (among others: Marshal Badoglio, Undersecretary of War Federico Baistrocchi, Minister of the Colonies Alessandro Lessona, Generals Frusci, Bernasconi, and Tedeschini Lalli, Commander of the Air Force in Somalia Lt-Col. Virginio Rigolone, plus many others) either remained silent or continued to deny it. The only one who admitted it was, unbelievably, Rodolfo Graziani himself. In the first edition of his book *Il Fronte Sud* (1938), Graziani casually wrote that 'twenty-four bombers took off, six of which were carrying gas' (page 406), and 'I gave the order to proceed with incendiary and gas bombing of the nearby forests' (page 483), these two sentences were to disappear in the following editions.[4] Again, in 1947, while awaiting to be called to trial in Rome, Graziani prepared a memo for his lawyers that said: 'It's necessary to make the court aware that in those tragic eighteen months as Viceroy of Ethiopia, I was besieged in Addis Ababa. Draconian orders were sent from

Rome, they wanted a regime of terror. I had to resort to heavy air bombardments and, when the situation got worse, to the sprinkling of poison gas…' Once again, in 1949, before his second trial in front of the military tribunal, Graziani notified his lawyers that he had received a letter from Capt. Franco Freda. The marshal asserted that 'Freda was the only officer in charge of our chemical service in *Africa Orientale Italiana* [AOI, Italian East Africa] and is therefore the only person who can tell us if and when gas was used. Freda is at our disposal, he's a friend, he can come and testify.' His lawyers never used his memo and neither did they ask Freda to testify, for the very good reason that during Graziani's court hearings, Ethiopia was hardly ever mentioned and nothing was said about poison gas. That was an old story, in 1948–49, Graziani's charge of treachery and collaboration with the Nazis was of greater importance. A real shame. Freda had quite a lot to tell. For instance, that the chemical service in AOI utilised four types of gas: suffocating gas (phosgene, diphosgene, chloropicrin), blistering gas (lewisite, Yperite and ethyl sulfide, secret serial number C/500-T), toxic gas (benzene), and tear and sneezing gas (chloroacetic and various forms of arsenic). Or, that the squadrons under his command, named the 'Kappa service', made sure they fertilised the ground after every bombing so that not even the advancing troops knew what had happened.

Uncomfortable truths are often wilfully ignored, it is better to lie as it is more reassuring and puts one's conscience at ease. In 1958, Alessandro Lessona had the gall to say that 'we only used gas once in Abyssinia as a reprisal, and it was just with three, I repeat three small bombs'. And here is the crucial point of an interview given by Pietro Badoglio in 1947 to Indro Montanelli, published by the famous journalist in the *Corriere della Sera*.[5]

> *Montanelli*: 'Listen Badoglio, did we really use gas in Abyssinia? Abroad they're convinced of this, they say that…'
>
> *Badoglio*: 'Never. Except once, by mistake and without any effect. At the battle of Endertà. On their own initiative, a battery fired an Yperite bomb. However, the bomb deteriorated and there were no consequences. It would have been foolish to use gas in Abyssinia. Worse than that, it would have been a disaster'.
>
> *Montanelli*: 'Foolishness, ruin. Because of the scandal it would have caused?'
>
> *Badoglio*: 'No, no. Because of the cost. Even wars are about numbers. The war in Abyssinia was beautiful because it cost us only 976 soldiers. A reasonable price for an Empire'.[6]

Pietro Badoglio has already been disproven by Angelo Del Boca (*Gli Italiani in Africa Orientale*, page 487 onwards). On the Northern Front, Badoglio made ample use of gas, and in the south, Graziani behaved no differently. Today we have the proof. There is a trunkful of documents that were taken in 1944 by US Intelligence, hidden away for years in who knows what US archive and then handed back to Italy in 1947—currently residing in the Central State

Archive. If they were alive today, the two marshals could say in their defence that they zealously followed Mussolini's orders, which were apocalyptic. But as we know, this is not an extenuating circumstance, but an admission of complicity.

Before we can analyse the aforementioned documents, it would be useful to tell the story from the beginning and to explain in what capacity Graziani took part in the Italo-Abyssinian war.

We left Graziani as he was returning from Cyrenaica to command the army of Udine. He did not stay there long, but just long enough to be decorated with a silver long service medal (twenty-seven years in the army) and to be promoted to *generale designato d'Armata* (general of an army). On 20 February 1935, Mussolini made him governor of Somalia and sent him back to Africa. Graziani boarded the *Vulcania* and set sail for the Horn. From his diary: 'How wonderful, I have an entire apartment to myself, I feel like a Lord'. When he arrived in Mogadishu, he discovered that he had been swindled. His new task was to build an immense network of trenches around the city and to stay put. Everything was set against him. His distance from Italy: 8,000 km away. Somalia's geography: savannahs, large desert areas, and a steep coastline unsuitable for docking ships. The climate: rainy from March until April. The meagre tools at his disposal: 200 lorries, thirty cannons, and some old aircraft to support 20,000 native and 12,000 Italian soldiers of the *Peloritania* Division. Converting this state of defensive immobility into one of rapid offensive movement was Graziani's undisputed military masterpiece.

Operation Southern Front began with a series of private messages sent to the *Duce*. Unable to stand still, the ambitious Graziani argued in favour of attacking. But what about logistical problems and the lack of roads? No problem. It was simply a matter of purchasing 'caterpillar' vehicles in the US, which were 'slow but could drive at any speed on all sorts of terrain'.

Graziani's report to Mussolini, March 1935:

A picture of Graziani and Badoglio in 1934 which appeared on *La Domenica del Corriere*. Before the Ethiopian war, they still got on well.

We must consider that a caterpillar tractor of 75 hp with two trailers can carry 500 kilos. Therefore, we can deduce that fifty tractors with 100 trailers can carry 20,000 kg. Now then, 20,000 kg of food are the equivalent of one million rations weighing one kg each, which is thirty days' worth of food for 30,000 troops. We would need 1,000 tractors—given that one tractor can carry 20,000 kg—in order to obtain an adequate load capacity. Further reasons for using the caterpillars are: fifty tractors working on two shifts only need 100 drivers; the tractors use naphtha so we can save on fuel; the tractors can only do 8 miles per hour but they can drive through forests and muddy terrain (apart from the winter, it rains all the time here); for the troops on the march, a convoy of tractors and lorries represents a depot and a fortalice all rolled into one; the expenses for all this can be covered by the colonies' funds without weighing on the state's finances.

The *Duce* thought this idea was pure genius. Mussolini now always wore military uniforms and played the role of the great strategist in front of a large map of East Africa dotted with arrows and flags. Even though the general staff was not in agreement (the offensive had to come from the north, from Eritrea, where 300,000 men under the command of Emilio De Bono were gathering. However, Pietro Badoglio had already been chosen to replace him) the prospect of a new second front down south appealed to the *Duce*. He told his wife, Rachele: 'That darned soldier, he's really done it this time'. He gave Graziani the go-ahead and allowed him to open an account with the Morgan Guaranty Bank of New York and had the 1st Libyan Division sent to Somalia as well.

In Italy, those were days of nationalistic exaltation. The propaganda was incessant, and the Fascist slogans went viral: '... we have a right to a place in the sun'; 'we need to avenge Adwa'; 'In Ethiopia there will be work for everyone'. The picture postcards showed topless Ethiopian girls, which pleased the recalled servicemen of 1911. No one sang '*O Baldissera, non ti fidar di quella gente nera*' ('Oh Baldissera, don't trust those black people over there') anymore, the song in vogue was '*Faccetta nera, bell'abissina*' ('Pretty black face, beautiful Abyssinian girl'). The western democracies made two crucial mistakes (the sending of British ships to the Mediterranean, the threat of sanctions on behalf of the fifty countries adhering to the League of Nations), which brought grist to the mill of Fascism. Great Britain, which possessed the largest empire on earth, wanted to teach Italy how to behave? The League of Nations took sides with the Negus, a ruler who tolerated slavery in his country? The people of Italy were indignant. Many volunteered to fight, leading the way were Achille Starace, Galeazzo Ciano, Mussolini's two sons, Vittorio and Bruno, the academic Tommaso Marinetti, Alessandro Pavolini, the federal secretaries, and ordinary members of the Fascist Party. At the Vittoriano, Queen Elena slipped off her golden wedding ring and gave it to the nation, 250,000 spouses followed her example. People pulled off gates and handrails from their homes so that the steel could be used to make cannons, the industrial world created substitutes for everything: rayon instead of silk and hibiscus tea instead of coffee. This was autarchy, but it was an autarchy which people happily tolerated, a bit like the car-free Sundays of 1973.[7] Mussolini gave a speech a day, he kissed widows and orphans, and he cooked up a motto a minute. The latest ones were: 'Italy will go it alone', 'Proletarian struggle against the plutocracies', 'Proletarian and Fascist Italy stands tall'. This world cup-like atmosphere ended up influencing even certain anti-fascists: the syndicalist Arturo Labriola asked to be allowed back into Italy, and former prime minister Vittorio Emanuele Orlando made it known that he was 'on hand'.[8] The majority of the clergy was supportive as well. Everywhere priests were blessing banners and pennants, Cardinal Ildefonso Schuster of Milan wanted to personally salute 'this enterprise, which at the price of blood, opens the doors of Ethiopia to the Catholic faith and Roman civilization'. On 2 October, war was declared. From Palazzo Venezia, the *Duce*, with his fists clenched at his sides, pronounced the famous 'We've been patient for forty years, enough is enough!' Bells were ringing, sirens blaring, and crowds went crazy. Never had Fascism enjoyed such widespread consensus.

In Mogadishu, because of all the work, Graziani slept on a field cot in his office. Aligned on the port's quay, alongside masses of material, were the notorious caterpillar tractors commissioned by the Cairo branch of Ford, behind them, the trailers, and further back, thousands of gigantic special Ford lorries with long-weave tyres for muddy terrain. Mogadishu looked like a building site and the Somalians did not mind the hard work ('because we pay them, we aren't slave-owners'), the

The propaganda against the league was intensified. A drawing by Galantra which appeared on *Marc'Aurelio* in 1935. Caption: 'Everything they put in it, turns into gold for the arms dealers'.

organisation was precise like that of an accountant. Graziani even went as far as to forge fake documents in order to provide his army with adequate supplies. By August, he had bypassed the sanctions (officially enacted on 10 February 1935) by sending a few officers in plain clothes and with counterfeit documents, purporting them to be Spanish merchants, to Yemen and Kenya. And so, thanks to a few helpful private companies, Graziani always obtained new supplies of food, clothing, and equipment.

By September, he was ready to move.

The Abyssinians had followed Graziani's flurry of activity with great apprehension and the league's observers were perplexed. The newspapers of half the world had been targeting the Italian general since May, orchestrating a denigratory press campaign, which alternated between jibes, made-up stories, sensational hit-pieces, and malevolent insinuations. It was an ugly page in the history of journalism.

> 13 May 1935. From Graziani to the Italian Legation in Cairo and to the Royal Consul of Italy to Jerusalem. The Jewish magazine *Hatikvah* of Alexandria has published an article with a picture of me claiming that I am an Israelite. Being of the Catholic faith in the eyes of God I would appreciate it if you could act on my behalf and deny the claims of the *Hatikvah* and *Haevri* magazines, from which *Hatikvah* got the story in the first place. Such claims, given my role as Governor of a predominantly Muslim country, are clearly designed to discredit me.

> 14 May 1935. From Graziani to Minister of the Colonies, Lessona. The Jewish press continues in its vile speculations against me. Apparently, I am one of them. Do something! I will never be a Jew.

> 25 May 1935. From Graziani to the Minister of the Colonies Lessona. All denials have been useless. My position as a Jew amongst the Muslims is difficult. I am embittered. What more can they add to this array of denigratory defamation?

Day after day, 'Graziani the Jew' became a leitmotiv of the Jewish and non-Jewish press. In London, the *News Chronicle* published an article on 'the noteworthy Jewish General Rodolfo Graziani', in Paris the Jewish writer Itamar Ben-Avi wrote a pamphlet entitled 'An unexpected fellow Jew, the Fascist General Graziani'. To reassure the natives, Graziani put on sandals and went to the mosque in Mogadishu, he entertained dignitaries in the governor's residence, and he altered the rations of the Somalian soldiers ('Because I am a great friend of Islam') arranging for the meat to be butchered 'according to the teachings of the Koran'.

Despite all this, his troubles with the newspapers were only just beginning. In July, to explain Graziani's hatred for 'the inferior races', the fairy-tale about the 'family massacre' resurfaced again. Everyone joined in with tear-jerking titles such as 'The wife-killing and parricidal Roman general who did it for love', or 'The Italian who killed his wife and daughter to spare them an even worse fate'. Absolutely enraged by these 'disgusting lies', Graziani managed to arrange for Mussolini to publicly receive Ines and Vanda at Palazzo Venezia. On 5 August 1935 (on instructions from the Ministry of Press and Propaganda: 'publish with photographs') the story was broadcast by the Stefani News agency with this brief and insignificant bulletin 'Lady Ines Graziani, Consort of the Governor of Somalia, together with their daughter Vanda, have today visited the Head of the Government and presented him a few African relics'. It would all be in vain. Abroad, this news bulletin was interpreted in a different manner: 'Today Mussolini received Graziani's second wife, given that, as is widely known, he killed the first one etc....'

In September, the 'family massacre' widened to include none other than Graziani's parents. From Copenhagen's *Nord Press* (8 September 1935): 'We have learnt that the Fascist General Graziani, as well as killing his wife and daughter, also killed his mother and father in order to spare them the tortures of the Libyan rebels'. This lie soon made the rounds of the world's newspapers, with few changes, even to the point of being republished (5 February 1936) in the *Giornale degli Italiani d'Australia*. 'It's not true,' affirmed the director of the periodical, Franco Battistella, 'that Graziani killed his own wife and daughter. What is true is that the general's father, a valiant man who fought at Adwa in 1896, had to finish off his wife so that she wouldn't fall into the hands of the barbarous Menelik'. Battistella would be the only journalist who amended the story and sent his apologies to Graziani.

After the Mogadishu post office had gone into overdrive sending off the general's denials, he wrote in his diary: 'to honour the memory of my poor parents who have been so outrageously insulted, I have made dispositions for a tomb to be built in Affile. Up until now they had been laid to rest in the bare earth'.

We have narrated Graziani's misadventures with the press for two reasons: because they explain his love-hate relationship towards journalists, and because it justified the incredulity of Italian and foreign public opinion towards the use of poison gas. When newspapers start exaggerating and going over the top their reliability flounders, even if in the end, they are telling the truth.

On 3 October 1935, twenty-four hours after the declaration of war, Graziani ordered the *Milano* plan to be put into action. This consisted of small offensive actions meant to size up the opposing forces. His force (50,000 men with 1,585 machine guns, 112 artillery pieces, 100 caterpillars, 1,800 lorries, seventy tanks, and seventy-six aircraft) was facing two Abyssinian armies. The first, which was 40,000 strong and garrisoned in the Sidamo-Borena area, was led by the emperor's son-in-law *Ras* Desta Damtew.[9] The second, which was located in the Ogaden, was made up of 30,000 men commanded by *Dejazmach* Nasibu Zamanuel, a young Ethiopian commander aided by the expert Turkish General Wehib Pasha.[10]

From the very start, the fighting went in the Italians' favour. The towns of Dolo and Dagnerei fell, Gorrahei resisted and so it was levelled by the air force. The only thing *Grazmach* Afarwaq could muster up against the Italian aircraft was a small 37-mm Swiss Oerlikon anti-aircraft gun, he clung to this piece for days. After being wounded, he would die of gangrene on 5 November. The road towards the Ogaden seemed open. However, *Ras* Desta decided to take the initiative and advanced on Dolo, 400 km away, defended by a ring of trenches. In mid-October, 40,000 Abyssinians left the heights of Bale, went beyond Neghelli, and descended on to the plains. This was a march towards death. They walked through deserts and savannahs, there was no adequate supply line, and they were harassed by enemy aircraft. They arrived at the outskirts of Dolo on 30 November 1935, and there were only 15,000 left. For Graziani, it was time to take the initiative. He sent off three columns from Dolo's trenched perimeter: the first had to go up the Dawa Parma river, the second the Ganale Doria, and the third along road that led to Filtu and then to Neghelli. The tractors advanced like slow trains, on the lorries there was everything, food, weapons, ammunition, and drinking water in the measure of one litre per man a day, the famous 'Neghelli litre'.

Against the Abyssinians who used dum-dum bullets, Mussolini authorised the use of gas 'as a retaliatory measure'. Graziani was unleashed. He used gas as a retaliatory weapon and as a final solution. The slaughter started in December and ended on 15 January with the battle of Ganale Doria. The war correspondent Sandro Volta met the governor of Somalia at Lugh Ferrandi (he had gone there to follow the military operations more closely) and described him in euphoric terms: 'He was a giant. His white safari jacket reminiscent of the heroes of ancient Greece. He repeated: "No passive resistance. I'm like a man whose been assaulted in a brawl and fights back with his bare fists. And because I have long arms, with every punch I take away a few acres of land from the Negus. It happened in the Ogaden and it will happen here!"' His forecast of the events was correct. When the famished and thirsty stragglers of Desta's army tried to reach the waterways, the Italians were waiting for them. Sandro Volta noted: 'They came in waves and we cut them down with machine gun fire eighty centimetres from the ground'. Gen. Agostini of the forestry militia, who was a poet at heart, wrote: 'They fell like tired quails'. Graziani, from a telegram to Gen. Frusci: 'Let's go and take Neghelli, we have nothing to fear'.

'Nothing to fear,' said Graziani, he was right, and he knew it. Ethiopia was a feudal kingdom of 2 million slaves and 13 million inhabitants. Corporal punishment, chains, and irons on guilty men's feet were still in force. Each *ras* governed his own territory and had his own personal army, which were in fact just undisciplined and irregular brigands. Like a medieval king, the Negus lived an isolated existence in the Imperial Ghebbi at Addis Ababa, a city within a city. Only he had a regular army of 35,000 men at his disposal, armed with modern weapons and trained by Belgian officers. Everyone in Europe knew this, but Graziani knew more. He surrounded himself with able collaborators and had at his disposal the best intelligence officer the Italian army had to offer, Maj. Alberto Mazzi of the Royal *Carabinieri*. In December 1934, after having broken the code of the Abyssinian cyphers, Mazzi

A drawing from the newspaper *Marc'Aurelio* from 1936. A British merchant sells dum-dum bullets to the Negus of Ethiopia.

was able to intercept all radio and telegraph communications in Ethiopia. All the messages intercepted by Mazzi amount to almost four volumes and give us a synoptic view of the difficulties faced by the Abyssinians. The armies of the various *rases* lacked everything, from weapons, ammunitions, and vehicles. Addis Ababa in 1935 was a hive of merchants. For the right price, they would sell the Abyssinians miscellaneous brands of rifles: Mauser, Mannlicher, Lebel, Gras, Schwarzlose machine guns from the First World War, run-down lorries, shoddy aircraft, and odd and unmatching ammunition. Unfortunately for the Italians, these merchants also sold the Abyssinians dum-dum bullets, primarily meant for big game and designed to expand on impact. Alongside this information, here are some tragicomic radio messages intercepted by Maj. Mazzi in the period preceding the start of hostilities:

> I am *Grazmach* Afarwaq, your devoted servant. I inform you that my men have diarrhoea and want to go home. I kiss your feet and humbly ask what to do.
>
> *Dejazmach* Nasibu here, I tell you that the white soldiers are as numerous as the heavy rain. I need coins because my warriors haven't received their pay and are thinking of leaving, I kiss your shoes.
>
> *Balambaras* Embaie speaking. Oh King of Kings I beg you, send me a cannon so I may take down the iron birds.

This is *Dejazmach* Ighezu, adviser to his Majesty the Negus Neghesti. Message to everyone. Try to avoid taking prisoners because I think the international laws forbid killing them after they are captured.

The great quantity of information supplied by Mazzi to Graziani (and from him transmitted to Eritrea, firstly to De Bono, and then to Badoglio) on a daily basis was so copious that it was like seeing all the opponent's cards. In the days of the taking of Neghelli (16–20 January 1936), Maj. Mazzi managed to lure the Ethiopian High Command into a trap with an operation whose echo resounded all over Italy and went down in history as 'the Neghelli bluff'. A platoon of Blackshirts managed to take control of *Ras* Desta's radio station at Cogorù and Mazzi, after having substituted the Abyssinian radio operators, continued to transmit messages for forty-eight hours managing to divert the enemy columns and send them straight into the jaws of the Italian troops.

Was it war? The British historian George L. Steer asked himself the same question. It is fair to say that it was a typical colonial war, fought between asymmetrical forces. This is also confirmed by a neutral source, one certainly not favourable to the Italian cause. We are alluding to the report of the American Maj. Norman E. Fiske whom we have mentioned before. Fiske knew every minute detail of both opposing forces. He wrote: '… the Abyssinian armies are disorganized; their leaders often improvise. Supplies are non-existent, I encountered emaciated and malnourished soldiers.… On the other hand, the Italians have an excellent organization, the air force is their strong point…' Fiske continued by giving a detailed analysis of the Northern Front commanded by Badoglio, and he described the recreational activities of the Italian soldiers, which his Anglo-Saxon tastes found amusing: 'I've noticed that all they need to have fun is either a guitar or a harmonica and so they start singing happily around the bivouac fire…' In conclusion, he added:

> As regards to the Southern Front, I have to say that, on a strategic level, it was of less importance than the operations carried out in the north. However, whilst it's true that the brunt of the war was sustained by Pietro Badoglio and the troops advancing from Eritrea, it's also true that Graziani's march on Neghelli was spectacular and has thus made a great impression on the people's imagination. The fact that the Abyssinians had no air force and possessed few badly manoeuvred artillery pieces obviously made the Italian army's job much simpler. Therefore, I believe that absolutely no comparison can be made between the Italo-Ethiopian conflict and conflicts between western armies.

And now the much-promised documentation on the use of poison gas. All these documents are authentic. They are, for the most part, telegrams preceded by those words ('urgent', 'very urgent', 'secret', 'very secret', 'personal message', 'to be deciphered by recipient') which are characteristic of coded messages from military commands and political ministries.

We have found these documents browsing through mountains of documents, leave papers, ship and aircraft loading lists, orders and counter-orders, all historically insignificant but indispensable for the organisation of an army on the move. We publish them alongside official communiques of the Ministry for the Press and Maj. Mazzi's interceptions.[11] Starting off in chronological order, the first hint of the use of poison gas comes from an Italian source:

> 14 September 1935. Rome. Undersecretary of War. From Federico Baistrocchi to Rodolfo Graziani, Governor of Somalia. Urgent, secret. I have arranged for the urgent formation of a chemical company. The requested 30,000 masks will arrive by the end of the month.

> 22 *meskerem* 1928 [3 October 1935]. Radio interception. *Grazmach* Afarwaq of Gorrahei here speaking to *Dejazmach* Nasibu, Governor of Harar and its province. This morning the Italians started dropping many disgraces [note by Major Mazzi: 'by disgraces he obviously means bombs']. When the disgraces blew up, they spread sulphur and a sort of flour that looks like mushy peas. Those who smelt it got an upset stomach and their heads started spinning.

> 25 *meskerem* 1928 [6 October 1935]. Radio interception. From *Dejazmach* Nasibu to *Grazmach* Afarwaq. Come on, be strong. The disgraces which fell on you will soon fall on us as well. There was a smell of poison? Bring me a bit

After sanctions were imposed on Italy by the League of Nations, the Fascist regime wanted to Italianise many foreign words which had entered the Italian vocabulary in the previous century. A drawing from *La Domenica del Corriere*: 'How would you say cocktail in Italian?' 'Stomach-ache.' (*Erodoto TV*)

of that flour, I will send it to have it analysed in Addis Ababa. Be prudent and if you cannot resist, behave like brigands and attack the Italians with ambushes. Afarwaq severely reprimands the warriors who shoot at the aeroplanes with their rifles. They are wasting bullets and offering themselves to death. May the God of Ethiopia protect you.

6 October 1935. Rome. Ministry of the Press and Propaganda, foreign press section. To all newspapers. Foreign correspondents in Harar are dishonestly reporting that during the bombardment of Gorrahei of the 4th, our pilots dropped venomous gas. Underline the falseness of this report.

19 October 1935. London. From Italian Embassy to Ministry of Foreign Affairs. Today, the *Times* published an interview with Nasibu, the Governor of Harar. Nasibu claims that the Italian Air Force is using aggressive chemicals and talks about a thick veil of yellow substances which burn the skin. We have denied all accusations.

11 *tekempt* 1928 [22 October 1935]. Radio interception. This is Haile Selassie, Negus Neghesti of Ethiopia speaking to *Grazmach* Afarwaq of Gorrahei. We are aware that previously these types of bombs were also dropped on Adwa. However, no one saw the exact location where the bombs fell. Only smoke was seen. Perhaps they were just smoke bombs. Who knows if it wasn't God himself who did this.

24 October 1935. Lugh Ferrandi. From Graziani to Lessona, Colonies. Private message, to be deciphered by recipient. I notify that the English Lt Howard Henry of the Somaliland Camel Corps has today been received by Capt. Busi at Garowe. The English officer, who is sympathetic towards Italy and the Duce, tried to find out whether we had the necessary equipment to defend ourselves against possible Abyssinian gas attacks and if we would make use of gas ourselves. Capt. Busi obviously replied in the negative.

27 October 1935. Rome. From H.E. Head of the Government Benito Mussolini to H.E. Governor of Somalia Rodolfo Graziani. 12409. Secret. Very urgent. 29th is good day for action. I authorize use of gas as last resort to overwhelm enemy resistance and during counter-attacks.

28 November 1935. Rome. From SIM to H.E. Badoglio and H.E. Graziani. Informed by reliable sources, our military attaché in London tells us that the current British Government has authorized the export of tear gas and yperite gas to Abyssinia. It was not possible to ascertain whether the gas will be shipped in bullets or in containers.

15 December 1935. Lugh Ferrandi. From Graziani to Badoglio, Adigrat, and Lessona, Rome. Very urgent. 1475. Against the barbarian hordes advancing towards us and are ready to commit any atrocity, we should not spare any weapons. I therefore ask for the liberty to use poison gas given that there is no risk of harming the local population as they have all fled into our territories or to Kenya.

16 December 1935. Rome. From H.E. Head of the Government Benito Mussolini to H.E. Governor of Somalia Rodolfo Graziani. Very urgent, very secret, to be deciphered by recipient. I reply to your 1475 with my 14551. Use of gas is ok if Your Excellency deems it to be necessary for supreme reasons of defence.

17 December 1935. Lugh Ferrandi. 6168. Governor Graziani to Gen. B.A. Bernasconi, Commander for the Air Force in Somalia. H.E. the Head of the Government authorizes the use of poison gas whenever I deem it to be necessary for supreme reasons of defence. The attack which is underway across the entire Somalian front itself necessitates supreme defensive measures; I order that poison gas be used wherever you deem it to be necessary.

17 *tahesas* 1928 [17 December 1935]. Radio interception. *Ras* Desta here asking to be put through to Addis Ababa. Starting from today the Italians are dropping gas bombs which rain down like hail. The smell of the gas forces us to leave our trenches. The great foreign medic doctor Hylander has warned us to be careful

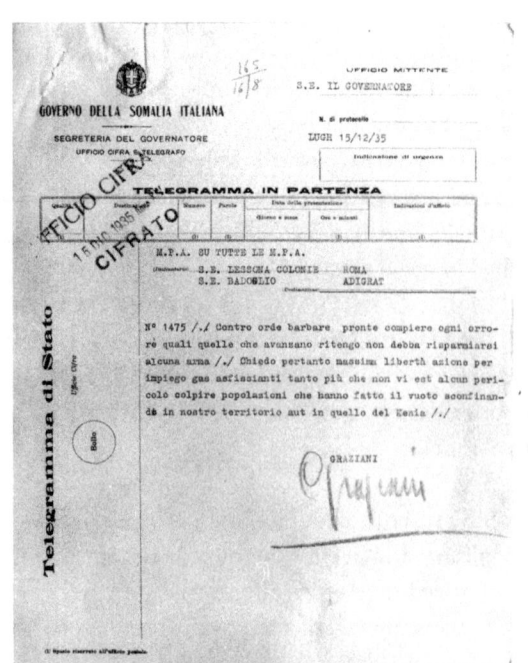

In this telegram from 15 December 1935 to the Minister of the Colonies and Badoglio, Graziani requests 'the liberty to use poison gas'. A revealing telegram which rebukes the claim that gas was only used as a 'retaliatory measure'.

as it could be poison gas. Even when the lesions caused by the gas are light, they become infected and grow into great sores. We are worried.

27 December 1935. Dawa Parma. From Gen. Frusci to Governor. Personal message. Urgent. One of our aircraft has been shot down. The fate of pilot Tito Minniti has been sealed. It seems he has been tortured, eviscerated, and decapitated. I believe it to be right and proper to proceed with a gas attack on Sassabaneh Bulale [Graziani's pencilled-in note: 'Agreed. An eye for an eye. I will talk about it with Bernasconi'].

29 December 1935. Lugh Ferrandi. From Graziani to Badoglio, Asmara, and Lessona, Rome. 2085. Very secret. As the pilot captured at Dagabur has had his head cut off, placed on a pike and taken as a trophy to the Abyssinian Headquarters, I have ordered a retaliatory attack. Our aircraft will also drop tricolour leaflets saying: 'You killed our prisoner, cutting his head off against all human and international laws in which prisoners are sacred and deserve respect. You will be given what you deserve.'

30 December 1935. Mogadishu. Air Force in Somalia. Gen. Bernasconi to Governor. Personal correspondence. Orders executed. Today, four of our aircraft have bombed the Abyssinian encampment and field hospital at Malca Dida. Leaflets were also dropped. Subsequently, during two bombing raids, six capronis bombed the enemy dropping one 250 kg bomb, six 100 kg bombs, ten 50 kg bombs, four 31 kg bombs, thirty-two incendiary bombs and twelve 21 kg yperite bombs.

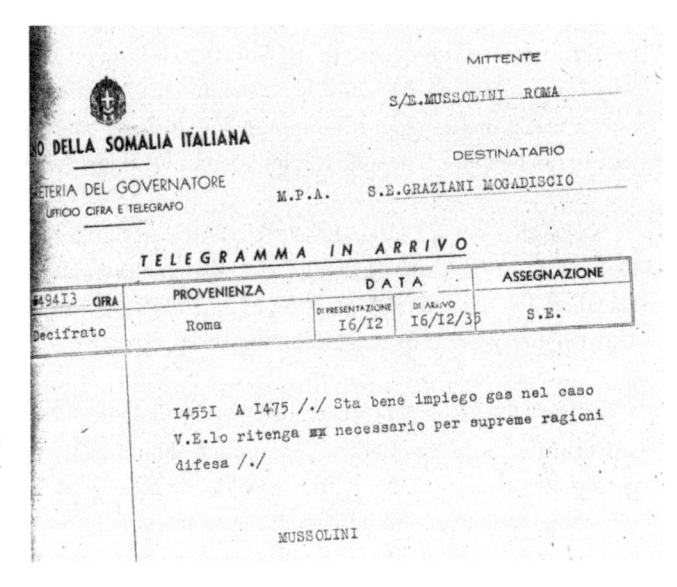

The following day, Mussolini himself replied to Graziani, authorising him to use gas 'if Your Excellency deems it to be necessary for supreme reasons of defence'.

32 December 1935. Mogadishu. Air Force in Somalia. From Gen. Bernasconi to Governor. Personal correspondence. I would like to specify that another eight aircraft have dropped 300 incendiary bombs and forty-eight yperite bombs on the enemy in the Dagabur and Sassabaneh Bulale area. Strong enemy reaction. Tomorrow we will repeat this action with twelve yperite bombs and all remaining explosives.

20 *tahsass* 1928 [30 December 1935]. Radio interception. From *Ras* Desta to His Majesty Haile Selassie I, Negus Neghesti of Ethiopia. Many aeroplanes came today and dropped countless bombs injuring the great medic of the Red Cross. [...] The enemy has totally destroyed all our wounded who were in the hospital. This week our enemies dropped the venomous bombs.

31 December 1935. From Graziani to Badoglio, Asmara, and Lessona, Rome. 2095. Very secret. Retaliation completed using gas bombardment on the Juba and Ogaden front. Seeing that *Ras* Desta has sought refuge in a small field hospital near Cogorù to shield himself from air attacks, I have ordered that these tents also be bombed. A medic was wounded during one of these raids, a certain doctor Fritz, Swedish.

31 December 1935. Lugh Ferrandi. From Graziani to Badoglio, Asmara, and Lessona, Rome. Secret. 2156 to 15231. Gen. Bernasconi has been ill with kidney stones for quite some time, he needs to be urgently operated on. I propose Lt-Col. Virginio Rigolone as his temporary replacement for Commander of the Air Force in Somalia. Has news of our reprisal leaked out?

21 *tahesas* 1928 [1 December 1935]. Radio interception. This is *Ras* Desta, put me through to *Blattengeta* Heruy, Minister of Foreign Affairs. I report that the Abyssinian Army of the South has been under violent enemy bombardment for over a week, including gas bombings. The Italians have destroyed the Swedish Red Cross hospital. The nine foreign medics working there have been killed.

31 December 1935. Mogadishu. Air Force in Somalia. Lt-Col. Rigolone to Governor. A Squadron of seven capronis has flown another bombing raid on Dagabur. 1,826 kg of explosive bombs and 231 kg gas bombs were dropped. We also dropped more leaflets. The action was effective. None of our aircraft was hit.

1 January 1936. Rome. From Minister of the Colonies Lessona to H.E. Graziani, Governor of Somalia. Retaliation against the infamy committed on our pilot is completely justified. May Your Excellency please send me more information regarding the accidental damage done to the small Swedish field hospital and the personnel therein. Exaggerated stories spread by Sweden.

2 January 1936. Rome. From H.E. Head of the Government Mussolini to Governor of Somalia Graziani and for reference to Marshal Badoglio. Very urgent. I fully approve of the reprisal bombings and from this moment on I approve of all future bombings. However, we do need to avoid hitting international organizations such as the Red Cross.

23 *tahesas* 1928 [2 January 1936]. Very urgent, from *Blattengeta* Heruy, Minister of Foreign Affairs of the Ethiopian Empire to Secretary General of the League of Nations, Geneva. The Italians have made widespread use of poison gas. We vehemently protest. Italy continues with its inhumane and so called 'mission of civilization' with impunity. We renew our protests against the criminal actions of the Italian government which are in flagrant violation of international agreements.

3 January 1936. Rome. Ministry of the press, Italian press section. To everyone. In response to the protests of Ethiopia and the League of Nations, emphasize the barbarous acts committed by *Ras* Desta's soldiers. Underline the Italian public's disdain. Ridicule the indignation of the British and North Americans. Remember that Sweden has a socialist government. Accentuate the fact that if Ethiopia's barbarity continues then we might well have to resort to using aggressive chemical weapons.

3 January 1936. Lugh Ferrandi. From Graziani to Badoglio, Asmara, and Lessona, Rome. Very secret. Very urgent. Avoid hitting the Red Cross at all costs. However, I would still like to point out that on the Swedish Red Cross lorries we found Mauser rifles and twenty-seven ammunition crates for Mausers made in Belgium by the Herstal company. We also found dum-dum bullets, courbashes for floggings and in their tents, chains for slaves.[12] I believe we should remind Geneva of Abyssinian atrocities and also that in order to flee from the offensive they paint Red Crosses on their tents and buildings.

4 January 1936. Addis Ababa telegram to London. Intercepted by SIM. Henry A. Young to *Diocles Press*. Only Doctor Hylander was wounded in the bombing of the Swedish Red Cross. I interviewed him. He said it was murder plain and simple. The Italian aircraft flew thirty metres from the ground. No one in the hospital was armed. Correspondence follows.

4 January 1936. Rome. Ministry for the Press, supervision of the newspapers. In the previous few days, our Air Force in Somalia flew some bombing raids over the enemy lines in retaliation for the capture and beheading of pilot Tito Minniti. Three thousand leaflets signed by Governor Rodolfo Graziani were also dropped during the bombardment. A few bombs hit the tent of the Swedish

SELLASSIÉ, al leone di Giuda: — Lascia fare. E' l'unico mezzo per salvarti la pelle.   (Dis. di Gamerra)

A cartoon from *La Domenica del Corriere*. The Italian newspapers claimed that the Ethiopians painted red crosses on their tents to avoid being bombed. In this drawing, the Negus paints a red cross on the Lion of Judah. The caption reads: 'Trust me, this is the only way to save your skin'.

Red Cross by mistake, and it seems that one Swedish person was wounded. *Ras Desta's* telegram where he claims that all the members of the Swedish mission were killed is untrue. It's untrue like everything which comes out of Addis Ababa and finds wilful listeners in the foreign press who have taken up the noble mission of defending Abyssinian slavery. And so, the denigratory campaign commenced by Geneva against Italy is to be ridiculed. The question remains as to why the League of Nations remains silent about the dum-dum bullets and the atrocities committed by the Abyssinians. Insist on this point.

4 January 1936. Mogadishu. Air Force in Somalia. From Lt-Col. Rigolone to Governor. Private message. We have repeated the bombing of Dagabur with eight capronis. We dropped 2,430 kg of explosives and 350 kg of gas. The area has been completely razed. The operation was a success.

4 January 1936. Rome SIM, review of the foreign press. The journalist Mr Wilson telegraphed the *Associated Press* in London from Addis Ababa. He says that,

according to Abyssinian sources, twenty-eight Ethiopian patients died during the bombing of the Swedish Red Cross. However, he says that information from the Ethiopians is usually inaccurate and that due to the inaccessibility of the roads, he cannot check for himself. He's waiting for Lt Frére, *Ras* Desta's Belgian military adviser, to return to Addis Ababa so he can find out more.

4 January 1936. Radio interception. This is Armand Frére speaking from Cogorù. For Col. Reul, Head of the Belgian Military Mission to Addis Ababa. The fighting started in the outskirts of Dolo. They are attacking us with a large number of tanks, so if you cannot send us any special lorries with many Oerlikon guns, weapons and cannons manned by artillerymen, then we won't be able to defend ourselves. Enemy aircraft fly over three times a day and drop large bombs and gas bombs.

5 January 1936. Rome. SIM, radio interception service. Full text of the telegram sent today by Prince Karl of Sweden to the Emperor of Ethiopia: 'The Swedish Red Cross and its president express, with deep respect to Your Majesty, their gratitude for the noble message we received after the ignoble aggression against the Swedish ambulance. We deplore the loss of so many valorous Ethiopians lives entrusted to our care and placed under the protection of the Red Cross.'

26 *tahesas* 1928 [5 January 1936]. Radio interception. This is Wolde Selassie Heruy, urgently calling from Neghelli. Doctor Hylander whom I questioned regarding the poison gas, told me that no gas was used where he was. Hylander was given a medical check-up by Major Arwilopilos [Maj. Mazzi's note: 'Greek medical officer, head of the sanitary services of the Ethiopian army']. His wounds do not seem serious.

5 January 1936. Rome. SIM, survey of the foreign press. The correspondents from Addis Ababa are insisting on the poison gas story. According to the article of a Mr Holmes of the *Nord Press* of Copenhagen our bombers destroyed the ambulance of the Egyptian Red Crescent.

5 January 1936. Rome. From H.E. Head of the Government Benito Mussolini to H. E. Badoglio, Makallé, and H.E. Graziani, Lugh. Very urgent. 180. Suspend all use of gas until the meetings at Geneva start, unless it is necessary for supreme necessities of offence or defence. I will give you further instructions in this regard.

5 January 1936. Rome. Ministry of the Press, Italian press section. To all newspapers. Stop all mention of our possible use of aggressive chemicals as a retaliatory measure. Talk about Abyssinian atrocities. Regarding the use of dum-dum bullets, underline England's involvement in this, given that these bullets are produced by Eley Brothers and Kynoch Ltd. companies from Birmingham which are associated with

the Imperial Chemicals Industries. It would also be useful to cite George Bernard Shaw's article which recently appeared in the *Times*. Especially where he writes: 'The League of Nations must not only ensure collective security, but also collective civilization. If a country is uncivilized, then it is the duty of the nearest civilized country to intervene. This is how the British Empire was built.' A fitting rebuke which can easily be applied to the situation between Italy and Ethiopia.

9 January 1936. Rome. From H.E. Head of the Government Mussolini to H.E. Governor of Somalia, Lugh. Urgent. 334 to 333. All good regarding your announcement. I am certain that everything will go as Your Excellency wishes. Stop. I authorize Your Excellency to utilize any means possible where necessary. Stop. A cordial greeting.

10 January 1936. Lugh. Personal message. From Rodolfo Graziani to Gen. Bernasconi. In the next few days, I shall launch an attack to throw *Ras* Desta's army back towards the north ... therefore the participation of the air force needs to be intense. The last bombing raids have demonstrated the effectiveness of poison gas...

12 January 1936. Mogadishu. From Air Force Command of Somalia to Governor. Private. Urgent. Bombers started taking off at six and continued to do

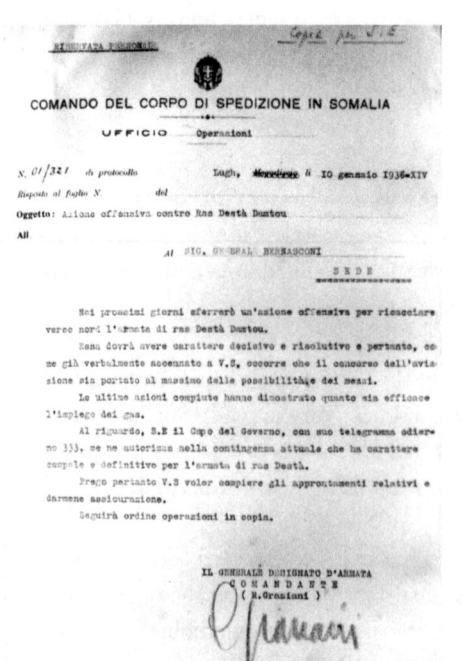

Dated 10 January 1936, a telegram from Graziani to Gen. Bernasconi. In it, he states: 'The last bombing raids have demonstrated the effectiveness of poison gas'.

so until twelve. One took off every half an hour. Twenty-four aircraft took part in this action, six carrying gas ... Gas was dropped on Bander and the left-bank of the Ganale Doria as far as Baccarà. Bombings with gas and explosives will continue in the afternoon and in the following days.

After dropping hundreds of thousands of kilos of explosives and conquering Neghelli, Graziani stopped using gas. There was no need for it anymore, *Ras* Desta was fleeing, and his scattered soldiers were hiding in the forests in small groups. But the foreign newspapers would not give him any credit. After every battle, the journalists would always bring up the use of chemicals. Every time the Ethiopians were defeated, it was always due to poison gas. Even the Abyssinian war bulletins constantly denounced the 'barbarous use of gas by the Italians'. At the beginning of March, Tzahai Ewotion, president of the Association of Ethiopian Women, wrote an emotional plea to Edouard Herriot, president of the French National Assembly: 'Help us,' exclaimed Tzahai, 'our sons are burned alive and reduced to shreds by the jaws of the toxic gas which the Italians drop on them like demons from the skies...'

On 30 March 1936, *Reuters* wrote: 'The communiqués from Addis Ababa continue to accuse Italy of utilizing aggressive types of chemicals. British public opinion is very shocked. Lord Cecil of the House of Lords and Anthony Eden of the House of Commons have condemned the use of poison gas as violating the Hague's convention n. 4 of 18 October 1907 and the Geneva protocols of 17 July 1925'. In April, the British Government sent a harsh formal protest to Rome:

8 April 1936. Rome. From Colucci, Colonies, to H.E. Rodolfo Graziani, Governor. 4245. Secret. To be deciphered by recipient. The international scene continues to accuse Italy of using gas. Is this true? Please confirm or deny.

9 April 1936. Dolo. From H.E. Graziani to Colucci, Colonies. Secret, Urgent. It is patently false.

10 April 1936. Rome. From H.E. Head of the Government Benito Mussolini to H.E. Governor of Somalia Rodolfo Graziani. Very urgent. Very secret. Do not, I repeat, do not make use of chemical weapons until further orders.

14 April 1936. Rome. From Colucci, Colonies, to H.E. Graziani. Very urgent. 4246. British delegation has notified the League of Nations ... The Swedish ambulance declares that there were seventy-one cases of burns caused by gas treated by the Swedes last December; The Norwegian ambulance declares that twenty-one cases of burns caused by yperite were due to one bomb on 29 March. To rebuke British claims may Your Excellency urgently provide information and make observations.

16 April 1936. Dolo. Graziani to Lessona, Colonies. Urgent, secret. I have not made any use of gas. The Abyssinians are liars and ignorant. Perhaps the burns were caused by flamethrowers. Our Foreign Minister ought to denounce continued use of dum-dum bullets by the Abyssinians. The valiant Lt-Col. Liberati was hit by a dum-dum round and has a horrendous gash where the bullet came out. I shall send photographs. I would also like to notify further torture and eviscerations.

27 April 1936. Rome. From H.E. Head of the Government Benito Mussolini to H.E. Governor of Somalia Rodolfo Graziani. Very urgent. Very secret. Given that the Abyssinians continue to use dum-dum bullets, I authorize Your Excellency to utilize gas as a retaliatory weapon, excluding yperite bombs. Only if Your Excellency deems it to be necessary.

Graziani did not deem it to be necessary, and certainly not for humanitarian reasons. Only because the war was drawing to a close. On 2 May, the Negus, with the court and his family, escaped to Djibouti, bound for London via Alexandria.

A comical drawing from *La Domenica del Corriere* entitled: 'The Abyssinian Julius Caesar'. The caption reads: 'Haile Selassie: "Son of a Tigray, now you will tell me what you have done." Ras Desta: "I came, I saw, I ran."'

On 5 May, Badoglio entered Addis Ababa, and on 9 May, after having conquered Harar, the vanguard of Graziani's army reached the capital. But now the guerrilla war had begun, a bloody, insidious, and tenacious war. Mussolini would be infuriated. Three times, between June and December 1936, the *Duce* reconfirmed the order to utilise gas against the Ethiopian rebels. Again in 1937 (4 October and 10 December), he sent a coded message saying, 'finish off the rebels by making large-scale use of gas.'

Graziani did not agree, his position and the determination with which he had fought permitted him to do so. He was notorious for being tough. A genocidal phrase, which he probably never said, has often been attributed to him: 'The *Duce* will have Abyssinia, with or without the Abyssinians'. No weakness was allowed in his book. However, Graziani did not agree, simply because (as he wrote in a private message to Gen. Tedeschini Lalli, commander of the air force in AOI, 6 October 1937), he believed that incendiary bombs were 'a lot better, they destroy the harvest and the areas inhabited by the rebels'.

Nonetheless, in October 1937, the viceroy continued to follow Mussolini's directives. He equipped a dozen planes with evaporators, he ordered them to fly at low altitudes so that they could sprinkle the ground with thin poison rain. However, due to the dry season, the results of this operation left much to be desired. Graziani had foreseen this and decided he might as well stop.

8 November 1937. Addis Ababa. Viceroy of Ethiopia to Superior Air Command for AOI. 7132. Cyphered. I confirm that the use of gas must only be used in exceptional circumstances and only when multiple favourable conditions consent its use. Otherwise, it's just a waste. As regards the operations taking place in Gojjam, known as great policing operations, the use of gas has proven to be ineffective as a consequence of the arid and bare terrain. And also, its rapid evaporation during the day due to the high temperatures. Given the above conditions, using gas has become a real joke.

This is the story of the use of poison gas on the Southern Front and the subsequent normalisation phase of the empire. It is the story of how and why it was used and how and why its use was stopped. It was not a 'real joke'. The Abyssinians had also committed atrocities, but Mussolini and his generals felt no hesitation nor had moral scruples. They used gas as long as it was useful, and only stopped when they deemed it to be useless and even harmful. 'Everything will go down the drain,' Graziani explained with macabre humour.

5

Marquis of Neghelli and Executioner of Addis Ababa

In 1936, Neghelli was a village of 500 inhabitants. Capital of the Galla people, 'door to Addis Ababa', and an important settlement of the Great Lakes region. Back then, there were only two brick buildings: the Coptic church and the HQ of the Belgian military mission. Yet, on 20 January, when the first convoy of caterpillars ploughed through the Somalian undergrowth and appeared on the plateau, Italy went wild. Graziani had reached the victorious troops thanks to an emergency landing near the village. He soon became a hero and received thousands of letters, telegrams, and postcards in thanks. Neghelli had been more than just a military venture, it had been a sports exercise. Apart from fighting the Abyssinians, the Italians had overcome the desert, long distances, unforgiving weather, and tropical diseases. They had won on their own against the whole world, dragging themselves to the top of a 1,441-metre-high plateau, and with them, water, the most important resource for any army.

Among Graziani's papers we have found a series of letters and telegrams that he received during this victorious period. Just about everyone wrote to him. From Vittorio Valletta to Elena Flamini ('Rodolfo, It's me, your old nanny. Bravo, you've beat them! Please respond, my address is viale Vaticano 40 in Rome'); from Don Lorenzo Jella, his teacher and confessor at the seminary in Subiaco, to the old *carabiniere* constable Andronico Pietro ('Most Excellent Excellency, pardon me if I use my typewriter'); from his neighbours at via Paganini 7 to his uncles, Peppino and Augusto ('Up and at 'em Rodolfo! We're always with you'). Leafing through at random, we find letters from schoolgirls, messages of praise from veteran associations, from the League of Fascist Women, workers' societies, greetings from the bowls club of Busto Arsizio and the mountain guides of Plan Rosà. The people of Filettino worked for weeks on creating a fine handmade parchment in dedication: 191 people signed it and it was then personally presented to their beloved *paesano* 'by the most revered Capuchin monks Ippolito from Velletri and Lodovico from

Frascati who are journeying to the land of the Galla as missionaries of the Roman faith'. Mussolini's telegram was nothing short of Napoleonic grandeur: 'Your Excellency, in Harar you will find the Marshal's baton'.

Even in Neghelli, Graziani kept a diary which today can be read at the Central State Archive. However, there is nothing truly relevant in it, only hastily written notes. Interestingly, they always start off by invoking the saint of that particular day: '6 February 1936. Saint Dorothy. Help me, Saint Dorothy, in my daily trials'; '24 April 1936. Saint George. In the name of Saint George, I shall defeat the dragon'.

Then come his personal thoughts, 'I really miss Ines', along with daily mundane events such as 'It's Sunday, mass in the camp and lunch with the officers', nagging health problems in the way of 'I have a temperature, let's hope it's not the malaria coming back'. There is little content referencing the war. However, Graziani mentions it exclusively on 22 January when his Libyan soldiers had celebrated by 'carrying me on their shoulders,' and where he then adds: 'If I had two motorized divisions, I could occupy Addis Ababa. Instead, I have to go to Harar. Hands off Addis Ababa.... Badoglio's private property!' A premonition and possibly the first hint that his friendship with his colleague from his times in Libya was going sour.

At Jijiga, on 6 May 1936, Graziani had a near-death experience. From his diary:

> Today the Coptic clergy played a murderous trick on me. Whilst my soldiers, in a final 400 km push set out to cut the road from Dire Dawa to Harar, I decided to visit the cathedral of Jijiga which the Abyssinian war bulletins claimed had been destroyed. I entered through one of the two main doors and as I walked down a few steps I placed my foot on a mat and suddenly felt the floor missing under my feet. There was a hole six m deep with a sharp pole in the middle, on which I was clearly meant to be impaled. I then fainted and when I regained consciousness, I tried to climb out using my elbows like a chimneysweep. As I arrived at the top I was nearly out of strength when I managed to grab hold of the hand of Capt. Burkler, my adjutant, and finally see the light. I got out of there alive, but I ended up with a bad bruise along with a suspected fracture, my right hand dislocated, and abrasions everywhere, in particular on my right knee. The doctor prescribed a few days of total rest.

At the end of hostilities on May 9, Graziani was bedridden and recovering in the Ghebbi of Jijiga ('a rathole, a disgraceful shack with a corrugated metal roof which reminds me of protestant missions'). It was here that he heard Mussolini's speech on the radio: 'Oh legionaries, lift up your banners and hearts to salute, after fifteen centuries, the return of the Empire to the fatal hills of Rome!' It was also from the radio broadcast that he learnt of his promotion to marshal of Italy. From his diary: 'I'm a Marshal and I'm aching all over. It must be like this all the time: success and pain simultaneously. The story of my life, *maqtub*'.

Again, from his diary on 20 May 1936: 'Badoglio has urgently called me to come to Addis Ababa. My head is bandaged, my arm in a sling, I can hardly walk. But I must go. I cannot miss the parade of our victorious troops'.

From his diary on 21 May 1936:

At Villa Italia, previously the seat of our embassy. Here I met Badoglio. I was full of stitches; he was bursting with health and happiness. He hugged me and then listened to the misfortune which occurred to me at Jijiga, he then explained to me the real reason for my urgent summon. These were his words: 'Dear Graziani, officially I'm briefly going to Rome on leave. But actually, I'm not coming back. These 2,600 m of altitude are not for me, here in Addis Ababa I can hardly breathe. As soon as I'm in Italy, I shall propose you for Viceroy, Governor General and Commander-in-Chief. Happy?' I can't have seemed very joyful—the situation in Addis Ababa was chaotic—because he soon added: 'You're ten years younger than me, soon everything will sort itself out. Don't worry!'

From his diary on 22 May 1936:

With Badoglio at the airport. He left accompanied by his son Mario, a diplomat. He's radiant, his term as Viceroy has lasted less than a fortnight. An enthusiastic welcome awaits him in Rome. In the car during our drive to the airport, he confided to me: 'I'm also going to settle some old scores. Baistrocchi tried to get one over on me and he'll pay for this. You see, Graziani, I strangle my enemies slowly, with a velvet glove!' As he tightened his closed fist. To be honest, his departure seemed more like an escape to me.[1]

Perhaps it was not an escape, however, it was certainly a very elegant way of getting out of a messy situation. At Addis Ababa, there was an unspoken state of siege. During their rapid advance towards the capital, the Italians had left behind them tens of thousands of armed Abyssinians, and now those Abyssinians were all there around the city—on the Entoto hills. Graziani called together all his military officials and civil servants to ask for statistics. He now realised that he had inherited a very troublesome situation from Badoglio. In the capital, there were 426 officers and 9,934 soldiers with 100 rounds each. Rations were also scarce, fuel was missing, and there was almost no possibility of bringing in supplies: the rebels had cut off the French run Addis Ababa–Djibouti road, the only cement motorway in the whole country. All in all, the Italians only controlled the urban area of the city and the surrounding eucalyptus forest, a defensive perimeter of 39 km in all. They were both victors and prisoners at the same time. The patrols which went out every morning encountered signs affixed to trees in Amharic which incited the population to rise up and 'beat the Italian invaders to death', or other rhetoric such as 'devouring them in a single bite'. The posters were signed by the Association of

Above left: Rodolfo Graziani in 1916 with his wife, Ines, and their daughter, Vanda. He is on leave after being fifteen months on the front line. He would become the youngest colonel in the Italian army.

Above right: Maj. Graziani pictured in the trenches on the San Michele mountain, 1916.

Below left: Libya, 1929. Pietro Badoglio, newly appointed governor of Tripolitania, with Graziani.

Below right: Graziani riding a *mehari* camel during the pacification of Libya, 1928. It was with these camels that in January 1931, Italian troops would march on Kufra, the last stronghold of the Senussi 'rebels'. (*Archivio Centrale dello Stato*)

Above left: Graziani dressed in a Tuareg cape as he talks with an Arab informer in the oasis of Hun, 1929. (*Archivio Centrale dello Stato*)

Above right: Omar al-Mukhtar pictured here after his capture. He was a valiant man who led the Libyan resistance for nine years. To catch him, Graziani and Badoglio devastated Cyrenaica with concentration camps, flying tribunals, and a long frontier wire along the border with Egypt. (*Wikimedia Commons*)

Below: Omar al-Mukhtar fell into Graziani's trap. The Italian soldiers were jubilant. The rebel leader behaved with dignity when he was brought to Benghazi in chains for a lengthy meeting with Rodolfo Graziani, then vice-governor of Cyrenaica. In less than three hours, a military tribunal would try him and sentence him to death.

Omar al-Mukhtar was sentenced to death by hanging and went to the gallows on 16 September 1931. Before his death, he said: 'We come from God and to God we return'. His execution took place at Soluch concentration camp in front of 20,000 prisoners. (*Wikimedia Commons*)

A light artillery battery manned by Somalian *askari*. In 1935, Italy declared war on the Ethiopian Empire. Graziani, governor of Somalia, commanded the Southern Front. His victory and conquest of Neghelli would render him famous and earn him the prestigious title of marquis. (*Wikimedia Commons*)

Graziani on the Southern Front next to a radio transmitter. The radio played a crucial role in the Italo-Ethiopian War. After cracking the code of the Abyssinian cyphers, the Italian intelligence service could intercept all Ethiopian radio communications. For Badoglio and Graziani, it was like seeing all the opponent's cards. (*Archivio Centrale dello Stato*)

Graziani and his general staff planning the capture of Harar, 1936. (*Archivio Central dello Stato*)

Above left: The conquest of Neghelli truly captured the public's imagination. Here, a drawing by Vittorio Pisani illustrates the submission of the Ethiopian notables. However, no one in Italy was aware that Graziani had used poison gas against the Abyssinian soldiers, most of whom were barefoot and armed with primitive weaponry.

Above right: Another illustration by Vittorio Pisani. The war was finished, and Addis Ababa had fallen. The artists, with naive rhetoric, depicted the meeting between Graziani and Badoglio 'The Two Great Warriors', while in the background, the female embodiment of victory holds the fasces. In actual fact, the guerrilla war had just begun, although the regime preferred to keep this under wraps.

Rodolfo Graziani mounted on *Uarr*, his white horse. At the end of the Ethiopian war, Mussolini promoted him to marshal of Italy and made him viceroy of Ethiopia. *Uarr* (which means 'difficult' in Arabic) would later be sold at an auction in Rome in 1944.

An Ethiopian boy working in a field kitchen. In the summer of 1936, the living conditions in Addis Ababa were dreadful and the city lacked basic necessities, even water.

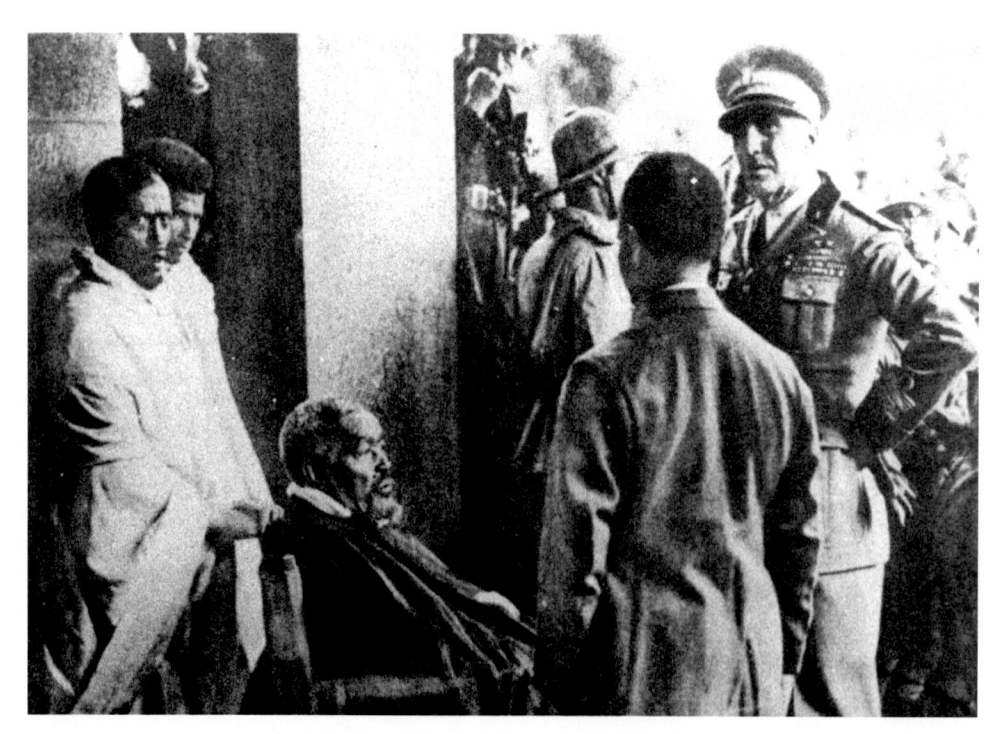

Graziani pictured meeting a member of the Coptic clergy. In the first months of the empire, the viceroy tried to ingratiate himself with the notables, the clergy, and the common people. But Mussolini believed that only a policy of 'terror and extermination' could defeat the rebels. Graziani complied and followed the dictator's orders with ferocious determination.

Above left: The obelisk of Aksum today, where it stood at the start of the Italian conquest. The Italians in East Africa destroyed many vestiges of the past and plundered the treasures of the Negus. This ancient monument was taken to Rome in 1937 on the *Duce*'s orders. Only in 2005 was it returned to Ethiopia by the Italian Government. (*Wikimedia Commons*)

Above right: Haile Selassie, Negus Neghesti of Ethiopia a year before the Italian invasion. On 2 May 1936, after realising that all resistance was futile, the Negus escaped to London with his family. When Haile Selassie returned to the throne in 1943, he proved himself a fair and just ruler. He did not seek revenge on the Italian colonists who remained in Ethiopia and abandoned the idea of having Graziani tried as a war criminal. (*Wikimedia Commons*)

Below left: A convoy of military lorries on the Asmara–Addis Ababa motorway. Built by the Italians, the road connected Eritrea with the capital of the empire, therefore ensuring the regular flow of supplies. On 10 August 1937, Graziani wished to personally inaugurate it. 'Excellent trip,' he telegraphed to his wife, 'I drove all day.' During his time as viceroy, Graziani also completed the road from Addis Ababa to Mogadishu, which covered all of Somalia.

Below right: On 19 February 1937, during a ceremony in Addis Ababa, the Ethiopian resistance attempted to assassinate Graziani. A bomb explosion peppered the right side of his body with 350 pieces of shrapnel. Shown here, the viceroy is being carried to safety. The Italian retaliation was horrific. For three days, the fascist squads devastated entire neighbourhoods, killed thousands of innocent people, and burned down Saint George's church. Despite being wounded, Graziani was consistently informed of everything. This is demonstrated by the telegrams he sent to Mussolini on 19 and 20 February.

Scenes of Horror: gallows on the outskirts of Addis Ababa. After the assassination attempt on the viceroy, the violent repression continued for months. Mussolini's orders were draconian: 'I ask Your Excellency to utilize the politics of terror and extermination against the rebels and the populations which shelter them'. Graziani zealously and ferociously followed the *Duce*'s orders. (*Ian Campbell*)

Executions in Abyssinia had become a regular occurrence. 'All rebels which are captured must be shot,' Mussolini telegraphed. Graziani carried out these instructions to the letter. The verbs which appear most frequently in his orders to his subordinates are 'eliminate', 'destroy', and 'liquidate'.

Above left: The body of a 'rebel' hanging from a tree.

Above right: Graziani's blood-spattered uniform. As a result of the attack, the viceroy injured the ankle of his right foot which became permanently dislocated. From then on, he needed to wear an orthopaedic shoe.

Right: A procession of Coptic clergymen and Abyssinian notables through the streets of Addis Ababa. The majority of the Abyssinian notables had made an act of submission to the Italian government and considered themselves to be immune from reprisals. Despite this, Graziani ordered that many of them be sent to Danane concentration camp, in Somalia, or exiled to Italy on the islands of Asinara, Ponza, and Giglio.

Graziani in ceremonial uniform with his wife and the officers of Addis Ababa's garrison. It was October 1937 and Vanda, the viceroy's daughter, is about to be married to Count Sergio Gualandi. (*Archivio Centrale dello Stato*)

December 1937, Graziani managed to extinguish the flame of revolt with brutal methods, and now, the colonists could finally relocate to Ethiopia. Here they arrive, with their uniforms, suitcases tied up with twine, and the village patron saint.

Italian colonists in Libya. They arrived in their thousands, all of them chasing the dream of 'a place in the sun'. (*Wikimedia Commons*)

Above left: Mehari camel riders on guard at Palazzo Venezia. It was 1937, the year of Fascism's greatest splendour. Mussolini wore the uniform of first marshal of the empire and the people of Italy looked to Africa as the promised land. They knew little about the guerrilla war being fought in Ethiopia. They heard nothing of the reprisals, the rounds ups, or the repression ordered by Graziani.

Above right: In 1938, Graziani receives the marshal's baton in Piazza del Campidoglio, Rome. The regime had organized great celebrations for his return from the empire.

Above left: Ines Graziani (centre) during a Fascist ladies' reunion. Mussolini wanted women to take part in events organized by the party. The participation of families during patriotic ceremonies was important, it reinforced the regime's image and demonstrated Fascism's popularity.

Above right: Rome, 1939. Mussolini and Graziani during a public ceremony in front of the Vittoriano.

Below: Graziani during the 1939 military manoeuvres in Piedmont. Next to him are the dukes of Pistoia, Bergamo and an unidentified general.

Above: Egypt, November 1940. Italian anti-aircraft batteries await the onslaught of the RAF. The end is near. Sidi Barrani would fall on 10 December 1940, in less than two months, the entire Italian 10th Army would be annihilated. After losing Cyrenaica, Graziani would become a disgraced general in the eyes of the *Duce* and would return to the fore only after the creation of the Italian Social Republic. (*Archivio Centrale dello Stato*)

Right: Graziani as military commander of the RSI. In 1943, he decided to join Fascism's desperate last stand, a decision he took against his better judgment. Pictured in 1944, the marshal gives the Roman salute during a military parade. His uniform is embellished with the collar tabs of Army Group *Liguria* with the gladius, which in 1944, had replaced the royal stars. Standing next to him, wearing a beret, is Prince Junio Valerio Borghese, commander of the *Decima MAS*.

Visiting the *alpini* of the *Monterosa* Division at the Münsingen training camp in Germany. The trip was a propaganda success. However, when these divisions returned to Italy, the Germans refused to deploy them on the frontline against the Allies. Thus, thousands of soldiers deserted. *From right to left*: Mussolini, Gen. Mario Carloni, and Graziani. (*Istituto Luce*)

April 1945, Graziani turns himself in to the Americans. He is wearing an army greatcoat without badges or rank slides and he has aged terribly. In his left hand he holds a 'communist' beret given to him by the partisans of San Vittore prison. Sandro Pertini wanted to have him executed as a war criminal. However, with the help of US Army Captain Emilio Daddario, he managed to escape execution. The marshal would spend 1945 to 1950 in prison, firstly in Algiers, then Procida and finally in Forte Boccea.

Right: Graziani in Rome's court of Assizes which prosecuted him for high treason. He denied any responsibility in the anti-partisan war. After seventy-nine hearings, in March 1949, the court ruled that he should go before a military tribunal. Thanks to many mitigating circumstances, Graziani would be sentenced to nineteen years in prison 'for collaborationism'. However, after various amnesties and reductions of his sentence, the former marshal would be freed from prison soon thereafter.

Below: Graziani pictured after the war. Alongside Mussolini, he had lived through the final agonising days of the regime and managed to come out alive. He pensively looks at a portrait of himself from the good old days. However, his days were numbered: he would pass away in January 1955.

Above left: The marshal lying in state.

Above right: Embaie Tekle-Haymanot, the loyal Ethiopian *shumbashi* who followed Graziani like a shadow. He had been alongside the marshal in Ethiopia, North Africa, the RSI, and during his adventurous escape from San Vittore Prison. Here he is at the funeral, being helped up by two MSI members after fainting. After this, Embaie was never heard from again.

Left: Filettino today. As of 2021, the local park still bears the name of Rodolfo Graziani. The marshal rests next to his wife and parents in the small cemetery in Affile. For more than half a century, he was all but forgotten. Only in 2012, with the construction of a new monument in his honour in Affile, has Graziani's name become once again the centre of controversy.

Young Ethiopians or the officer cadets of the Military Academy of Oletta who had come to the aid of the armed bands who had refused to surrender. The rebels were led by *Ras* Imru, *Dejazmach* Gebremariam, *Ras* Desta, *Dejazmach* Beyene Merid, and *Ras* Kassa's sons, Aberra and Asfawossen Kassa.

Graziani's diary ends abruptly on 25 June 1936. However, between the end of May and mid-June, it is lined with dispirited and worried comments.

> 26 May. I am waiting for the *Tessitore* Column, 20,000 soldiers who are my lifeline. Unfortunately, the start of the rainy season means the roads will become quagmires.
>
> 28 May. Pouring with rain. I go and lodge in the small Ghebbi which the Negus had built for the visit of the Crown Prince of Sweden. At least it's clean. Unlike the great Ghebbi which is disgusting and was sacked by thieves and vandals.
>
> 4 June. God bless my caterpillars. They've managed to drag out the cannons and lorries of the *Tessitore* Column which were stuck in the mud. If we're able to reinforce and reconstruct our supply line, it'll be thanks to them. *Post Scriptum*: Today His Majesty conferred on me the Knight's Grand Cross of the Order of Saints Maurice and Lazarus.
>
> 7 June. Last night, we repulsed an attack by rebel bands. Rome refuses to acknowledge the truth. They prefer to believe that Ethiopia is Eden.
>
> 12 June. A courtesy visit to the foreign diplomats. Herr Strom, German legation, cordial. Mr Patrick Roberts, British embassy, cold. To me, the nicest were Mr Bodard and his wife Madame Pierrette of the French Embassy. Not only owing to their excellent champagne. The Americans, sanctionists to the bone, closed their legation in protest. The Japanese are only interested in doing business, they want to import their Abugiadid cloth into Ethiopia.
>
> 17 June. My problem is I need to resist and consolidate my position until the end of the rainy season. How is the main issue.
>
> 24 June. I'm having to deal with hundreds of Abyssinian notables, former councillors of the Negus, civil servants, merchants, scribes and schoolteachers. All ask to have their previous rank back, and above all their salary reinstated. I await instructions from Rome.[2]

The instructions from Rome were muddled and as contradictory as one could imagine. Orders, counter-orders, pleas for peace, exhortations to use harsher measures, inclusion requests for Ethiopian notables in the government, or their explicit exclusion.

On 11 May 1936, forty-eight hours after the occupation of Addis Ababa, Mussolini had already telegraphed twice. The war was over, it was time to build a lasting peace, but the *Duce* was worried about insignificant issues such as philology and eugenics. The first telegram stated:

> Title of Negus Neghesti obviously cannot be attributed to His Majesty the King even in the indigenous language. In official documents the title of Emperor assumed by His Majesty must be translated into the Ethiopian *Qesar za Itiopia*, so reutilizing the title of *Qesar* which the Ethiopians used to address the Emperors of Rome. The title must also be translated simultaneously into Arabic as *Qaise al Habashak*.

In the second telegram he said: 'In order to tackle the terrible and soon foreseeable effects of race-mixing early on, I have decided that no Italian man, either military or civilian, must remain in the colony for more than six months without his wife'. The *Duce* of Fascism then merrily went on to say:

> 19 May. I authorize the spending of seventy million lira for the construction of the main Government building. The new Addis Ababa must be grand and beautiful.

> 2 June. Urgent. Secret. To extinguish the flames of rebellion, rebels who are captured must be shot.

> 5 June. Newspaper of Nazism highlights the reopening of the Zalù Pharmacy in Addis Ababa. Excellent. In general, it's good to humour the Germans.

> 8 June. In agreement with Lessona, Minister of AOI, a law of fundamental importance has been passed for the Empire. The five governors of Eritrea, Somalia, Amhara, Jimma and Harar will be subordinate to the Viceroy. Collaboration with local elements is favoured as long as they are subordinate and kept in honorary roles.

> 16 June. To reach the objective of normalization I suggest appealing to common Christian faith.

> 29 June. Disregard previous order about allowing participation of locals in the government. It's premature.

> 8 July. Very urgent. Secret. I ask Your Excellency to utilize the politics of terror and extermination against the rebels and the populations which shelter them. If we do not use the law of an eye for an eye on a large scale, we shall not be able to heal the wound in a timely manner.

Marquis of Neghelli and Executioner of Addis Ababa

Being propelled from left to right by these contradictory orders, a confused Graziani held the uncertain reins of the empire. He did everything as instructed and then would subsequently forsake what he had just done. Such indecision inevitably disappointed both those who wanted to live in harmony and those who demanded ferocity. Graziani attempted to win favour with the clergy by supporting one of their most ancient aspirations: the independence of the Abyssinian Coptic Church from the Coptic Church of Alexandria in Egypt. However, a massacre of Italian aviators at Lekempti and a night attack on the capital by the armed bands of Aberra Kassa prompted him to execute the *Abuna* Petros, the Coptic pope, for conspiracy with the Kassa brothers. He tried to improve relations with the Ethiopian nobility by openly embracing the *rases* who were more willing to submit, notably *Ras* Seyum Mengesha and *Ras* Hailu Tekle-Haymanot.[3]

However, fearing that these acts of submission were just for show, he exiled half of them to Danane in Somalia, or to the island of Ponza in Italy. He tried also to gain the sympathies of the country's downtrodden by handing out alms to the poor. But then, he issued a proclamation threatening execution for those who did not spontaneously hand over their weapons to the authorities. Back then, nearly all Ethiopians owned some sort of rifle or sabre, it was a symbol of prestige so he may as well have executed all of them. In fact, while initially executions were infrequent happenings, they soon became a normal part of life in the colony. In January 1938, when Duke Amedeo of Aosta replaced him as

June 1936. The Ethiopian notables submit to Italian rule. However, after the assassination attempt, this gesture would prove meaningless. Graziani had nearly all of them deported to Italy or to the concentration camp of Danane in Somalia.

viceroy, Graziani's name had already become infamous.[4] Fittingly, the Ethiopians called him 'Graziani the Executioner'.

In order to illustrate what the living conditions in Addis Ababa were like during what became known as 'the year of the Empire', we will take a look at the first-hand observations of Ciro Poggiali, a professional journalist for the *Corriere della Sera*. In 1971, when all was long forgotten, Poggiali put together his secret diary entries in a book. They were 'secret' because the regime's censorship had prohibited their publication on the daily columns. In mid-June 1936, Poggiali's train journey from Djibouti to Addis Ababa seemed like something from the American Wild West. There were machine guns on the platform roofing and on top of the wagons. At Mojo, 1,000 Abyssinians on horseback tried to assault the train, which relentlessly continued to steam ahead amid explosions and gunfire. Half the passengers lay face down on the floor and the other half were busy firing from the windows alongside the soldiers. When he arrived in the relative safety of the capital, Poggiali checked in at the Imperiale Hotel, the best in the city. It was somewhat akin to a filthy run-down bathing establishment, and the food on the menu was bound to result in food poisoning. Here are a few of his choicest annotations:

14 July 1936, Tuesday. It's total chaos here, we're still in a state of war but you can't write about it. People have been terrified of a full-on assault on the city for about a week now. At night it's dangerous to walk about. I go to bed with two bombs next to my bedside.

15 July 1936. Wednesday. I witnessed a Military Tribunal in the market square. Unenthusiastic, tired, and bored judges. The sentence was written before the trial. The interpreter, a certain Marciano, struggled to translate the lawyers' follies into Amharic, such as: 'I hereby request that, in this instance, the counterparty confirm that the information submitted in the course of the investigation phase is correct.' The defendants were five natives accused of possessing weapons. Four were sentenced to death and one was acquitted. The indifference of the condemned is striking. The acquitted man covered the shoulders of the youngest of the condemned with his own cape. The young man was half naked, proud and beautiful.

17 July 1936, Friday. Ceremony at the Ghebbi for the passage of power from Federal Orazi, who is going back to Rome, and Federal Cortese who is replacing him. Graziani gives a rousing speech but looks sad and tired.

18 July 1936, Saturday. A *Carabinieri* marshal by the name of De Martini tells me that he and his men routed a large group of rebels and captured about twenty of them. When they had to cross a turbulent river, some prisoners refused to do so. To make things easier they were shot. The remainder were taken to Addis Ababa in a camp near the radio station, Graziani ordered their immediate

execution which occurred on the shores of the Kabana river where the fast-flowing waters washed away the bodies.

21 July 1936, Tuesday. In the morning, review of the *Tessitore* Column which has arrived from Dessie. It took them fifty days to cover 400 km. The Viceroy led the troops through the streets as a show of strength. Then he talked to the natives announcing brutally oppressive measures.

24 July 1936, Friday. The *Sabauda* motorized Column arrived today. Graziani walks amongst the locals and lets them parade before him. Such a thing has never happened before in Ethiopia. A marriage of force with political astuteness. In Abyssinia, a great leader has never come in contact with the crowd.

28 July 1936, Tuesday. Night attack by the rebels. Scenes of terror, people frantically running to safety, mass arrests of adult natives herded around the church of Saint George. Exceptionally brutal treatment given by the *Carabinieri* who hand out lashes and pistol-whippings like candy. This evening I also kept a rifle by my bedside. Another attack is expected at dawn.

4 August 1936, Tuesday. At the market prices are sky high. But above all no one knows whether to pay in thalers or lira and what the exchange rate is.[5]

6 August 1936, Thursday. Executions continue. They have now become a routine occurrence. Weekdays: executions and aperitifs at Café Fiammetta. Holidays: executions, Holy Mass, and aperitifs at Café Fiammetta.

23 August 1936, Sunday. A sad spectacle at the Ghebbi: distribution of six thousand talers to three thousand vagrants. Their repulsive and frightening facial expressions reveal their total human misery. The notables also attended the ceremony because, before the handing out of money, there was the celebration of *Ras* Burru's submission. During his speech Graziani said something quite interesting to the submitting Ras: 'See how you are treated by the government of the great and powerful King and Emperor of Italy. Unlike your former Master who used to kick you up the arse.' He turned to the interpreter: 'Heard that? Translate that I said "up the arse."'

27 August 1936, Thursday. At four in the morning there's an infernal bombardment lasting about an hour. The rebels led by *Dejazmach* Balcha, an almost eighty-year-old eunuch, have managed to infiltrate the city. Our artillery easily shells and annihilates the advancing hordes. 250 corpses lie just outside the city.

28 August 1936, Friday. It's absolutely prohibited to telegraph Italy about the attacks on Addis Ababa. A useless restriction because the world will soon know:

the consuls and the other foreign representatives continue to send cyphered telegrams. But Italy mustn't know.

6 September 1936, Sunday. The locals seem gob-smacked by the sight of our war wounded. Wooden legs. Glass eyes. The natives think this is something diabolical, they then kneel and pray. We burst out laughing.

14 September 1936, Monday. Marshal Graziani calls together all the officers in command of indigenous troops to the Ghebbi. They all feel calm when they arrive but are then attacked by an extremely violent speech. Without a lot of formalities, he reads anonymous letters in which the indigenous battalions are described as being tired due to their long service and their Commander, Gen. Gallina, is portrayed as a wimp and a cretin. Gallina, who is in the Ghebbi, takes the punches in silence.

16 September 1936, Wednesday. Birthday of the Crown Prince with a reception in the Ghebbi. Dancing, music, and refreshments. Finally, we can eat like human beings.

18 September 1936, Friday. The firing squads have moved to the suburbs. Too often the condemned yell 'down with Italy,' 'so this is the civilization you've brought us,' and so on. All these things have made a bad impression.

2 October 1936, Friday. Horrifying stories. On the road to Maychew the bodies of the executed have been put together with the gravel for the roads in order to fill in holes. Alessandro Lessona, Minister for East Africa, arrives today. Graziani telephoned to tell him to bring sheets, table linen and cutlery. There's nothing here.

17 October 1936, Saturday. Lessona and the Minister for Public Works Cobolli Gigli have ordered the toppling of the mausoleum and Menelik's statue in Saint George's square, which occurred during the night. What stupidity! Can we perhaps deny that before the war Abyssinia belonged to the Abyssinians?

11 November 1936, Wednesday. The King's birthday, reception at the Ghebbi. *Abuna* Qerellos was noticeably absent. Perhaps he's protesting the execution of his predecessor, the *Abuna* Petros, decided by Graziani in half a day. But Graziani offers a gift to *Abuna* Qerellos, a beautiful shepherds' cane with a golden pommel. And so, peace is restored.

19 November 1936, Thursday. In the afternoon, the Viceroy reviews the Eritrean battalions. *Fantasia* around Graziani, he is cordial with the *askari*, the speech he gives is soldierly and it resounds with the troops. Despite the violence he is

The number of Ethiopians who resisted Italian rule ran into the hundreds of thousands. Graziani had these leaflets dropped by aeroplane in rebel strongholds, inviting them to submit to Italian rule.

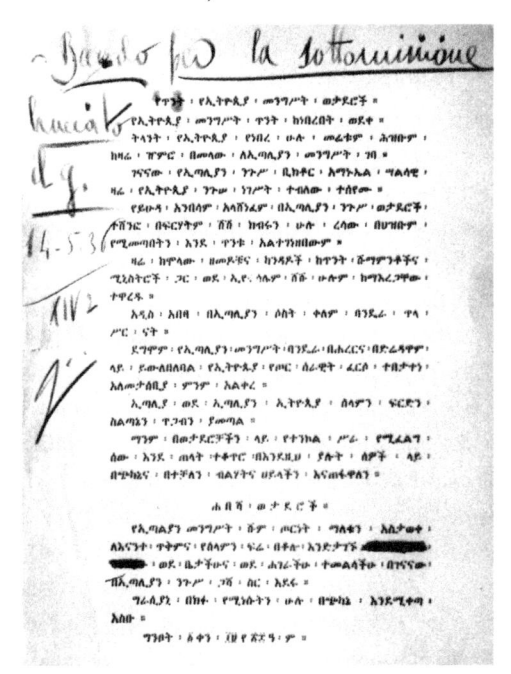

forced to dish out, deep down he is a sentimentalist. The heart always triumphs over the brain.

We doubt whether Graziani was a sentimentalist in Ethiopia. What is certain is that, apart from executing rebels, suspected rebels, and the relatives of rebels, he was also involved in more peaceful activities. Together with Cobolli Gigli, he had put together a vast program of public works for the reconstruction of Addis Ababa according to a new regulation plan. All over the empire, the construction of roads, bridges, railways, power stations, schools, hospitals, and leprosy clinics were well underway. He cleaned up and renovated the great Ghebbi, forbidden city of the emperor, by replacing the pre-existing wooden shacks with a series of elegant buildings which crowned the dais, the Negus's pavilion. He befriended an important *Ras*, Hailu Tekle-Haymanot, crown king of Gojjam, whom he trusted blindly to the point of letting him retain an armed band of 4,000 Ethiopian collaborationists. *Ras* Hailu would never betray Graziani, in the eyes of the Italian 'conquerors' he represented the other side of the coin. He was praised highly as a 'good' Ethiopian, unlike the 'bad' ones who had to be punished— an example and a warning to the local population. Graziani's *shumbashi*, Embaie Tekle-Haymanot, always claimed that he was the nephew of *Ras* Hailu, therefore, an Ethiopian of the noblest blood. Was it true? It is impossible to confirm as Tekle-Haymanot is quite a common surname in Ethiopia, and even a district of Addis Ababa is called Tekle-Haymanot. In any case, Embaie, whose conversations we have published according to the testimonies of the old people of Piani di Arcinazzo, would always be by the marshal's side. He was much more than a servant; he would compete with Concitella in canine devotion and would not abandon his 'master' even in front of the gates of San Vittore prison. The last photo, taken in January 1955 at Graziani's funeral, shows him among the group of crying family members. He was comforted by the neo-Fascist politician Roberto Mieville. After this, Embaie was never heard from again.

In the autumn of 1936, with the end of the rainy season, the Italian troops went on the offensive. The tactics were identical to the ones tried in Libya: mobile columns, round ups, and aerial reprisals against villages in the interior which had aided the rebels, essentially not much carrot and a lot of stick. The viceroy had won the bet he had made with himself: he had managed to resist inside the besieged capital and had strengthened his position. Now, in the five governorships, Graziani had 113,000 men at his disposal: the garrison of Addis Ababa alone numbered 5,318 Italian soldiers, a few thousand *Carabinieri* and finance guards, 4,006 Blackshirts and 22,025 Eritreans and Libyans. Under the supervision of Alberto Mazzi, who had been promoted to colonel and appointed chief of staff, the identities of all the Abyssinian notables were catalogued and put under surveillance by Col. Azolino Hazon, commander of the *Carabinieri* in AOI and Maj. Giordano Vicino Pallavicino, head of the military intelligence. Each *ras* who was still on the loose had a bounty on his head: 'dead or alive, as long as he is recognizable', was written on the posters. The highest price was for *Ras* Imru, the most prestigious guerrilla leader (he had studied in France and had attended the Military Academy of Saint-Cyr): a bounty of 20,000 thalers. Imru would be the first to fall into the hands of the Italians. On 21 December 1936, trapped on the right-bank of the Gojeb river, *Ras* Imru surrendered to the colonial brigade led by Lt-Col. Minniti. He was then taken to Col. Malta's headquarters in Bonga. We will examine the capture of *Ras* Imru, as a few foreign newspapers picked up the story (followed by Italian publications in 1945–1946) and wrote that Graziani had him shot after promising to spare his life, therefore breaking his promise. Nothing could be further from the truth. Here is the text of the radio messages sent by the viceroy to Col. Malta along with some telegrams sent to Rome.[6]

21 December 1936. From Addis Ababa to Bonga, via radio. Graziani speaking, is this Col. Malta? for Imru, let me have all the information so I can judge whether a summary execution is in order. Please tell me your point of view in this regard as well. Over. Excellency, this is Malta, I have understood. To express my views, I would have to know whether Imru is responsible for the slaughter of the Gondrand construction site. Over. You're absolutely right. I will take it upon myself to ask for this information from the *Carabinieri*. Over and out.

22 December 1936. From Rome, urgent telegram. From H.E. Head of the Government Benito Mussolini to H.E. Viceroy of Ethiopia Rodolfo Graziani.

Ras Imru is to be considered a prisoner of war. No execution. He will be interned in Italy. I express my most heartfelt congratulations to Your Excellency.

22 December 1936. From Addis Ababa, urgent telegram. From H.E. Viceroy of Ethiopia Rodolfo Graziani to H.E. Head of the Government Benito Mussolini. I thank you *Duce*. Your voice and your iron will command me.

22 December 1936. From Addis Ababa to Bonga, via radio. Graziani speaking, listen to me, Malta, I have received instructions from Rome. Here is what you must do with Imru: spare his life on condition that he submits unconditionally. Reassure him about his fate. I will send an aeroplane to come and get him. Over and out.

23 December 1936. From Bonga to Addis Ababa, via radio. This is Malta, I want to speak to the Viceroy. Excellency, I have informed the prisoner who is just recovering from a deep moral and physical depression. Imru is willing to submit, but first, he would like a meeting with Your Excellency, he says he admires you. Over. Have you made any promises? Over. On the first day I told him to put his hopes in God and the Italian Government's justice system. Over. Watch him, don't scare him and treat him well. We need him alive to convince *Ras* Desta to surrender. Over. I am treating him very well; I have even given him a bottle of champagne Over. Perfect. Christmas coming up soon, I will send a crate full of champagne by aircraft. Over. By the way Your Excellency, any news from the *Carabinieri*? Over. Yes, he has nothing to do with the slaughter at Gondrand. Over and out.

Ras Imru spent the years to follow exiled on the island of Ponza. In a twist of fate, at Ponza, he was lodged in the very same building which housed Mussolini for a few days after his toppling in 1943. When Haile Selassie returned to the throne, Imru was given the esteemed post of Ethiopian ambassador to the United States.

But let us return to December 1936. Despite the capture of *Ras* Imru, the rebel chiefs, and in particular *Ras* Desta, refused to surrender. The guerrilla war and its rosary of horrors would go on for quite some time yet, for the whole of 1937. However, Addis Ababa was no longer in danger. The rebel bands continued to roam around the countryside of the capital but never dared attack. Assured that all was well on the guerrilla front, by the new year Graziani—who had had his family come over—decided to dedicate himself to the colony's much neglected civil administration. As always, he was a shrewd administrator of public finances and a severe judge of other people's behaviour. He began financial inquiries into: the Salus pharmacy, the Italia cinema, 'La Rapida' transportation company, and the treasury of the local section of the Fascist Party. He also asked for a judicial investigation into the merchant Guido Mazzetti because 'he supplied the army with low-grade soap,' and the Anglo-Indian lubricant company Mohamedally & Co. 'suspected of shipping contraband currency with the Kenyan branch of the same name'. He opposed the construction of the Torre Italia, a monumental project by Florentine architect Flavio Dessy favoured by Lessona: '7,750 rooms and higher than the Eiffel tower and the Empire State Building'. He ordered the repatriation of two officers 'they challenged each other to a duel', of three male and two female civil servants 'caught fornicating in their offices during working hours,' and of two chief maniples of the Militia 'they were aware of corrupt activities but complacently remained silent'. He involved himself in everything: censorship, charity, the correct use of the Pro Opere Impero funds, in relations between the provincial governors, the managing of the Italica Gens hospital and in handshakes. The abolition of handshakes was one of the many brilliant ideas of Achille Starace, secretary of the Fascist Party. One of his circulars from 4 February 1937 stated: 'In the Empire, handshaking is prohibited; only Roman salutes are allowed. Handshakes are unhygienic and reveal political defects'. Even though it was ridiculous, this instruction needed to be applied. Graziani made sure it was. From Rome, the viceroy received a never-ending stream of complaints and problems. Two of these are of a particular importance, the 'problem of Jewish careerists' and the 'problem of madamism'.

The 'problem of Jewish careerists' began on 16 January 1937 with a telegram from Lessona which read: 'The German press has made unfavourable comments about Jews in AOI who have obtained posts of high responsibility. The case of Captain Modiano is considered indicative. Without resorting to antisemitism, may Your

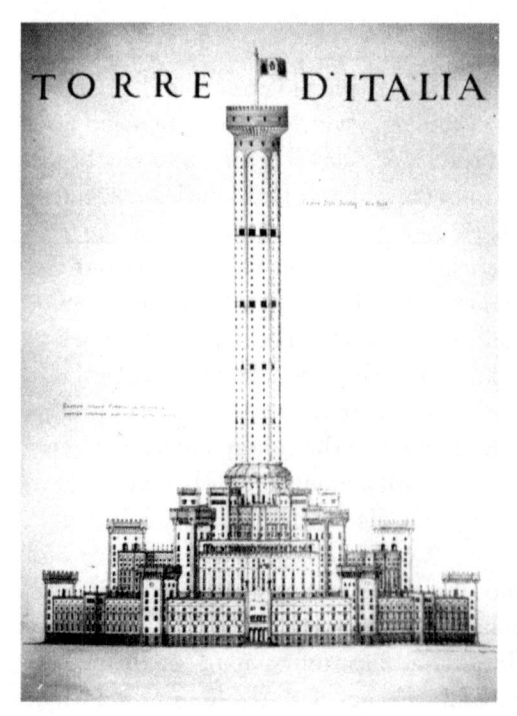

Mussolini wanted the new Addis Ababa to be 'grand and beautiful'. Above, a drawing of the 'Torre Italia', a building which was meant to be taller than the Eiffel tower. Graziani botched this pharaonic proposal.

Excellency in the future please prevent the rapid career and promotion of Italian citizens of the Israelite race'. Here follows Graziani's rapid inquiry and blunt response:

> Captain Modiano is a fictitious person invented by journalists. The Jews residing in the Empire are as follows: Cesare Banon, a soldier in the medical services and now a storekeeper for the Francesco Faranda company in Asmara; Federico Sforza, an accountant in the offices of the Governorship of Addis Ababa; Israel Norbert, a doctor; Osvaldo Pietro, a typist for the military tribunal; Alberto Rimini, a merchant; Loris Ottolenghi, former militiaman of the 221st Legion *Fasci all'estero* and currently representative of Mohamedally & Co.; Ilia Spizzichino, volunteer and currently cereal merchant. Six other Italians of the Israelite race and religion are currently serving in the Blackshirt *Tevere* Division. May Your Excellency in the future please desist from intervening on the basis of false information from the press.

The 'problem of madamism' was far more serious. The man who had invented this curious neologism was Mussolini himself. Many Italians, as soon as they had arrived in Ethiopia, had taken local girls as their lovers and mistresses and hastily called them 'madames'. 'I've got hold of a madame', 'I have a madama', people would confide to each other in their various dialects. Was this not one of the main reasons they had gone to war in the first place? The famous song '*Faccetta Nera*' ended with these words 'My darling little black face, a family we will have'. But such talk displeased the *Duce* and so he announced the 'fight against madamism'. Lessona's telegram to Graziani on 13 February 1937: 'His Excellency the Head of the Government disapproves of unions and cohabitation with native women, not because of a dislike for black people, but for racial differentiation. He demands that something be done about this'. Graziani saw to it. The viceroy's order of the day to the employees of the colonial administration (15 February 1937): 'Starting from today all employees must sign a document stating that they will make an effort not to start relationships with women of colour. For the salvation of the white race and for its prestige, long live the King, long live the *Duce*!' Cries of anger rose up. The soldiers protested, as did the workers intent on building the Addis Ababa-Asmara motorway. Mussolini also did not want Italian prostitutes in the Empire. 'The Italic woman,' he said, 'must appear to the natives in a dignified manner. Not as a prostitute.' And so? The viceroy, apart from giving the soldiers and employees a severe reprimand ('Get your wives or your girlfriends to come over'), was forced to pretend to be a pimp and recruit Madame Brunette, owner of the best brothel in Addis Ababa, to import Greek, French, Spanish, and Portuguese prostitutes. Of course, the Italians continued to make love with the young Ethiopian women, but cautiously, like political dissidents, knowing that they were putting their careers at risk. Graziani was unswerving, before his time as viceroy was over, he even repatriated three of his most worthy collaborators because they had Ethiopian mistresses: Maj. Pallavicino of the SIM, Maj. Quercia and Capt. Moroni of the Royal *Carabinieri*. But above all else, he was concocting a plan (which was never put into practice), for the separation of the races 'in public places and on public transport'. Basically, Graziani theorized the concept of apartheid twenty years before South Africa.

On Friday 19 February 1937, the Imperial Ghebbi was embellished with flags, to celebrate the birth of Prince Vittorio Emanuele of Naples, the only male son of Crown Prince Umberto and his wife Maria José of Belgium. Those invited and gathered around the garden were important civil servants, Abyssinian notables, and Coptic priests led by *Abuna* Qerellos. Pressing against the gates of the enclosure, guarded by three officers and ninety-three *Carabinieri* in dress uniform, were the poor and homeless awaiting for the customary handing out of thalers. At midday, while the waiters were serving refreshments and the band was playing the *Marcia Reale*, a bomb exploded. This signalled the start of the assassination attempt. Immediately following in rapid succession, seventeen hand grenade explosions rained down upon the viceroy and the small group of dignitaries. Graziani had the right side of his body peppered with shrapnel, while alongside him *Abuna* Qerellos, four generals, Col. Mazzi and many others were thrown to the floor and severely injured. Count Gherardo della Porta, government commissioner at Addis Ababa, witnessed the whole scene whilst taking cover behind a column. He proceeded to coldly count the wounded, fifty-two in total, then gave the order to barricade up all the entrances while inside the Ghebbi, the panic-stricken guests scurried like ants. Some tried hiding, others tried to climb over the gates of the enclosure, all of whom were beaten back and shot at. Capt. Di Dato seized Basciaured Aptewold and Hagi Batasso, two former cadets from the Military Academy of Oletta, and killed them both with a shot to the back of the neck.[7] The *Carabinieri* were shooting at a group of civilians who had just returned from ransacking the Ghebbi's armoury and the forecourt was covered in corpses. And amid the chaos ambulances began to arrive. From Graziani's autobiography:

> I found myself under a canopy roof, I was greeting the guests. At that very moment I had noticed nothing, I thought they were just fireworks, or the midday cannon shot. After the second explosion I went out into the open and as I looked up, the third bomb explosion hit me. I fell and I felt the weight of other bodies falling on top of me. I yelled; 'A car, a car! Take me to the hospital!' Gen. Gariboldi, Federal Cortese and *Carabinieri* Capt. Mossuti all came to my aid, my uniform was spattered with blood, they stretched me out on the back seat of Danilo Brindelli's car, a photographer for the Istituto Luce. In the hospital Doctor Tarquini blocked the haemorrhage by tying my right femoral artery. I got through the operation well and never lost consciousness.

The Italian reaction was immediate and swift. For forty-eight hours, from the afternoon of Friday 19th to the afternoon of Sunday 21st, Addis Ababa was set ablaze in a mad 'hunt for the darkies' in which a thousand or a few thousand Ethiopians were brutally killed. *Tukuls*, houses, and churches were ransacked and demolished.[8] A retaliation attack similar to those of the *Waffen*-SS. Abroad they exaggeratingly talked about 6,000 or 10,000 people slaughtered and entire areas of the city wiped out. Again, in 1948, when the marshal was about to be put on trial by the court of assizes in Rome, the French journalist Victor H. Boccara wrote: 'Graziani is the man who wiped out every sign of life in a suburb of Addis Ababa ... to his *aide-de-camp*, whilst drawing a circle with a red crayon, he said: "In twenty-four hours' time, I don't want to see anything standing in this area, not even a tree."'[9]

During the Fascist period, the gravity of the reprisal was either denied or minimised, for obvious reasons, and afterwards, to maintain Italy's respectability. Only the journalist historian Angelo Del Boca has told the facts as they really are, but all these are quite uncomfortable truths. They contradict the image of 'the good Italian'. The current unofficial version shifts the blame to 'the Fascist squads'. This is true, but only in part. The Fascists wreaked havoc, but behind them were also officers and soldiers in civilian clothes. Many civilian functionaries and workers, all of whom were terrified of being massacred and were overcome by an extreme ferociousness. What is also false is the claim that, when the bombs went off, the viceroy was 'trembling with fear'. Concerning the dynamics of the assassination attempt there were five eyewitnesses (Federal Cortese, Birindelli the photographer, Count della Porta, Capt. Mossuti and Poggiali the journalist): all agree when affirming that 'no one felt afraid because there was not even enough time for that'.

Ciro Poggiali, who was at the Ghebbi on 19 February and suffered two slight injuries during the explosion, wrote in his diary, not only about the attack, but also of the repression which followed the assassination attempt.

> ... I can hear the echo of the firing squads in the hospital where they're treating my wounds. The retaliation against the natives has begun. Despite my limp, I go out and see what's going on. The Italian civilians in Addis Ababa, about 3,000, have initiated their vendetta putting into practice the most authentic methods of Fascist *squadrismo*. They go around armed with batons and steel bars, taking out any native they see. There are mass arrests: hordes of negroes are herded together with courbash whippings. In a short period of time the roads around the *tukuls* are dotted with corpses. I see a driver, who after beating down an old negro by hitting him with his club, uses a bayonet to pierce through his head. It's quite obvious that only innocent people have been the victims of this slaughter. They will later say that without the swift and violent reaction of the civilian population, the thousands of inhabitants of Addis Ababa could have risen and massacred us. At night, they start another retaliation by burning some *tukuls*...

Saturday, 20 February:

I return to the Ghebbi. The notables who have been arrested have all been herded together in the throne room, they are either sitting, standing up or lying on the steps. The captives form a unique spectacle with their opulent clothing. The former director general of the Ministry of Foreign affairs is in a tuxedo and a former minister is even wearing a fur coat. The servants form a separate group, as do the Muslim notables who are gathered in another hall.... I learn that during a search they found a large warehouse with rifles, bombs, and ammunition. Rumour has it that the plot was organized by *Ras* Desta whose armed bands are not far from the city. So naive. The rebels believed that after eliminating our leaders, chaos would reign and then they could occupy the capital.... I also went to see inside Saint George's church, devastated by a fire ordered by Federal Cortese and carried out under his supervision. All the paintings are lost, the *Sancta Sanctorum* has been opened, and the baldachin containing the tablets of the law has been burned. About fifty deacons who were in the bell house were tied together and left to burn alive: a colonel of the grenadiers intervened and stopped the massacre. In the evening I try to obtain Col. Mazzi's permission to telegraph the newspaper. The orders from Rome are unequivocal, no one in Italy must know. Luckily, I am able to send a telegram to my wife telling her simply that I am ok. Apparently, the radio has issued a short communiqué on the assassination attempt, inviting Italian citizens to deck out their houses with flags. Mazzi rebukes the claims that machine guns were found in Saint George's church, showing how its burning was unjustified. Throughout the whole night the *tukul* burning continues, with a greater intensity than the previous night. The tragic sight of great flames soaring high into the night sky. The natives are all out in the streets. Shocking indifference of the women and children huddled in their small crowds around the smoking rubble. Not even a yell, not a tear, not an insult. The men hide because they risk being beaten by the death squads. Horrifying episodes of senseless violence. They tell me of an American citizen who was beaten by the *squadristi* because he went to the aid of an injured Abyssinian. There is a crackling fire in the eucalyptus forest with flames reaching the skies. The natives are fleeing the city, their backs buckled under the weight of household belongings. The death squads seek out chickens and the little sacks of coins which are found in every *tukul*.... Many savage scenes have been photographed. All the diplomats of Addis Ababa are moving around, armed with cameras. The foreign press is going to have a field day...

Sunday, 21 February: 'I went to the eleven o'clock mass at the palazzo. The Viceroy wasn't there, he was in hospital, Vice Governor Petretti, the Governor of Addis Ababa Sinischalchi and Chief of Staff Italo Gariboldi were also injured. The Federal spread the word that all violence must cease, that at 21.00 all the whites must go back home. It would seem that there are no chickens or coins left to steal'.

At this point, it must be ascertained who ordered and tolerated this indiscriminate manhunt and why the army did not intervene. According to the marshal's supporters, his innocence is out of the question. 'He was lying in bed, in a chloroform induced sleep,' so Titta Madia claimed. In his autobiography, Graziani denies that he was sleeping and admits having ordered the punishment of those responsible, 'Anyone else in my position would have done the same.' He declared that the events of Addis Ababa were unknown to him and cites the testimony of *Abuna* Marcos. 'Despite nominally holding command,' he explained, 'on the same day of the 19th he [Graziani] transferred all civil powers to Arnaldo Pedretti [Petretti] and military authority to Italo Gariboldi. In the afternoon, as soon as I saw Federal Cortese, I pleaded with him to come to an agreement with Gariboldi and I told him "No excesses of violence."' Even according to the marshal only the Fascists were responsible for these 'excesses'. In October 1947, one of his notes for his lawyers smacks of complaining and recrimination: 'If I could use the documents which were taken from me by the Americans,' Graziani wrote, 'I would be able to prove that it was Rome that wanted an extermination, when I always struggled to soften the harshness of the orders I received.'

Today, the documents are available and can be consulted freely. They demonstrate that it was Mussolini who wanted an extermination and that the marshal was fully cooperative. He did not try to soften anything, on the contrary, he often went above and beyond Rome's orders. All of Ethiopia's intelligentsia, graduates, officer cadets and members of the Party of Young Ethiopians were shot. He exiled most of the Ethiopian notables. He conjugated the verbs eliminate, destroy and liquidate in the present and future. He even proposed the complete destruction of the old quarter of Addis Ababa and the rounding up of its inhabitants in a concentration camp.

On 19 February at 3 p.m.: Lessona had just been informed of the assassination attempt and he received a telegraph from Petretti containing a list of those injured and the medical report written by Gen. Bedei and Captains Borra and Pala of the Army's medical corps. The two worst cases were the viceroy's ('multiple injuries caused by bomb shrapnel to the soft tissue of the lower right limb with a wide lacerated and contused wound in the popliteus region with subsequent massive haemorrhage'), and Gen. Aurelio Liotta ('Traumatic amputation of the right leg and lesions to the right eye').

On 19 February, at 3 p.m.: In the headquarters of the Fascist Party of Addis Ababa Federal Guido Cortese assembled his men. He said: 'I have just come back from the hospital, Marshal Graziani has his entire body riddled with shrapnel, he is lucid in mind and spirit. I've told him that we've formed fifteen action squads made up of twenty men each. We'll start moving in twenty minutes'.

On 19 February at 8 p.m.: With an urgent telegram, Graziani informed Mussolini about his health and the measures which had been taken. In it he stated: 'I continue to maintain military and civilian control through Vice Governor

Petretti and Chief of Staff Gen. Gariboldi on whom I have bestowed full powers for the defence of the capital. I have ordered exceptional police measures to maintain order within the city. Two hundred arrests have been already carried out. I have telegraphed the commanders of the bordering regions ordering them to rigorously weed out rebels'.

On 19 February at 9 p.m.: 'The journalist Mario Appelius was allowed to bypass the regime's censorship and telegraph the Stefani news agency to break the news of the assassination attempt. The viceroy has suffered slight injuries; groups of civilians have formed vigilante squads to help maintain public order.'

On 20 February, Graziani woke up with a high temperature. During the night, the medics removed about 100 of the biggest pieces of shrapnel from his chest and his right leg (the remaining 257 fragments would remain lodged in his flesh for the rest of his life). However, after the operation and his chloroform induced sleep, there was an inflammation of the lungs. The doctors and Lady Ines, who was at her husband's bedside, insisted on rest. But the iron-willed marshal refused: he wanted to be informed minute by minute of what was happening, he wanted to be in command regardless. He read through the well-wishing telegrams which arrived during the night, one sent by the king, and the other sent by the *Duce* which ended with the words 'And now start the clean-up'. He received his collaborators; he called the provincial governors to reassure them and examined one report after another. One of these by the commander of the *Carabinieri*, Col. Hazon, put his mind at rest. It said:

> The situation is under control. Fifty individuals arrested. 2,000 stopped and searched. 200 killed because of the colonists' reactions or victims of various accidents. A few *tukul* have been burned, as well as the interior of Saint George's church. Soldiers of the *Granatieri di Savoia* Division have executed thirty natives on the outskirts of the city because they were found with weapons and ammunition on them.

At midday, on 20 February, Graziani sent two cyphered telegrams to Mussolini, numbers 8934 and 8935. In the first one, the viceroy told the head of the government that 'I have blocked all the journalists' correspondence and I have interrupted the foreign embassies' radio communication.' In the second telegram he specified that: 'The city is absolutely calm. 2,000 individuals are being held, amongst them are all the chiefs and members of the clergy. Currently, rigorous and repressive measures are being enforced in the areas where the assassins would have received support'. The *Duce* gave an immediate response: 'None of those being held or those who will be taken in the future must be released without my order. All civilians and clergymen who are suspects must, in any case, be executed by firing squad without delay. I await confirmation'.

Despite all of this, 20 February ended with some good news for Graziani: two columns led by Gen. Natale found the rebel headquarters at Goggetti, a village approximately 50 km away from Addis Ababa. A battle ensued. *Ras* Desta managed to escape, *Dejazmach* Gebremariam killed himself rather than surrender and *Dejazmach* Beyene Merid was taken prisoner and then executed. The booty was immense: four cannons, thirty machine guns, and 5,000 rifles. From his hospital bed, the marshal ordered: 'On to the chase. *Ras* Desta's on the ropes. He must be captured and shot'.

On 21 February, while masses were being held in Affile and Filettino to thank God for 'the great *paesano*'s narrow escape', Dr Cesare Frugoni and surgeon Vittorio Puccinelli landed at Addis Ababa airport. Mussolini ordered that the viceroy be treated by the finest doctors in Italy. The two luminaries of medicine rejected the need for any further operations and confirmed the army medics' diagnosis. Graziani's health was not in danger. There were no abscesses on his eyes, and the inflammation in his lungs was healing by itself. Above all, the patient was in a state of shock and needed rest. That Graziani was 'in a state of shock' was an understatement. He had transformed the hospital into a bunker, there were even machine guns placed on the windows of the operating theatre. He could not and did not want to rest. He read a report by Maj. Pallavicino which worried him. The report stated:

> There is much disapproval amongst the foreign community for the reprisals and the violence which was committed against the natives in the city. Even some Europeans were harassed. The action squads, with the support of civilians, officers, and soldiers, were technically responsible for many abuses as well as theft. As a result, many foreign citizens intend leaving Ethiopia and going to nearby Kenya. Old grudges held towards us are resurfacing. I am informed that the embassies have sent exaggerated reports to their governments. It is my opinion, as head of our military intelligence, that it is time to call a halt to all this.

The marshal agreed. Through his chief of staff, Alberto Mazzi, he ordered that all reprisals cease 'within and not after 21:00'. This order was countersigned by the head of the political secretariat Giovanni Sindico and delivered by hand to Café Fiammetta in piazza Littorio where Cortese and his boys had set up their HQ. On Sunday afternoon, a car with a loudspeaker drove through the streets of the city. '*Camerati!*' exhorted Cortese 'it's time to go back to base. The Party thanks you for your work.'

Still at midday on the 21st, the inexhaustible Graziani prepared a report for Mussolini ('dictated from the Italica Gens hospital, 16:00 o'clock, my temperature: 37.8'). The end of the message reads as follows: 'In these last few days I have ordered mass searches to be carried out and the execution of those who possess weapons, plus the burning down of their homes. As a result, a thousand natives have been executed and as many *tukul* burned'. This letter coincided with a secret and urgent telegram from Mussolini which had just arrived. The *Duce*'s telegram read: 'All males in Goggetti above eighteen years of age need to be executed by firing squad and the village destroyed'.

CAMERATI!

Ordino che dalle ore 12 di oggi 24 febbraio XV cessi ogni e qualsiasi atto di rappresaglia.

Alle ore 21.30 i fascisti debbono ritirarsi nelle proprie abitazioni.

SEVERISSIMI provvedimenti saranno presi contro i trasgressori. Le auto pubbliche, private, ed i camions (meno quelli in servizio di Governo e Militare) debbono cessare la circolazione alle ore 21.

IL SEGRETARIO FEDERALE

Graziani, worried by the reaction of the foreign community residing in Addis Ababa, ordered the end of the reprisals. This poster by the Federal of Addis Ababa Guido Cortese reads: '*Camerati!* Starting from 12:00 of 24 February, all reprisals must cease. At 21:30 all Fascists must return to their homes. Anyone who does not obey will be severely punished'.

The number of documents which the U.S. Military Intelligence Service gave back to Italy is vast, they span the entirety of Graziani's time as viceroy. To make things easier, we will only publish the most important documents which are relevant to our story:

22 February 1937. Setting up of special tribunals with attached firing squad.

23 February 1937. *Carabinieri* and SIM start a formal inquiry into the assassination attempt to identify those who are guilty, their conspirators and to understand how the attack was carried out.

24 February 1937. 'Capt. Tucci to Viceroy. 06:00. today my column has captured *Ras* Desta Damtew and forty of his men at Egia. In accordance with your orders the prisoner has been shot at 17.30. The medical report will follow soon.'

25 February 1937. Private correspondence for the Viceroy. 'I have ascertained the death of the native Desta Damtew. His death was immediate. He was hit by twenty-three shots, three of which were fatal. The body is still in our possession. Medical Lt. Doctor Giuseppe Candela.'

26 February 1937. In a short piece published on the *Corriere dell'Impero*, Addis Ababa's newspaper, Federal Cortese publicly thanks the *camerati* 'who took all the necessary steps to clean up the city and teach good and valuable lessons.' 3,000 of those taken prisoner were released, however, exile awaited 250 notables who were still being held in the Ghebbi.

28 February 1937. SIM, review of the foreign press. According to the foreign newspapers six to ten thousand people were executed in Ethiopia. Two articles from the *Times* are indicative. The first started off with the words 'Graziani's cruelty has, sadly, become notorious...' And the second, bore the title: 'Graziani personally commands the firing squads.' The Marshal, who was slowly recovering from pneumonia, wrote on the package of newspaper cuttings: 'disgusting!'

1 March 1937. Urgent Telegram by Mussolini to Graziani. 'I approve the banishing of the 200 notables. I once again re-confirm my order to have them all executed if they are in any way suspect. However, I am contrary to the mass burning of the *tukul* and the establishment of concentration camps which Your Excellency has proposed. Such a thing would cause great repercussions abroad. It is better to inspect the *tukul* and burn them down individually.'

3 March 1937. From Lessona to Viceroy of Ethiopia. 'Here are the following places of exile which have been chosen for the notables: the islands of Asinara, Giglio and Ponza. Each exile will be given one thousand lira a month and be obliged to write home every week. This has been decided because enemy propaganda claims that we do not exile them but throw them out of aeroplanes into the ocean. The less important exiles can be sent to the penal colony of Danane in Somalia. No salary, they must be only assured a diet of 1,800 calories a day. Medical experts suggest: one lemon a week, 400 grams of meat twice a week, a 650-gram loaf of bread and a hot pasta or rice meal a day.'

3 March 1937. From Viceroy of Ethiopia to Minister for AOI Lessona. 'No problem regarding the exiles. I will make sure I send a list as soon as possible. In the meantime, I am sending you a cinema reel of Addis Ababa filmed by the Luce institute. Its purpose is to demonstrate that all is calm here.'

5 March 1937. From SIM to Viceroy. 'The bombs arrived via Berbera and were deposited at Mohamedally & Co. The assassins, ex officer cadets of the Military Academy of Oletta, were—according to reliable sources—housed as guests in the Coptic monastery of Debre Libanos.'

7 March 1937. From Rodolfo Graziani to Gen. Ruggero Tracchia. '... all of the clergy of Debre Libanos and the surrounding population are accomplices.... You can, therefore, easily understand why I don't give a damn about the well-wishes of the Coptic clergy for the good health of the Viceroy and their deference to the government.... I therefore give the *Carabinieri* complete freedom to investigate and to penetrate where penetration is needed. I assure you that the monastery of Debre Libanos is going to pay for what they've done.'

8 March 1937. The Mohamedally firm was shut down by the authorities. All the foreign staff who were not suspected by the police, had been expelled from the Empire. The *Carabinieri* confiscated packages full of posters in Amharic which read: 'Only a few people have committed evil acts.... The Italian maul anyone, good or bad.... Long live the Negus.'

9 March 1937. The first group of exiles, including eight women with two boys, departed for Italy.

14 March 1937. The *Carabinieri* Command of Addis Ababa sent a generic report to the Viceroy on Debre Libanos. It is the largest monastery in Ethiopia, with 297 monks and 129 deacons, they venerate the remains of the Tigrinya Saint Tekle-Haymanot. It is a famous pilgrimage site.

19 May 1937. From Rodolfo Graziani to Gen. Pietro Maletti. 'Just this minute a military lawyer has relayed undeniable proof of Debre Libanos's monk's collaboration with the assassins. Execute all the monks without distinction, including the Vice Prior…'

24 May 1937. From Rodolfo Graziani to Gen. Pietro Maletti. 'I've talked to *Ras* Hailu who confirms the monastery's responsibility. I therefore order Your Excellency to execute all the deacons of Debre Libanos by firing squad, minus the boys. When you have finished, send me a message with the words "LIQUIDATION COMPLETE."'

In order to shoot so many Coptic Christians, Gen. Maletti had to resort to using machine guns and the 45th Muslim Battalion.[10] The mass execution (only 304 boys were spared) took place at Debra Brehan, in the valley of Fiche, which was then transformed into a mass grave.

The massacre of Debre Libanos was the climax, while simultaneously, the end of Mussolini and Graziani's reign of terror in Addis Ababa.[11] It is true, the firing squads continued to do their work, but less frequently. The remaining rebel bands sought refuge in faraway Gojjam. Enough blood had been shed. The marshal had other things to worry about. Things were not going well with respects to his health. As he got out of bed, Graziani discovered that he had a limp. The ankle of his right foot had dislocated, therefore, to walk he would need a special orthopaedic shoe. On top of this, in Abyssinia and Italy rumours were mounting. It was said that Graziani 'is only half a man' as he had been completely eviscerated by a rogue bomb fragment. Upon hearing such scurrilous claims, the viceroy exploded with uncontrollable rage, his shouting was heard throughout the hospital's corridors. He railed against Lessona who refused to open an inquiry into 'the slanderers', he railed against Gen. Pirzio-Biroli, governor of Amhara, when he casually mentioned during an informal meeting that: 'Our Marshal is very much in need of mental and physical rest'. Graziani abruptly replied: 'The only one in need of rest is you, I'll rest in the grave'. Graziani's telegrams to Lessona then became more and more frequent:

Graziani: 'I demand the punishment of the slanderers, typical representatives of a *petit bourgeois* mentality'.

Lessona: 'These are all rumours from anonymous people. An inquiry would be illogical'.

Graziani: 'Then I will punish the gossipmongers. I am not a finished man, nor am I ready for the scrap heap!'

Lessona: 'No one is saying that you are finished. Your Excellency knows that you are held in the highest esteem by the Head of the Government and by me personally'.

Graziani: 'I thank you and I would like to tell Your Excellency that even though my right foot is incapacitated, it won't stop me from kicking the backsides of those who slander me with impunity'.

In April 1937, the 'kicking people's backsides' reference would become the marshal's obsession. As he came to learn that some ministers and party officials had also criticised him, believing the reprisal of Addis Ababa to be 'out of proportion', he shouted over the phone: 'It's easy to dish out judgements when you're thousands of miles away!' and threatened them with kicks up the backside. Word also got back to him that Badoglio described the conquest of Neghelli as 'a bluff'. He took it as an offence ('I wouldn't have expected it from him'), he talked about it with Col. Mazzi and promised further boots up the rear. He had the visitors' register taken to his room from the reception of the hospital, so as to leaf through it and tick off the names of his 'fake friends' (foreign diplomats, Ethiopian notables, untrustworthy collaborationists). He wrote in the margin: 'the evening before the attack I was at a reception at the French Embassy: Mr Bodard, usually quite affable, seemed embarrassed, his wife avoided eye contact.... It's clear, they could tell something was afoot.... They are all in need of a good kicking'. At the end of April, Graziani summoned *Ras* Hailu and talked to him man-to-man: 'You need to persuade the natives,' he said, 'that they need to stop it with their fantastic conjectures.' On 6 May, after being bedridden for seventy-eight days, the viceroy finally left the hospital. He returned to his bunker-like home with sentries and machine guns everywhere. However, he now had the impression that the natives and the colonists smiled at him mockingly. Given his suspicious nature he saw a double meaning in every sentence and gesture. 'Operation persuasion' had failed. On 7 May, the viceroy applied to receive the War Wounded medal. Count della Porta who received his application naively remarked 'Of course, who deserves it more than you?' Graziani nearly manhandled him. On 9 May, he took the podium during a military parade near the airport and improvised a sort of jig for the cameras. He then telegraphed the Minculpop to say that they could tell the newspapers to publish one, or maybe two photos 'where I am in good shape with ample physical strength to jump and give speeches'. His constant flexing of his muscles soon became ridiculous. The marshal himself realised this and on 19 May 1937, he audaciously decided to have a medical commission examine him and photograph him naked. Among many tales of horror, the story of the naked marshal is an especially amusing one.

On 19 May:

> From Viceroy of Ethiopia H.E. Rodolfo Graziani to H.E. Minister of East Africa Alessandro Lessona. Today, ninetieth day since the assassination attempt, considering the catastrophic rumours which are going around the mother country regarding my mental and physical health. Stop. Whilst Your Excellency knows that I have been working without interruption. Stop. I have deemed it necessary to undergo a legal medical examination the report of which I will send immediately on the first outgoing plane. I will also send photographs of the ceremony of the 9th of May, my latest portrait and photos of the physical exercises which I practise daily. Sent also to the Head of the Government.

Africa Orientale, by Diego Pettinelli, 1936.

On 20 May, after having sent that letter, he wrote another to Mussolini justifying himself. He said: 'You must understand *Duce*, I have every right to defend myself. Far too many rumours have been circulating about me: I have diabetes, nephritis, tuberculosis, I am having a mental breakdown. Utter vile nonsense! You're well aware that I did not relinquish the reins of power for one second…' After having read the letter, Mussolini's suspicions were confirmed. The marshal was in shock and maybe, as many were suggesting, it would be better to replace him. However, Graziani remained vigil.

On 26 May: 'From H.E. Viceroy of Ethiopia Rodolfo Graziani to Mr Osvaldo Sebastiani, secretary for the Head of the Government. There are rumours that I am to be replaced. Any news? Tell me the truth'.

Meanwhile, his test results had come through. The report stated:

> The military medical Commission, headed by Lt-Col. Doctor Signorino with as its members Maj. Doctor Tarquini and Capt. Doctor Pala has put the Marshal of Italy Rodolfo Graziani through a meticulous medical examination and has ascertained that:
>
> Medical history: 1911: snake bite on the index finger of the left-hand. 1912: Malaria contracted in Eritrea. 1915–1918: intoxication caused by poison gas, slight wounds to right arm. 1935: abscesses on tonsils. 1936, January: intestinal infection. Bruises and abrasions caused by falling into a ditch.
>
> Recent medical examination: As a consequence of the attempt on his life of the 19th of February Marshal Rodolfo Graziani has been perforated by 350

pieces of shrapnel to his right hemithorax and his lower and upper limbs. Ninety-three fragments have been extracted. During the post-operation period there were abscesses caused by suppuration and a lung inflammation which disappeared after a few days.

Current medical visit: he is an individual with a strong and robust physique. His numerous wounds have not affected any vital organs. The heart, the liver, the lungs and the spleen are in perfect condition, his nerves are intact, and his scars are superficial. The only case of mutilation concerns his right foot which has caused him to limp. The latter has been corrected by using an orthopaedic shoe. The examinee is declared fit for regular military service.

As soon as he got this report, Graziani called the photographer Danilo Birindelli and had himself photographed in eighteen different poses: on horseback, on parallel bars, on a mule, on a bicycle, walking, running, and dancing. The last three stills show him naked, in profile, and looking straight at the camera with his scars and genitals on show.

On 30 May 1937, six top-secret parcels were sent by aeroplane to Italy to be delivered to Mussolini, Lessona, Achille Starace, Count Volpi, the president of the Senate Luigi Federzoni, and Duke Amedeo of Aosta. They contained copies of the photographs and of the medical report. The accompanying letters are either in an impersonal or confidential manner, according to how well Graziani knew the recipient. The letter to his friend Count Volpi reads: 'Dear Volpi, here is proof that I have not been eviscerated as the legend would have it. I just laugh it all off! My foot is still dislocated but as you can see, I can walk, run, ride a horse or a mule and kick people. I can also dance, and I will, God willing until I'm ninety...'

The medical report, the letters and the telegrams are now public domain, however, the photos have disappeared.[12] One can imagine Mussolini's face and that of the other recipients the moment they opened their parcels. Eyebrows would certainly have been raised, as it was an era which demanded virility, not the ostentation of his male attributes as if he were a Riace bronze statue. The *Duce* never replied to Graziani. Only Volpi, Lessona, and Amedeo of Aosta acknowledged receipt via brief, cold responses and without lengthy comments, a polite way of expressing disapproval. From then on, however, the chit chat about the marshal's supposed mutilation ceased.

Now we move on to the months that followed, the last of Graziani's days as viceroy, which, in general, went quite well. Graziani appeared pleased as he felt certain that better days were ahead. He was laying down foundation stones, he was a witness to numerous weddings, a godfather at numerous baptisms, and present at inaugurated public works. On 10 August, together with Mr Pini, director for the state-owned road-works company, the viceroy travelled by car from Addis Ababa to Asmara (he telegraphed his wife, Ines, 12 August 1937: 'I've driven all day. Fantastic journey. Tomorrow I will be in Eritrea. The new asphalt road is beautiful. Love and

The tree of Lacqueth by Bruno Colori, Ethiopia, 1938.

affection to you and Vanda. Rodolfo'). On 13 October, for Vanda's marriage to Sergio Gualandi, who the king had made a count seven days before, Mr and Mrs Graziani hosted a great reception with many guests who came over especially from Italy. On 26 October, the marshal founded a charitable trust named after his mother Adelia Clementi Graziani. Authorised by Victor Emanuel III, the charity was founded to help the families of the fallen soldiers of the *Tevere* division. It could also boast of a 1.7-million-lira patrimony from the Pro Opere Impero fund.

But what about the guerrilla war? It continued; however, it was more akin to a writhing, dying animal. Against the Italian army, which in April had been reinforced by a black army of 300,000 collaborationist Abyssinians, the rebels could do very little. Their ambushes were as useless as they were counterproductive. One August morning, four officers and one NCO were found like this: Capt. Soldatini, decapitated; Lt Barra and Sergeant Del Mastro had died slowly due to multiple stab wounds; Capt. Paternostro, had been tied to a horse and dragged through a bramble bush; and Maj. Liverani had killed himself to avoid capture. Before such bloody spectacles, the soldiers did not need much inciting. They went, they killed. On 11 September and again on 2 November, the main rebel army, 2,000 men on horseback, managed to approach the capital. Three regiments came out to face them, the trail of fire from the incendiary bombs dropped by the air force exposed where the enemy was fleeing to, towards the Gojjam and the lands of Amhara. 'We must liquidate the rebels,' Mussolini telegraphed, adding: 'Hurry up, this is not a war or a guerrilla war, it's simply a great policing operation'. The *Duce* wanted to wrap everything up, all over Italy people were waiting to move to the Empire. To speed things up, Graziani was free to use whatever means he deemed necessary, including, as usual, poison gas. He utilised it a few times albeit with disappointing results, then resorted to using scorched earth tactics. A telegram the viceroy sent to Gen. Belly (9 November) communicated how things had to be rectified: it begins with the words 'ban on compassion, armed conquest excludes all sentimentality', it ends with the obsessive repetition of the verb 'to eliminate'. The day afterwards from Jimma, Belly relayed: 'Rebels have been beaten. Fifty-three prisoners taken and then executed. Everything within sight has been burned'. It was the end. Submissions to Italian rule multiplied in the regions of the Showa, Nono, Guduru, and Ginde Beret. The noose was tightening around Aberra and Asfawossen Kassa, and so they decided to give themselves up to the collaborationist *Ras* Hailu: he entrusted them to Gen. Tracchia who had them shot.[13]

With the death of the Kassa brothers, the last flames of revolt disappeared. Perhaps Graziani thought he could rest on his laurels. He was wrong. The 'normalization' of Ethiopia also meant the end of his tenure. On 11 November 1937, with suspicious swiftness, Mussolini gave Graziani the sack. He wrote:

> ... with the liquidation of all rebellious unrest in Amhara and in the Showa now imminent, your job can be considered finished.... For nearly three years you have been one of my most precious collaborators and one of the creators of the African victory. I have chosen as Your successor H.R.H. the Duke of Aosta.... The Prince will arrive in early December. Your Excellency will meet him at Addis Ababa to hand over the baton.... I wish to kindly convey my cordial friendship and express the gratitude of the Nation...

Graziani was deeply hurt. He wrote on the *Duce*'s message a tragic '*Consummatum est*', he complained to Volpi that he had been the victim of an underhanded manoeuvre 'and in which I recognize the hand of the clique of party officials deceiving Mussolini. I know that Badoglio is jealous of my successes, that Balbo badmouths me even in front of porters. I don't give a damn...' He actually did give a damn. He put his foot down and penned report after report to support his view that 'the changing of the guard is not ideal'. At the end of November, Attilio Teruzzi (Lessona's successor as Minister of AOI) had received a large report which contained statements from Abyssinian notables thanking Graziani for 'the wise work which he has carried out', and pleas from native officials daunted by the idea losing 'a strict but fair leader'. Letters from various *rases*, including *Ras* Hailu, claimed that 'Graziani's departure will cause the rebellion to gain strength'. Hailu even impertinently said: 'Already, the good Ethiopians are in mourning and the bad Ethiopians shout "Jellem Graziani," Graziani has fled'. The dossier had absolutely no effect on Mussolini. He had taken his decision and he would not allow interference or second thoughts. In a conversation with Teruzzi, the *Duce* said: 'The title of Marquis and great celebrations are all ready for Graziani. So don't worry about him...'

On 10 December 1937, fresh from the king's royal patent letter, the newly appointed marquis of Neghelli was resigned to his fate as he waited at Addis Ababa airport to receive Duke Amedeo of Aosta and his consort Anne of Orléans.[14] To come were many farewells, embraces, speeches, toasts, welcome, and farewell dinners. On 2 January 1938, during the farewell ceremony, Graziani left Addis Ababa by car with his wife, his escort, and a trunk full of luggage, seventy-nine cases in all.[15] Before leaving Ethiopia, he wanted to see once again all those places which were close to his heart, such as the plateau of Neghelli and the Great Lakes region. While in the Arsi territory, the former viceroy asked for, and was granted, a 465-acre plot of land 'ideal for growing coffee, tobacco and cereal'. On 10 January, he arrived at Mogadishu thanks to the new Somalian motorway. At the port, the people then gathered to bid their farewells as Graziani boarded the *Crispi* for an unforgettable voyage home. At Massawa, crowds chanting his name arrived at the port: as Graziani walked among the populace, a group of Eritrean *askari* carried him on their shoulders and he was given flowers and gifts. On board the ship, the EIAR (a news station) announced that Messina, Naples, and Rome were preparing great receptions for the 'undefeated African hero'.

On 25 January, while on the seas, he received a wireless telegram from his daughter, Vanda, telling him that 'number one is on its way'. He was deeply moved

A fine parchment granting Graziani honorary citizenship of Milan.

and replied: 'Thank you. I will become a grandfather. I am happy, and at the same time, agitated and astounded'. When the ship anchored at Messina, Graziani was in bed with a cold. It was hard luck having to postpone the celebrations. Graziani rested in the San Domenico hotel of Taormina. When his cold passed, on 16 February 1938, the marshal disembarked at Naples amid the howling of sirens and the waving of handkerchiefs. He went to Rome on a beflagged train and at Termini station Mussolini was there to greet him. They embraced and then the *Duce* told him: 'Go, this is your moment'. Piazza Esedra and the via Nazionale were chock full. More than 100,000 people had come to greet him, and the motorcade struggled to pass through the dense crowds. Everyone wanted to see the marshal close-up, congratulate him, and express their admiration. At Palazzo Vidoni, seat of the Fascist Party, Graziani had to come out onto the balcony nine times: an emotional moment at receiving such a grand ovation, he waved modestly at the crowds as he found himself unable to speak, choking on his words.

It was an authentic triumph, which in the months following his return, resulted in myriad honours, ceremonies, and the bestowing of all sort of titles. The king bestowed him with the Great Sash of the Military Order of Savoy, tiny San Marino gave him the Medal of Military Valour of the Republic of the Titans, and Mussolini granted him the honorary position of governor general of Italian East Africa for life. Every town hall across the country competed in granting him honorary citizenship, and out of eighteen candidates, Graziani chose Rome and Milan. At the Campidoglio, Graziani received the marshal's baton from the mayor of Rome. It was the handiwork of sculptor Alfredo Ravasco, paid for by the comrades of the Blackshirt *Tevere* division. It was made of gold and adorned with ornaments, fasces and eagles.

At the entrance of Palazzo Madama, a marble bust of him was unveiled. Honorary memberships included: CAI, Touring, the Royal Geographical Society, and many other esteemed associations. He was more popular than a film star; hundreds of parchments, commemorative signs, and plaques were dedicated to him. Through a public appeal, the people of Filettino prepared a grand gesture for their famous *paesano*. They purchased the house where he was born in from its residents and thereafter refurbished it from top to bottom and then placed a marble cross where 'he let out his first whimper' ('his first roar, if you will,' said the mayor of Filettino in the opening speech). When he arrived at his birthplace, Graziani found a functioning kitchen, a sumptuously laid out table, and, in the stables, a sorrel. Tears came to his eyes; he did not know what he could give in return, so he gifted them the drum of Menelik, the old Ethiopian emperor.

The letters that Graziani received in this period take up two full shelves. Letters from admirers and beseeches, postulants and verses, pamphlets, and booklets printed and paid for personally by the authors. The marshal received half a kilo of post per day and Capt. Burkler's hair turned white while attempting replies.

Deemed the land of poets and songwriters, even then Italy was true to her name. While looking through documents, we have found rhymes compiled by the *Corriere*

Above left: Upon his return to Italy, Graziani was welcomed as a triumphal hero. His face was presented on propaganda posters alongside those of Mussolini and Badoglio. The caption on this poster reads: 'Heroes of the Ethiopian gest'.

Above right: In 1938, Graziani's fame and notoriety were at their peak. He reportedly received half a kilo of post a day. For the 'Lion of Neghelli', many composed hymns, odes, songs, and poems. Here is the cover sheet of a poem sent by the Italian workers of Ethiopia to Graziani and Count Volpi. The two men are described as 'Great promoters of Italic industry in the world'.

dei piccoli ('Oh Negus what are you doing? Why don't you leave'; 'Row, row, Blackshirt and stop the ugly foot of the slavedriver from darkening the door of the Empire'), and then odes, *chansons*, songs of Africa, prayers, and slogans. We list a few here, as they are either naive or incredibly pretentious. Among the hymns are 'Hymn to the Italic Empire' (verses by Pietro Mazzario, elementary school teacher from Trebisacce, music by the maestro B. B. Blandi), the 'Hymn of Roman Addis Ababa' (lyrics and music by maestro Mario Giarratana from Corleone), the 'Imperial hymn' (by the former councillor for the Bank of Italy B. Bertoloni, from Imperia), the 'Hymn of the combatant' (musical composition by Antonio Cavicchioli, from Como), the 'Imperial Roman hymn' (authored by Giacomo Grignolo from Savona), and finally the 'Hymn of the Marshal' (music by the maestro Licinio Retice, from Frosinone). Of the odes, there were selections created by Aldo Magnani from Milan ('Ode of the assassination attempt'), Cesare Finocchiaro, head of the post office of Bulo Burti in Somalia ('Ode Abissinia', which must be sung to the same tune of 'Giovinezza'), Giulio Mazza from New York, blind war veteran ('Ode to Victory'), and Capt. Giovan Battista Pintus from Sassari ('African ode') 'to be recited to Beethoven's fifth symphony playing in the background'. We conclude with the 'Soldier's prayer', written by A. Bartolomasi of Italy's Military Chaplain's service.

There was a mountain of paper in tribute, if on the one hand it shows that there is no limit to exhibitionism, on the other, it shows that in 1938, Graziani had 1,000 reasons to be satisfied. Instead, after the first surge of commotion, he became unsatisfied and angrier than ever.

'Rome, 18 April 1938. To Count Giovanni Volpi of Misurata, Palazzo Quattro Fontane. You know how much I wanted to be a senator. Nothing. My legitimate aspiration has been refused with the excuse that I'm not yet sixty. But I...' And he then went on commiserating himself and deprecating human ingratitude.

'Rome, 25 May 1938. To Viceroy of Ethiopia H.R.H. Duke Amedeo of Aosta. Some criticisms regarding the charitable trust named after my deceased mother have got back to me. Some have been heard saying: "If only the Grazianis had put some money towards the whole thing." A despicable phrase. As despicable as the news I've heard that the portrait of my mother has been taken off the entrance of the foundation. When I created it, all I intended to do was remember her name, which is also mine and which some civil servant in Your staff dared brand "Executioner." ... I courteously ask for reassurance.'

The duke's reassuring reply came quickly ('I have personally visited the trust's offices. Everything is in order. The portrait of Your Lady mother is in its usual place'), but it was not enough to placate the fuming marshal. Rodolfo Graziani was always Rodolfo Graziani, whether rightly or wrongly, he continued to see plots and conspiracies everywhere.

'Rome, 25 September 1938. To Lady Ines Graziani, Grand Hotel Terme, Chianciano.... Despite it all, I have dedicated *Fronte Sud* to Pietro Badoglio. The book will come out with a nice preface by Mussolini.[16] The *Duce*, however, doesn't seem to need me anymore. I tried probing him, I told him that I intended moving to Kismayo, to my agricultural land in Somalia. He told me to grow lots of bananas because our market needs them. What do you think that means?'

Even in his autobiography, Graziani deplores Mussolini's sudden indifference to him. 'In 1938,' he wrote 'I was idle.' He then added: 'I was fifty-seven and I didn't know what to do', 'The Boss's spirit was distant from mine'. The marshal spent a long time deliberating and trying to understand the *Duce*'s disaffection towards him. Had his excessive popularity become harmful or was he not needed anymore? The former appears to be the more logical explanation. Mussolini was notorious for his *prima donna*-like mentality and wanted all the applause for himself. Graziani, so much less able and supple than he was, certainly could not upstage him. The fact is that the marshal was not a general for all seasons, he was a soldier used for doing the hard and dirty work. In 1938, peace reigned in Italy as it did in the rest of Europe. And as long as this peace lasted, Graziani was no longer needed.

6

Twenty Months on Lake Garda

Halb zog man ihn, halb sank er hin ('He was pushed a little and slipped a little'). A Berlin play on words used in the business world, referring to reluctant customers who need to be convincingly nudged rather than tempted. It was also the malicious comment made by Rudolf Rahn, German ambassador to Salò, regarding Rodolfo Graziani's adherence to the *Repubblica Sociale Italiana* (RSI, the Italian Social Republic).[1,2] This comment is also corroborated in the memoirs of German General Consul Friedrich Möllhausen, Rahn's collaborator.[3] 'The Ambassador,' wrote Möllhausen, 'skilfully alternated threats along with adulation in order to dupe the Marshal.' We will return to these German methods of persuasion, as they are helpful in understanding the most crucial decision the marshal took during his lifetime.

But why did Graziani decide to seal his fate with the final flames of Fascism? 'For honour and for The Nation,' he would declare until his last breath. Radio Bari, the main network of the Kingdom of the South, had a more sinister interpretation of the marshal's betrayal: 'it's because he was against the Monarchy', 'because the hatred he felt for Badoglio had blinded him', 'because he was pro-Nazi and yearned to fight with the Germans'.[4] During his trial, Graziani would indignantly refute all these 'base insinuations'. He would protest, condemn, and then justify his actions in the following manner:

> I wasn't against the monarchy, but I did become so afterwards. I come from a family which lived through the epic exploits of the *Risorgimento*, who considered the House of Savoy as a living and spiritual symbol. In 1900, after the tragic death of Umberto I, my father sent a poem *in memoriam* to Queen Margherita.[5] I have preserved the sovereign's sacred and kind response written in her own hand. Your Honour, you know why they accuse me of not being a good monarchist? Because in 1938, when I received the Marshal's baton in the

Campidoglio, I shouted, 'Long live the *Duce*' and I forgot to say 'Long live the King.' I was very nervous...

A further explanation followed:

The first time we met, Badoglio was already Marshal of Italy, Marquis of the Sabotino, Governor of Tripolitania. Could I really hate him? I, who was just a simple general? If today I despise him, and I say despise and not hate him, it's because Badoglio betrayed The Nation. I'm not just talking about the armistice. I'm talking about the campaign in North Africa. In Africa, Badoglio sent my soldiers fuel cans full of water, he is a traitor, yes, he's the traitor...

Following with:

If I had really been pro-Nazi, then at Salò I should have got on well with the Nazis. If the truth be known, I quarrelled with them every day. I was fighting for Italy, to save whatever I could from Hitler's rage. As for the slanderous accusation that I had already been conspiring to side with the Germans, it's so laughable as not to even merit a rebuke. What kind of plan could I have been cooking up given that I lived in the countryside, far away from everyone?

Here, the playing field was levelled in the marshal's favour, nothing was premeditated, it was a well-known fact, and he was not particularly friendly with the Germans. As we have seen from his diary, Graziani even suspected the Germans of having pushed for the Investigative Commission against him. So, the question remained: why then did Rodolfo Graziani join the RSI?

In order to explain the Fascist Republican Graziani, today's historians have produced two opposing hypotheses. The first group, including William Deakin, Giorgio Bocca, Max Gallo, and Giampaolo Pansa, underline the marshal's impetuous, ambitious, stubborn, and contrarian character. In simpler terms, Graziani went to be by Mussolini's side on Lake Garda because he was bumbling, reckless, desperate for a comeback and would have accepted any terms just so he could be in the limelight again. The second hypothesis, that of the journalist and historian Silvio Bertoldi, is based on one particular occurrence. Bertoldi wrote: 'On 22 July 1943, Mussolini chose, in a contradictory way, Graziani as Chief of the General Staff instead of Ambrosio. Later on, this would serve as the real reason for Graziani's loyalty to Salò. He was simply following Mussolini's appointment from two months before. The rest is all hearsay'.

If we carefully read Graziani's diary of 1943, we cannot really be certain of anything. In July, Graziani did hint at a possible appointment 'for the armed forces', a nomination suggested by secretary of the Fascist Party, Carlo Scorza. However, we know little of Mussolini's real intentions. In August, during the forty-five days of Badoglio's government, Graziani had a different interlocutor. He was in contact with emissaries from the House of Savoy, from whom he learnt that soon it would be his turn. He then proudly wrote to the duke of Acquarone to tell him that he was at 'the King's complete disposal'. However, the announcement of the armistice surprised Graziani at Piani di Arcinazzo. The marshal, who had just been visited by the Crown Prince Umberto of Savoy, complained that he was not considered worthy of even 'a scrap of confidence' from him, but despite his bitterness, he did not plan on taking revenge. After the war, his nephew, Giulio Cesare Graziani, torpedo-bomber ace and soldier of the Italian Liberation Corps, would tell Rodolfo of his meeting with Prince Umberto in Naples: 'On the 8th of September, His Royal Highness sent you a letter to which you did not reply'.[6] To which the marshal responded: 'I had no idea, I didn't receive it, I thought that the monarchy had abandoned me'. What then resulted seemed a murky and complex picture. A single explanation would not suffice to explain the Republican Graziani, one would have to contemplate what had already been ascertained, then dig far deeper.

However, it would seem safe to say that the marshal swore allegiance to the Italian Social Republic due to his impassionate character, to defy Badoglio, out of anger at the king's supposed abandonment and above all, because the Germans had simultaneously frightened and incited him. He did not make this decision lightly, he resisted. He proceeded in hopes to save himself and occupied Italy from the violent Nibelungen repercussions announced by the Führer. A diary entry attests to this state of mind: '23 September 1943 I have made the ultimate sacrifice!'

One might say that a diary, and especially one of a man being tried in a court of law, is not Gospel. True. However, it remains a veritable source worth considering. If it does not tell the absolute truth, then at least it tells an interpretation of the truth according to the author, as no one lies to their own diary.

We left Graziani on 16 February, the anniversary of his return from the empire, we continue from March, publishing the diary entries alongside official news and clarifications from Graziani's autobiography. The marshal's style of writing consisted of shifting from important facts to insignificant happenings from his daily life. The diary is certainly authentic and without a doubt, in the marshal's own handwriting. The fact he changed the colour of the ink from green to blue after 23 September, seems almost intentional so as to underline the start of this new chapter in his life.

It was on 22 March 1943 at Anagni. In the same building where Pope Boniface VIII had been slapped and humiliated by Sciarra Colonna, Prince Umberto had decided to set up his headquarters.[7] The king had recently appointed his son chief of Army Group South and Umberto, as he was a well-mannered gentleman, made sure he greeted the locals, authorities, and the area's prominent residents. Piani di Arcinazzo was not far away from Anagni, and so he thought it right to send a dutiful greeting to Graziani. He did so through his adjutant, Col. Roberto di San Marzano. Graziani was overjoyed by this visit and wrote about it excitedly in his diary: 'Today the Prince of Piedmont asked after me. It seems he's interested in my defence. Two years since my return from Africa and here is the first acknowledgement from the Royal Family'. At this time, Graziani had very little happening in his life and was so bowled over by this enquiry that he mistook a simple greeting of courtesy for genuine interest in his plight. In contrast, the prince had other things on his mind, the very thought of reading the marshal's defence statement embarrassed him. In fact, from then till June he made various excuses to avoid the marshal's requests for an audience.

And so, the marshal returned to his mundane life as a pensioner:

28 March. The stallions have arrived for the pairing with the mares. I have made a deposit for the purchase of 220 sheep.

29 March. This evening I'm going to the theatre, they're playing *Rheingold*.

2 April. At the theatre again, today it's *Siegfried*.

23 April. I visited Cardinal Jorio to thank him, the Sergio-Vanda situation is patching itself up.

8 April. Mrs Rao came to see me; she is quite surprised by my state of health. She says I look well, she heard I was ill. On a piece of headed paper, I wrote down a famous admonition from Tacitus: 'If one pays attention to satire which is intended as defamatory calumny, it grows in intensity. If one ignores it, it spreads.' I ignore it.

10 April. Uncle Augusto has died.

14 April. I have the flu.

27 April. Giulio Cesare Graziani, my brother's son, was here for lunch. He is about to leave for the operational theatre.

29 April. Whilst walking through Rome I bumped into Gen. Mezzetti and I didn't say hello to him, paying back his vile insults.

30 April. No rain. I'm worried about damage to the feed and the grain.

6 May. I accompany Vanda and my pupis to Ostia. They need the sea breeze.

14 May. Sheep shearing. Today, General C. of the *Carabinieri* came to visit me. I talked to him about the injustices perpetrated against me.

17 May. They have bombed Ostia. My friend Zingoni has taken the children to Affile. They will be safe there.

20 May. My Father died thirty-nine years ago today.

24 May. I have sent my defence to be read by the Prince of Piedmont.

25 May. Starace has come up here. We had a lengthy discussion about my predicament. He asked if he could borrow my lorry so he can move his things to Arcinazzo.

Achille Starace, whom the *Duce* had stripped of all positions in the Fascist Party, had moved to Piani di Arcinazzo in June as a guest at Villa Confalonieri. He remained for three months, and was then arrested on 30 August 1943, after

Badoglio seized power. Fifty *Carabinieri* surrounded his residence, with another fifty suddenly jumping out from the nearby forest of Monte Retafani. Starace was seized in his shorts whilst tending to his garden. He would later say that such a large deployment of troops had left him gobsmacked rather than frightened.

Returning to Graziani's diary:

29 May. Today, Bocca visits the new secretary of the Fascist party. Scorza is inscrutable. I don't care at all.

30 May. Vanda's birthday. Sergio has come back home. All is well.

1 June. Hooray, the Prince of Piedmont will receive me the day after tomorrow, Thursday 3, at twelve.

3 June. I have handed the final part of my defence to the Prince.

7 June. I must lament the attitude of the police commissioner of Rome who never came to talk to me.

15 June. I am negotiating a deal with the Santo Spirito hospital for a plot of land in the Pontine Marshes.

16 June. The grain harvest begins.

17 June. I moved the sheep to Casal Biancaneve.

20 June. In the fields. I take care of the harvest, the threshing and the reaping.

24 June. The pupis are here. Lunch on the grass, lots of fun.

Following, on 25 June 1943, Graziani confided in his diary of his sadness over the death of his beloved dachshund, Topolino. There was only one month left until the 25 July, the regime's days were numbered, the Allies had landed in Sicily, and the marshal continued to remain preoccupied with trivial family issues. Until 23 July, his diary is full of insignificant events such as the harvest, a dental appointment, the death of Fanny the horse, a trip with the 'pupis', and other minor details and happenings: '3 July. In the office at Palazzo dei Marescialli. No visits. The visitors are like a pendulum, they move with the wind'.

Although Italy was in a catastrophic state, Graziani continued to obsess over his defence that nobody wanted to read: '12 July. Even De Bono handed me back my defence with no comments'. Regarding financial problems caused by the war: '19 July. I'm at the Bank of Italy to be reimbursed for the damage done to my lost agricultural property in the Juba and Arsi territories'. Pertaining to himself and his loved ones: '21 July. There are refugees everywhere here. I've transported all the household belongings by lorry to our relatives' houses. I'm making sure I prepare everything for anything which might happen in the future. What will become of me?'

Finally, on 23 July 1943, the marshal's handwriting trails off the page and even covers the date of the diary. The secretary of the Fascist Party, Carlo Scorza, had asked for a meeting with Dr Magno Bocca to enquire to the marshal's availability for 'an important task'. Graziani, who on 29 May wrote 'Scorza is inscrutable, I don't care at all', was now admitting: 'this interests me'.

He felt rejuvenated, it was a gleam of hope for the future. What he did not know was that all of this had come too late, and events were precipitating.

23 July. Bocca called me this evening: I need to go to Rome tomorrow morning.

24 July. In Rome. I talked with T. about Badoglio's intrigues; he talks about everything going on at the moment. Tonight, meeting of the Gran Consiglio.

25 July: 11:00. Bocca told me what he learned from Melchiorri about the meeting of the Gran Consiglio. It lasted nine hours, from Saturday night until this morning. It would seem it was turbulent and violent. I called Ines; she's doing ok.

15:25, Bocca learned that Scorza wants to see him immediately and in uniform. I told him to go. Bocca called me back to tell me that Scorza has phoned the *Duce*. I wait at home for any new events.

18.00. Casually, I learnt from a friend who was just passing by via Salaria that Badoglio went in uniform to Villa Savoia. I tell Bocca, who telephones Scorza, who astonishingly tells him that the Duce is also at Villa Savoia and that he, along with other affairs, went there with my name for the armed forces. That Badoglio is also present evidently demonstrates that the King has put Mussolini before his own supreme decisions, as could obviously be deduced by Badoglio's frequent visits to the sovereign in the past few days. 23.00. The radio announces that the King has accepted Mussolini's resignation ... and has nominated

On 25 July 1943, King Victor Emanuel III had Mussolini arrested and appointed Pietro Badoglio as chief of state. Despite Marshal Badoglio announcing that the war would continue alongside the Germans, the Allies had no doubt that this was Italy's first step towards stepping out of the conflict.

Badoglio Prime Minister and Head of the Government, taking sole command of the Armed Forces. Soon afterwards cheering and loud noises can be heard in the streets. Bocca telephones me saying that outside Villa Badoglio people can be heard repeatedly shouting: 'We also want Graziani.' Of course, I say, but without Badoglio.[8]

The marshal wrote nothing else on that crucial day of 25 July. No mourning for the *Duce*'s fate; no grieving for the fall of Fascism and the toppling of its symbols. Even the fact that Scorza's 'job for the Armed Forces' had gone up in smoke did not seem to particularly phase him much. Did Mussolini really intend to propose Graziani for chief of the general staff when going to Villa Savoia? No one can say for certain. Buffarini Guidi would ultimately deny it, and the *Duce*, during the RSI, would not say anything further on the matter. The only confirmation comes from Graziani's personal secretary, Dr Magno Bocca. However, Bocca, who after the war penned a long and detailed report on the matter, would admit to only having negotiated with Scorza 'without ever talking directly to Mussolini'.

On 26 July, finally grasping the fall of the regime, Graziani wrote in his diary: 'Badoglio's proclamation on the radio, the war continues. I refuse to meet C. and anyone else. The Prince has given back the first part of my defence statement. In the evening, before leaving for the Casale, I sent a letter to Acquarone, Minister of the Royal Household'. The letter which the marshal sent to the duke of Acquarone (and the correspondence that followed) is historically significant, as it proved that Graziani had put fascism behind him and was now trying to reconcile with the monarchy. He was anxious to reassure the king of his loyalty. The following is the original text in full:

Rome, 26 July 1943.
Dear Acquarone,
People worthy of trust have told me, being authorized to do so, of your words which are to stay calm, given that soon my time will come. I am particularly delighted by this, especially where you state your esteem towards me, considering that yesterday, a highly respectable Lady from the Court told me that, 'there I am seen like the plague' as I am supposedly anti-monarchical. An interpretation which derives from the fact that in 1938, when I received the Marshal's baton in the Campidoglio, I am said not to have saluted the King. In these two years and a half of moral martyrdom I have not uttered a single word, all in accordance with discipline. As soon as I returned from North Africa, I asked for a dutiful visit to the Head of the Government after my being relieved from command became public: I was promised this would happen, but this promise was not kept, which stopped me from visiting the Sovereign soon afterwards. The point is that I did not want to infringe on the hierarchical order. So as that my behaviour wouldn't be misinterpreted, I explained what had happened to the Monarch's first *Aide-*

de-Camp. A year later, feeling no longer bound by this, I asked the very same *Aide-de-Camp*, Gen. Puntoni, to be granted an audience with my King, which I was denied. Such an accusation, which is incredible as I have had monarchist sentiments since birth, asserting them time and time again in my actions and in my words throughout my entire life, has convinced me to write to you today, yes, this very day, these aforementioned declarations, so that you might see the truth.

Warm greetings, Graziani.

Dated 9 August, the duke's response:

Dear Excellency,

Please forgive me for my late reply to your dear letter of the 26th, but I have been overwhelmed by the course of these unexpected events. I can assure you that you have been very misinformed: in this small and modest environment that is our Court, far and untouched by any political current, Marshal Graziani enjoys all the consideration which he deserves. I cannot even begin to think how they could have told you such rubbish! I am truly grateful that you have feelings of cordial friendship towards me.

Yours faithfully, Acquarone.

On 13 August, a new letter from Graziani to the minister of the Royal Household:

Piani di Arcinazzo, 13/8/1943.

Dear Acquarone,

I am incredibly grateful for your letter of the 9th, which restores my serenity. I am convinced that even this episode is part of the destructive and denigratory campaign launched against me (you will be aware of its various manifestations). You know whom I've always served loyally and who then tried to annihilate me in order to hide their own responsibilities during the first episode of the campaign in North Africa. For two and a half years I resisted the urge to react in any way. Now that things have changed, I am fully confident that the day will come when justice will be done on my behalf and the clarity of my actions will be shown to the people of Italy, who, for the most part, have always been on my side. My hope is that the Nation will able to overcome this supreme trial with the least harm possible and this thought today overrides any other personal considerations, and needless to say I once again confirm that I am at the complete disposal of the King and the Nation. Best regards, Graziani.

During the forty-five days of Badoglio's government, the marshal had other contacts with individuals close to the House of Savoy. We reveal two, both indicative of his renewed faith in the monarchy and of how little Graziani had learnt from his reading of *The Prince*.

On 31 July, Graziani received an unexpected visit from Professor Cavagnaro, an aid to the king's private affairs. Cavagnaro was an intimate friend of the sovereign who often used him to settle delicate matters. In this particular case, the monarch's agent wanted to learn of Graziani's thoughts, specifically: 'Whether or not to continue the war'. Graziani attested: 'The war must continue; our national honour is at stake. Nations can rise up from ruins, but not from dishonour. I am sure that His Majesty will take this path even if it would mean losing his crown'. Professor Cavagnaro, who expected an entirely different reply, at that point got up and walked out.

On 24 August, Graziani paid a visit to the new minister of war, Gen. Sorice. 'I saw him,' he wrote afterwards, 'to ask what the instructions were, should the Government relocate. He replied that the Marshals would simply follow the Government. I asked where, as presumably the King and the Government would retreat to Piedmont or Lombardy. After some slight hesitation Sorice replied: "To Piedmont or Lombardy, and you will have a villa at your disposal."' In his diary, these entries have notes next to them in red ink, written in 1944. Reading over these events once again, the marshal commented: 'They must have been laughing behind my back', 'What an idiot I was!', and 'Now I understand why everyone seemed embarrassed or stupefied when talking to me, totally incredulous at my foolish naivety'. Graziani would always be proud of this foolishness, as among so many cunning and underhanded people, he was the only one of pure intent without any hidden agenda.

That the marshal had no inclination of any scheme and was unaware of an imminent armistice has been proven. However, only his diary exhibits the exact degree to how little he knew.[9]

A caricature of Mussolini and King Victor Emanuel III from the *Daily Express*.

7 August. Dentist's appointment.

9 August. Thirtieth wedding anniversary, one hundred years since my father's birth.

10 August. Acquarone has replied to me. One of these days the Prince wants to see me for lunch.

11 August. My sixty-first birthday. With us at the Casale are Sergio, Vanda and the children.

12 August. Lunch with H.R.H. Umberto of Savoy. The Prince was very affable in the officer's mess and gave me a place of honour. He hopes to see me again, he wants to talk to me in private of a matter of utmost importance. I handed him the third part of my defence statement.

13 August. Second bombing of Rome. Fifty-six enemy aircraft flew over the mountains from the north-west, machine gunning and dropping one bomb. During broad daylight!!!

14 August. Parcel from M. He warned me about Badoglio. It seems I will be arrested.

20 August. The vet came, my horse is ill.

24 August. Today I saw Sorice.

26 August. Starace visited the Casale. He is also afraid he'll be arrested.

29 August. Funeral Mass at Anagni for King Boris of Bulgaria. Full uniform and decorations. The Prince also came.

30 August. Starace has been taken by the *Carabinieri*. The potato harvest has finished.

2 September. Radio Algiers lies and says that I've been arrested.

4 September. *Il Messaggero* published my disclaimer: 'I am in good health, I have not been arrested, my freedom is holy and inviolable.'

5 September. Call from P. The powers on high didn't like the sound of my disclaimer. P. tells me: 'The King knows that you are well, and if he knows that's all that matters.'

7 September. At Anagni I asked for His Royal Highness to intervene in favour of the airfield they want to build at Sant'Anna.

8 September. At Casal Biancaneve. In the evening, the radio announced the signing of the armistice with the Anglo-Americans. I tried to get through to the Prince's Command at Anagni but to no avail.

News of the armistice caught Graziani by surprise and like millions of other Italians, he was perplexed and worried. Had the war really finished, was it time to go home? Why did the prince not consider Graziani worthy of a 'scrap of trust?' Starting from 9 September, his entries were written in haste. In order to truly understand them, they need to be interpreted and placed in context. Interestingly, the marshal never mentions any of the events which are violently unsettling Italy, such as the king and Badoglio fleeing to Brindisi, the German occupation, and the fact that no one defended Rome. He avoided judgements, comments, and recriminations. He only references himself and his own tiny, private world.

> 9 September. Barrage of contradictory news.
>
> 10 September. The Germans have broken into my property. I barely manage to stop them from committing acts of violence. I decide to move my family. Arcinazzo is too isolated. Filettino is better.
>
> 11 September. Ines is at Filettino. She will be safe there. I gave Sergio some documents so that he may take them to Affile, I leave for Rome on the via Sublacense.

At Subiaco, the Germans were fighting against Italians, Tivoli was in chaos, filled with bedraggled soldiers. Graziani's trip was short but adventurous with detours along narrow, country lanes. He saw a Panzer column driving up the via Tiburtina, he then raced towards Guidonia and managed to get on the via Salaria where 'the *Piave* Division had halted in perfect order'. At 5 p.m., by turn of fate, he arrived at Villa Liotta.

'12 September. With De Bono and then Calvi di Bergolo.'

De Bono lived in via Massaua, 100 metres from Villa Liotta and would update Graziani on the latest news. Gen. Carlo Calvi di Bergolo was at the Ministry of War. After having negotiated the surrender of the capital, Marshal Caviglia, with German approval, had appointed him Commander of the open city of Rome.

Graziani only wanted to ask Gen. Calvi di Bergolo, the king's son-in-law, for a permit in order to be able to travel outside the city walls. 'The farm work is half done,' he said. 'I need to go back to Filettino and reassure my family.' Calvi shrugged, there was nothing he could do. The man in charge of permits was General Stahel, Rome's real commander. At the German embassy in via Conte Rosso, the marshal obtained his long-awaited permit. He had no problem as Stahel knew of him by name. He was amicable, and even told Graziani: 'Good news, we have just liberated Mussolini from Campo Imperatore'.

'13 September. Leaving for Filettino. When I got there, I learned that they ha stolen my lorry at Arcinazzo. I'm back in Rome at 21.30.'

Two platoons of German soldiers, who arrived at the Casale early in the morning, had commandeered the marshal's lorry. The farmer protested, and the soldiers simply replied: '*Es ist Krieg*.' Graziani rushed off to Ferentino where an SS captain repeated: '*Es ist Krieg*,' meaning, 'It's war.' However, he was then offered a motorbike escort. With them, Graziani went on to chase the lorry thieves, but to no avail. He later returned to Rome extremely tired.

> 14 September. At Volpi's. We examined the situation.
>
> 15 September. With Zingoni at the German embassy regarding the lorry. No one receives us, they push us away at the entrance. Calvi di Bergolo tells me to speak to Kesselring whom I don't know.

16 September. Marshal Kesselring says he has nothing to say to me and asks me to write down the reason for this meeting.

17 September. I refused to go to any meeting, and I insisted on my request. Either they give me back my lorry or they will have to buy me a new one. I sent Calvi di Bergolo the letter for Kesselring. He will forward it to him.

18 September. At Arcinazzo. All work at the farm has stopped, we need forage for the horses.

19 September. At Affile to repair the church adjacent to my house. Then to Biancaneve. Busiri is there. Together we go to Rome.

Clemente Busiri Vici, General Saverio Grazioli's son-in-law, was the bearer of an important message. Grazioli requested a meeting with Graziani immediately to discuss an urgent matter.

20 September. In Rome with Grazioli. Buffarini Guidi had offered him the supreme Command of the Fascist Republic's army which is being formed. Grazioli refused. He tells me that he asked straight away: 'What about Graziani?' To which Buffarini replied: 'The *Duce* doesn't want him because of

News Chronicle

ITALY SURRENDERS, UNCONDITIONALLY
Britain, U.S., Russia Approved Armistice Terms: Badoglio Tells Italians 'We Oppose Attack From Any Other Quarter'

ITALY has surrendered, unconditionally. At 5.30 last night General Eisenhower, Allied C.-in-C. in the Mediterranean, announced:

"The Italian Government has surrendered its armed forces unconditionally.

"As Allied Commander-in-Chief, I have granted a military armistice, the terms of which have been approved by the Governments of the United Kingdom, the United States and the Union of Soviet Socialist Republics.

Some minutes later Algiers Radio broadcast the text of a proclamation by Marshal Badoglio (later to be twice broadcast by Rome) in which he said:

"The Italian Government, recognising the impossibility of continuing the unequal struggle against the overwhelming power of the enemy, with the object of avoiding further more grievous harm to the nation, has requested an armistice from General Eisenhower, Commander-in-Chief of the Anglo-American Allied Forces. This request has been granted.

"The Italian forces will, therefore, cease all acts of hostility against Anglo-American forces, wherever they may be met.

"They, however, will oppose attacks from any other quarter."

More announcements were still to come from Algiers Radio.

The first was a call to the Italian people who now have "the opportunity of taking vengeance on the German oppressor."

Then Admiral Sir Andrew Cunningham went to the microphone and appealed to men of the Italian Navy and the Italian merchant fleet to make at once for Gibraltar, Tripoli, Haifa or Alexandria. Ships in the Black Sea should make for Russian ports.

And from the other end of the Mediterranean the C.-in-C. in the Middle East called to the Italian forces in the Balkans and the Ægean Islands to seize all points occupied by the Germans in the Dodecanese.

It was agreed that the armistice should come into force at the moment most favourable to the Allies.

That moment was 5.30 p.m. last night.

On 8 September 1943, Gen. Eisenhower announced Italy's unconditional surrender to the world. Hitler was furious and ordered that Italy be invaded and its people punished. Badoglio, the royal family and the government fled to Brindisi where they established the Kingdom of the South with the backing of the Allies.

Africa...' It's better this way. If they had asked me, I would have told them TO GO TO HELL!!! [these last words in Graziani's diary are in block capitals].

21 September. At Casale Biancaneve. Provisions have been made for the late start of the potato harvest.

22 September. At Casale Biancaneve. At around twelve the former federal of Benghazi Capt. Barracu arrived. He told me that the *Duce* has phoned Munich and designated me as Supreme Commander and Minister for the Armed Forces of the new Fascist Republican Government. I refused to accept his offer. I let him know that tomorrow I will be in Rome on personal business, and I would like to talk to Mezzasoma. I went to Filettino to update Ines. I then went to Rome where I arrived at 19:30. I telephoned Bocca who slept over at my house.

23 September. In Rome. In the morning I meet C. who informs me of how the Party is struggling to create a Ministry due to lack of men. Bocca telephones Barracu and arranges for the meeting to take place at my house at ten. Meeting at home with the aforementioned. I refused all their offers. Pellegrini intervened. We went to the German embassy. My name is already included in the list of ministers of the new Government. Lunch at the embassy. I have made the ultimate sacrifice!' (This last phrase is underlined).

This hurriedly put together sequence of events does not help the marshal's case. Technically, things really did go according to his diary, however, to understand how the marshal's 'no' became a 'yes', we will examine the accounts of those who were present. Specifically, the aforementioned memoirs of Friedrich Möllhausen and Ambassador Rudolf Rahn's autobiography.[10]

On the morning of 23 September, Graziani was having a heated debate with the two party officials at Villa Liotta. The marshal seemed intransigent. His adjutant Mario Zingoni could hear him yelling from the antechamber: 'You come asking me, me! Whom you've spent years denigrating?' At 10:30 a.m., the doorbell rang. It was Domenico Pellegrini, a likely candidate for Minister of Finance. 'Anyway,' said Pellegrini, 'you should come with us to the embassy, the Germans are waiting. If not, your refusal will be interpreted as fear.' Graziani stood up: 'I know what going to the embassy will mean for me, but do not think that I'm afraid. Let's go'. They went to Villa Wolkonsky, the seat of the German Embassy. The clock was ticking; at midday, the list of the new ministers was to be announced on the radio. Rudolf Rahn was incredibly skilful: he seated the marshal in his office, offered him a drink, then bombarded him with rhetoric. Gen. Karl Wolff, commander of the SS in Italy, acted as his cohort.[11] Rahn was as persuasive as Wolff was brusque. The ambassador began by badmouthing Badoglio. 'The day I saw him,' he told Graziani, 'Badoglio embraced me. He tried to put my mind at ease, there was no truth to the rumours of an upcoming armistice. He kept repeating: "Along with Pétain and Von Mackensen, I am one of the oldest marshals in Europe. How could you think that I wouldn't keep my word as a soldier?" Well then, that day was the 8th of September, the day of treachery, when the German ally was stabbed in the back.'

At this point, Rahn teutonically changed his tone and commenced outlining the consequences of this betrayal. 'They will be terrible. Italy will be treated like Poland.... worse than Poland.' 'The Führer's made it clear,' Gen. Wolff intervened, 'the fate of Italy will serve as a warning to the world.' In a conciliatory manner, Rahn returned to reassuring Graziani: 'because all good Germans know perfectly well that not all Italians are made of the same stuff'. 'There are Italians who are men of honour,' he added, 'and I am sure that you are one of them'. Although the marshal objected, Rahn had an answer for everything. 'The oath of loyalty to the King you ask? To what King, a King who flees and abandons five sixths of his country and his people? Such a King does not deserve loyalty.' 'The uncertain course of the war? These are just temporary setbacks. We will win, Germany is strong, our secret weapons are not a joke. Join us and you will see'.

'Either with us, or with the traitors,' Wolff harshly butted in, 'today no one can just sit and watch.' According to Möllhausen, this is when Graziani began to hesitate. 'Your name was suggested by Mussolini,' the ambassador added, continuing in his pursuit of the marshal, 'but it was Hitler himself who confirmed your appointment. This is what the Führer said: "If Italy must still have an army, there's only one man who can lead it, Graziani. As far as I'm aware, Marshal Graziani is of anti-German sentiment. However, I approve of him because no Italian general enjoys the same prestige or popularity. If Graziani accepts, I will abandon the idea of a mass reprisal, but if he doesn't..."'

Graziani was never the type of person who would be considered 'clever'. And now, hearing that the fate of occupied Italy depended on him alone, he did not know whether to feel flattered or afraid. 'But, but...' he uttered, trying to protect himself. There was then a knock at the office door and a secretary entered: 'It's time for the radio announcement'. Both Rahn and Wolff closed in on the marshal and asked, in unison 'So, yes or no?' And in one breath he replied: 'Yes. If the threat is so great, then I'm ready to serve the Nation'. It was only two minutes until midday, the ambassador concluded with, 'Now, let's eat.' While his guests were having lunch, Rahn wrote a report to send to Berlin: 'the operation has gone according to plan,' he wrote among other business, 'I managed to convince Graziani one minute before the radio announcement aired. It was not an easy task. *Halb zog man ihn, halb sank er hin.*'

First, a lorry arrived, then, the head of the police, Gen. Umberto Presti, appeared in a car escorted by two motorbikes. Under late-night rainfall in the courtyard of Villa Liotta, Graziani waited impatiently. He had spent the previous day, 13 November 1943, packing and wrapping his belongings while Ines had taken care of all the silverware and family heirlooms. Dr Magno Bocca, appointed chief of staff of the Ministry of National Defence, took care of the marshal's documents and letters, consisting of a dozen crates which—with the help of Embaie—had to be loaded on to the lorry. At 3 a.m., under the cover of darkness, the small convoy departed the villa for the nearby Basilica of St Agnes. Graziani was ready to reach the government of the RSI on Lake Garda, however, he did not want to leave without first stowing his valuables in a safe place. Before he left, he had the crates hidden in the catacombs under the Basilica, after begging the priest to take good care and look after them.

He then completed a dreadful journey via very poor roads, it took twelve hours just to get to Florence. From his diary: '14 November. Last night I must have caught a cold. I have a temperature. There's fog on the Apennines. As we drive on I see children going to school. I tell Ines, who's with me: "Even if a month late the school year has started. Somehow life goes on as best it can"'.

'Life goes on as best it can,' said the marshal, and he was right. After joining the RSI, everything had gone as best it could, and the first days had been euphoric and exciting. On 25 September, during a radio broadcast, Graziani gave a haranguing speech, a *j'accuse* directed specifically at the king and Badoglio. On 27 September, at Rocca delle Caminate, the marshal met Mussolini. The *Duce* seemed like a shadow of his former self: pale, thin, and poorly dressed. They embraced in silence, as if in tacit agreement not to dig up the past ever again. Later, on 1 October 1943, Graziani experienced a magical moment, the great rally of the Adriano theatre, an episode worthy of remembrance.

It was Sunday, and although under grey skies, the Roman autumn still held a light essence of summer. For two days, the speakers of the EIAR had been inviting the gentlemen officers to 'come to the Adriano theatre to listen to the voice of Marshal Graziani'. The capital was heaving with officers in civilian clothes. All young lieutenants and old colonels with mouths to feed. For the most part, they were southerners who could not return home due to the Allied advance. They walked idly about, stopping to look at the barracks which were now garrisoned by the Germans and talking downheartedly among themselves. The proclamations of the *Kommandantur* were bone chilling: 'show up or prepare for imminent punishment'. In essence, show yourself and risk being herded on to a train bound for Germany. Thus, the officers avoided the Germans at all cost. However, the 27th had passed, no salary was forthcoming, and it was difficult to afford lunch and dinner. Graziani's invitation arrived at just the right time. He could be trusted, as he was a soldier, a marshal of Italy, and had been viceroy.

And so, on a Sunday morning, 1 October, there was a throng gathered in the square just in front of the Adriano theatre. The fact there were no SS soldiers in sight was encouraging or at least alleviated some of the fear. Some 4,000 entered, some in uniform, as was Graziani, who still had the royal stars on his collar, with his chest decorated in ribbons. Bareheaded, his hair shaken by his oratory, he spoke unscripted, with spontaneity. He made a good impression on the officers who liked what they heard. There was no mention of Fascism or Nazism, but only a series of impassioned observations. 'Worse than betraying our ally, the King has betrayed our trust by leaving us without orders, pacts need to be respected, one cannot just jump so indecently onto the enemies' bandwagon. Are we or are we not men?' Thunderous applause spontaneously broke out. Encouraged by this, Graziani gave into rhetoric:

> ... the man who stands before you, is a Marshal of Italy, who during his long life as a soldier has encountered success and failure, and his armies have known the sun of glory and the shadow of ingratitude. Today, he has been called on by destiny to tighten his grip around the sword which will erase the shameful stain of treachery and dishonour which have defaced the flag of Italy.

He then quickly concluded: 'Italy will rise again, the army will rise again, under the banners of the republic you will find new duties, new dignity, and new higher salaries'.

The crowd then rose with a standing ovation.

Present on the stage was a crowd of unexpected guests: Farinacci, Pavolini, and Gen. Stahel. Stahel brought the *Wehrmacht*'s support to 'the old warrior who has had the strength to rise up against dishonour and who will give Italy back its rightful place'. They were only words, but to the officers who had nothing, they were enough. A procession then got on its way, and all proceeded to the Vittoriano, with the giant Graziani leading the way. The people who had gathered in the streets, watched on in silence. Some turned into alleyways, while some gave the Roman salute. The people of Rome did not seem phased; they had seen it all before. But was it starting all over again? It was indeed. The same evening 400 officers of the disbanded *Piave* Division asked to join the ranks of the newly formed Republican army. An unexpected success, Graziani rejoiced; 'Bravo' telegraphed Mussolini. This triumph and once again, the feeling of being the protagonist, would be short lived.

On 2 October, at Palazzo Caprara, where he had set up his office, the marshal received some catastrophic news. At Frosinone, Littoria, and even Rome, the

The front page of the Socialist newspaper *Avanti!*, 16 October 1943. The title reads: 'The anti-Nazi war is a people's war! The King and Badoglio have no right to be its leaders!' (*Erotodo TV*)

Germans were rounding up civilians to send as forced labourers to the front at Cassino. Graziani rushed to Frascati to see *Feldmarschall* Albert Kesselring. Kesselring was one of many Germans who loved Italy, however, despised Italians. He often said: 'The only Italian army which won't betray us is one that doesn't exist'. With such a preamble, Graziani had a lively discussion with Kesselring. Face to face, the latter asked Graziani to immediately enforce the following three measures: the disarming of the *Carabinieri* of Rome 'they are untrustworthy Badoglio-truppen'; the handing over of 30,000 labourers 'good for digging trenches'; and the deportation to the north of all officers living in Rome 'including the ones on leave, in the reserve and even the officer cadets'. The marshal begged and protested. Was this the real reason why he had been recruited in the first place, when he had accepted to serve the RSI? No, never. By taking these steps, the people would be brought to the point of exasperation and revolt. Nonetheless, Kesselring was unwavering: 'Either you do it,' he cut short, 'or we will. We need workers, we have no use for *Carabinieri* and army officers. We remember Naples, where they shot us in the back.' Graziani was on the ropes, 'I'll deal with this,' he said. He hoped to drag things out, and eventually find a solution. He returned to Rome daunted, and then found another barrage of bad news. The Fascists were impatient for the creation of a regular army and had started assembling armed bands led by makeshift commanders, on which the marshal received a constant flow of reports. In Veneto, Turin, Brescia, and Alessandria, old *squadristi* and young fanatics had reopened the federations, the *case del fascio* and had armed themselves with pistols and muskets. They stood guard at the offices of the party officials, half ushers, half soldiers. At Verona, Col. Facchini had established himself at the abandoned army barracks of Porto San Zeno and recruited volunteers as if he were a soldier of fortune. The outfits of his men were quite picturesque: windbreakers, crew-neck sweaters, Munari ski boots with a Vibram/tank-tread sole. Tragically, nearly all of them would die in Venezia Giulia fighting Tito's partisans. In contrast at Reggio Emilia, a sinister death battalion had appeared. The 'batmort' as the Emiliani called them, donned sweaters and black berets embellished with skulls and crossbones. They would set off in 1944 for the 'supreme sacrifice', but ultimately, they would all end up hiding at Castelbolognese. Bewildered, Graziani examined reports and documents and pondered: What did this increase in paramilitary forces, vigilante squads and acronyms mean? Why were the Germans doing nothing to stop them? He did not understand it, but as a man of law and order, he smelt the stench of anarchy.

On the evening of 2 October, instead of returning home, the marshal travelled to Monte Mario to pay a visit to his friend Marshal Enrico Caviglia who was on his way to Finale Ligure. Marshal Caviglia was eighty-two years old, he spoke freely, and considered himself beyond good and evil. Mussolini was aware of this, but he ignored it. 'Harmless aunties gossiping,' he concluded. In a scolding manner, Caviglia asked Graziani: 'what is the purpose of your Government if it's not capable of ending the German occupation which has no place being here?' And again: 'During the news reels I admired the first armed units. Some soldiers they are! You aren't going to fight a war with them'.[12] He was right, and Graziani could only agree. Testimony to his disappointment can be found on two notes written on 8 October 1943, which today can be read in the Central State Archive. The first takes the form of a question: 'Fundamental query. Do the Germans intend to treat Italy as an occupied territory?' The second is an answer to the previous question: 'The German authorities created the Fascist Government purely for internal German political interests'.

It was now too late to go back. Kesselring threatened 'to start the round ups again, to bomb the *Carabinieri* barracks, to take revenge on the families of the officers'. Graziani decided to move first, as it was better to solve problems between Italians, the Italian way—through a volunteer program he supplied Kesselring with the necessary workers, by organising a military labour inspectorate. In April 1945, the manpower recruited by the inspectorate would be 300,000 people. During his trial, the marshal declared that: 'If anything I prevented 300,000 unhappy souls being deported to Germany'. Graziani also managed to exempt the officer cadets, those on leave and in the reserve, so as only regular officers would be obliged to go. In 1948, the prosecutor would accuse him of having intimidated the officer corps, threatening them 'with a Saint Bartholomew-like massacre' if they did not obey. The marshal denied this, stating: 'It was the Germans who wanted bloodshed, I simply informed the officers of the risk they were taking'.

The *Carabinieri* of Rome were ultimately, all deported to Germany. A shameful incident which Graziani would struggle to overlook. Regarding that dramatic episode there are two contrasting versions.

Col. Delfino, interim commander of the *Carabinieri* in the capital, recounted:

> On 6 October 1943, in my presence, the Marshal signed the order to disarm the *Carabinieri*. In vain I tried to stop him. Fortunately, on the night between the 6th and the 7th, many deserted. On the morning of the 7th of October, the Germans rounded up the *Carabinieri* who had remained at their post and sent them by train to a concentration camp.

On the contrary, Graziani would claim:

> Delfino was unaware of previous events, only I knew of Kesselring's real intentions: On 6 October I implored the colonel to go with his men to Zara, besieged by the Yugoslav partisans. If the *Carabinieri* had been deployed in military operations, they would have been under the control of my Ministry, it was the only chance I had to save them. Delfino refused, fearing total disbandment. However, the collapse was already underway: either on leave or calling in sick, the *Carabinieri* of Rome went from 7,500 on the day of the armistice to 4,000 a month afterwards.

The colonel's refusal left me with no choice. The Minister of the Interior, Buffarini Guidi, refused to help: to him and the Fascists, the *Carabinieri* were the assassins of Ettore Muti and the accomplices of the 25th of July.[13] I ordered their disarmament. I had made a pact with the Germans: the *Carabinieri* would reach Fidenza and then be scattered to various commands operating in the North. On 7 October the SS accompanied 1,500 unarmed *Carabinieri* to the train station, they were herded onto a regular train, not a cattle car, and they were taken away. I then learnt that the train had not stopped at Fidenza but had gone directly to Germany. I turned Gen. Stahel's office upside down. He told me to calm down, that it was all a mistake, the order had been misinterpreted. I sent a commission to Germany led by Col. Chierico and I demanded the return of the 1,500 deportees and other 10,000 *Carabinieri* captured after the 8th of September. Sadly, the commission was knocked about from one place to the other, and after a month it returned to Italy empty handed. It's the truth, I swear.

Despite its exhaustiveness and the fact that it was deemed convincing by the military judges, the marshal's explanation would not be enough to dissipate suspicions: was Graziani tricked by the Germans or was he their accomplice? The answer to this question has never been settled.

On 11 October 1943, an urgent telegram was dispatched from Hitler's HQ, which read: 'Der Führer wishes to confer with H.E. Marshal of Italy Rodolfo Graziani, Minister of National Defence of the Italian Socialist [*sic*] Republic on the 13th, signed: Wilhelm Keitel'. The message from the warlord of Europe was not an invite, it was an order. On 13 October, together with Colonels Zingoni and Dollman, Graziani departed Guidonia airport and headed for Rastenburg in East Prussia. Hitler was awaiting his arrival from within his HQ, a bunker hidden away from enemy aircraft under the cover of a pine forest. The two knew each other only by sight, as they had once met in Rome in 1938 ('A Special Day,' in the words of film director Ettore Scola). Seeing each other again, their impressions were mutually pitiful. The Führer thought Graziani 'old and grey', and the marshal wrote in his autobiography: 'Adolf Hitler seemed as if he had aged fifteen years. His ash-grey jacket, of the Austrian type from the previous war, his long black trousers, his low-healed, shiny leather shoes made him look like a monk dressed in civilian clothes. He was hunched over, his eyes were not piercing, but almost colourless'. The 'monk', however, knew what he wanted. Initially, in front of the fireplace, he was extremely courteous: 'I am deeply sorry that you were given such a thankless job,' said Hitler, and, 'despite the unjust treatment you have received, it was right for you to accept this job. A soldier cannot be aloof from the field of action and honour.' Moving on from the thinly veiled acclamation, Hitler expeditiously became very harsh and got to the point. When the marshal stated that he intended to equip twenty-five divisions, the Führer silenced him with a blunt '*Nein*'. Graziani then whittled it down to four divisions, hoping he could go up to eight, then maybe twelve. Hitler was no longer listening. Wilhelm Keitel, chief of the *Wehrmacht*, insisted on labourers, explaining: 'One million Italian workers in Germany equals one million new German soldiers at the front'. His insinuation was obvious. The Germans did not care about Italian soldiers, Italians were only good for manual labour. The marshal dug in his heals and demanded at least four divisions, which led to a confusing and violent tussle with Hitler's generals. Matters were not helped by the fact that neither understood the other's language. In the end, thinking that he had obtained three important conditions (recruitment of Italian POWs in Germany, mixed Italo-German armaments, training in Italy), Graziani decided to sign a rough draft of a protocol, which stated the exact opposite. The soldiers of the RSI would be recruited among the very young, the Italian government would have to provide weapons, and the training would take place in Germany. The one who would eventually pay for the marshal's blunder was Col. Emilio Canevari, general secretary for the Republican armed forces. Canevari was charged with ratifying the agreement, but when he arrived in Berlin, he discovered the ruse, so he delayed signing and waited for further instructions. This enraged the Germans who demanded his immediate removal.

The dismissal of Emilio Canevari's meant the loss of one of Graziani's most valued collaborators. Since 5 October, he and the marshal had been working on the Republican army's foundational law. To call this law stupefying would be an understatement. Graziani's vision was that the Republican army had to be one, apolitical and national, for the defence of the nation and for the salvation of fundamental liberties. It was compulsory that all officers and soldiers be volunteers, and they were prohibited from joining any sects or political organizations. This, in a country where there was only one party, the Fascist Republican one. The service car and the attendant were abolished, and a theoretical equality between soldiers and officers was established: soldiers could now eat from plates instead of mess tins and would now receive the same type of rations as officers; regarding salaries, there would be absolute equality between both the Italian and the German soldier. In practice, an unmarried brigadier ought to have earned 9,610 lira a month, a divisional general with five children, 18,000 lira a month, these being salaries which in 1943 were a considerable amount. The law was considered stupefying, not necessarily because of its contents (the improvement of regulatory and financial conditions had been demanded by the lower ranks for some time), more so because of its principles. An apolitical army in German occupied Italy?

Confined to his office at Palazzo Caprara, Graziani was becoming detached from reality. On the other hand, in the post-war period, Graziani would say that that law fulfilled a noble purpose, to remove the Republican army from the fratricidal civil war. Should he be believed? It is still up for debate. In any case, it was quite odd that the Marshal, an expert of guerrilla and counter-guerrilla warfare, refused, from the very start, the idea of an anti-partisan army.

The Fascists did not accept Graziani's new law at all. Their opinions were diametrically opposed to his. They invoked the army of the party and shunned the idea of lazy demotivated squaddies. 'Let us do what Lenin did with the Red Army,' Nicola Bombacci kept repeating to Mussolini.[14] Alessandro Pavolini, national secretary of the Republican Fascist Party: 'The Militia is the new army, the army of the Blackshirts'.[15] From a logical point of view, Bombacci and Pavolini were right. The war was not about Italy as a nation, it was about one faction of Italians, the Fascists, against the external enemies, the 'plutocratic-Jewish-masonic democracies'. It was the Fascists against the internal enemies, the Badoglian subversives. It is known that in ideological wars, just as in wars of religion, it is only those with the most faith who fight. With this national and formally apolitical army, Graziani actually gave an involuntary contribution to the growth of the Partisan movement. Many of the young conscripts, who feared deportation to Germany, deserted. Many others, to escape the terrible draft of 1944, would go into hiding in the countryside. However, looking back at October 1943 after his return from Rastenburg, the marshal saw that Renato Ricci, *squadrista*, legionary of Fiume and former president of the *Opera Nazionale Balilla*, was stealing his thunder. He was supported by Pavolini and Farinacci, and he aspired to command the Militia, 'the real army of the RSI'. Graziani argued with Pavolini, insulted Farinacci, then antagonised Ricci. When Mussolini received both the marshal and Ricci, the latter announced: '*Duce*, I bring you the army of the Party'; while Graziani declared, '*Duce*, the people hate the Militia, it needs to be disbanded'.

Mussolini was tired. He agreed with them both. Believing the situation to have been already compromised, he thought that one army was as good as the other. Graziani and Ricci were engaging in a futile argument. At the Council of Ministers of 28 October, the *Duce* decided to settle things for good and approved Graziani's draft of a law which included call ups before 9 November and the incorporation of the Militia into the regular army. The marshal, aided by the chief of the general staff, Gastone Gambara, got immediately to work. Those born in 1924 and 1925, the eighteen and nineteen year olds, had to be recruited, given uniforms, equipment, and weapons. Equip them how, lodge them where? Graziani went from wishful thinking to feeling uneasy. Around him, he saw only ruin. From Enrico Caviglia's diary, who, on All Souls' Day, briefly visited Villa Liotta in Rome: 'Graziani tells me he can do nothing because he has no weapons and no uniforms, and the Germans have given him nothing. They take away everything and destroy what they cannot...'

Rodolfo Graziani, supreme commander, Minister of Defence, second only to Mussolini, yet in the autumn of 1943, he was essentially reduced to a hobo, forced to beg for weapons and uniforms on newspapers. '... one hundred lira reward for anyone who hands in a field-grey uniform,' an announcement said, '200 lira for a rifle or a musket, 500 lira for a machine gun.' His pleading would continue to the end. In February 1944, the *Gazzetta del Popolo* of Turin published a pathetic plea to its readers, imploring: 'Would you kindly donate, the money is needed to give a motorboat for our sailors and a fighter for the pilots of the *Graffer* squadron'.

And yet, what did in fact happen, was that the draft of 9 November turned out to be a success. The first and last in the Republic's short history with 87,000 answering the call at the recruitment offices. The province of Emilia exceeded all others with 9,876 men. All this without any collaboration with the Fascists, or any intimidation or threats (they would come later). The marshal had hit the bull's eye. He finally had an army, his army. He was even more successful with the officers: 300 generals and 40,000 lower ranking officers answered the call, just what was needed for 100 divisions. It was not possible to accept and pay for all of them. Many volunteers had to be sent home, a job that was headed up by a special commission responsible for the thinning out of the ranks.

However, no volunteers were to be found among the troops. The few that wanted to join preferred other special units, the most popular being the *Decima Flottiglia MAS* of Prince Junio Valerio Borghese.[16] This unit provided nice uniforms, good food, along with a certain arrogance to it all. Meanwhile, taciturn and suspicious draftees arrived in the cold and humid regular army barracks. No wine bottles, nor a song on anyone's lips. Each of the recruits kept civilian clothes in their suitcase, as part of their back up plan to be utilised if the right time for an escape presented itself. The officers settled them into work battalions, in the infantry and in the *Guardia Nazionale Repubblicana* (Mussolini had had second thoughts, he had disbanded the militia and invented the GNR, a fusion between militiamen and *Carabinieri*). Soon thereafter in December desertions began. On hearing the words 'we're off to Germany', hundreds would jump off the trains and into the wilderness. But on 14 November, Graziani was satisfied and kept telling his wife that everything was going as best it could.

However, none of this be found in the marshal's diary. His entries, written in blue ink, are generally just memos for appointments:

30 October. At Kesselring's.
  1 November. Dinner at the Grand Hotel.
  23 November. At the Casale. Settling claims for the requisitioning of cattle.
  25 November. Gardone, Council of Ministers.

From 11–31 December, he wrote just one phrase to cover everything: 'During these days, carrying out multiple affairs relating to my office'. The diary ends there. In 1944 and '45, he would not keep a diary at all.

Although sketchy, these following four entries merit further, in-depth examination. The first is from 5 October: 'I visit Thaon di Revel to reassure him'. The old duke of the sea who had presided over the Investigative Commission against Graziani was on a list of officers to be sent to the north. The marshal wanted to reassure him personally that no one would bother him. He also gave the same reassurance to Gen. Ago, a member of the very same commission. In other words, Graziani was not petty and did not abuse his position to enact revenge. He would demonstrate this even during the darkest months of the RSI when, at Lady Ines's request, he interceded in favour of soldiers and civilians arrested or persecuted by the Fascists or the Nazis. However, the only two who would thank him for this were Emilio Faldella and the journalist Indro Montanelli.[17]

His second entry is from 12 October: 'At Monseigneur Montini's regarding the Palatine guard question'. During that period, Giovan Battista Montini was the Vatican's secretary of state. Graziani had been introduced to him by Cardinal Jorio and would visit Montini on numerous occasions during this period. These frequent visits would give rise to the legend, put forward by some historians, 'that he, through high officials of the Church, was engaged in secret communications with the Kingdom of the South'. Nothing of the sort can be found within the archives and the marshal would always deny it, claiming, 'I am not a man of intrigue.' The explanations given by his wife, the journalist Carlo Silvestri and the rector of the Major Lateran Seminary—Monseigneur Roberto Ronca—were quite simple. Graziani and Montini held meetings to resolve issues of mutual interests between Italy and the Vatican. Discussions on the Palatine guard took place, as many Roman nobles aspired to join and have the honour of guarding the holy places. Furthermore, the SS had planned to blitz the Lateran Palace and capture the anti-fascists who had taken refuge there, such as De Gasperi, Nenni, Bonomi, Casati, Soleri, and Ruini. They spoke of avoiding possible territorial violations and finally, avoiding further perils for the open city of Rome, pressed between two armies. On 26 May 1944, for the last time, the marshal passed through the great bronze door: taking with him the promise, even in the name of Mussolini, that no fighting would take place in Rome. It is quite likely that Graziani used this occasion to entrust Vanda and his grandchildren to Montini's protection, as Graziani's daughter had refused to leave the capital. We assume this was the case, due to the evidence being only circumstantial (in the autumn of 1944, Lady Ines, worried about the fate of her family, would turn to Cardinal Ildefonso Schuster to 'have news of my dear ones at the Vatican's Secretariat'). On the record, there is only one letter sent by Monseigneur Montini in February 1946, requested by Marchioness Graziani, where the clergyman attests to 'the effective work undertaken by Marshal of Italy Rodolfo Graziani to spare Rome, seat of the Pontifex, from the horrors of war'.

Third entry: '19 November. Buffarini in my office with federal commissioner Bardi and Mr Pollastrini, commander of the vigilante squads, to whom I express, in harsh terms, my disapproval, inviting them to act in a more reasonable manner'. Gino Bardi and Guglielmo Pollastrini had gained a sinister notoriety in Rome, carrying out arbitrary arrests, homicides, and engaging in torture. Graziani tried to stop them, and on 26 November, he would write in his diary: 'it's absolutely necessary to dissolve that band'. However, he would not succeed, the 'villas of sadness', as they were called, and the gangs would multiply. And so, to disavow their violence, the marshal would ask to change the name of his ministry from the Ministry of National Defence to the Ministry of the Armed Forces, but essentially, nothing would change. However, this would come in useful to Graziani when he had to claim that the wild dogs of Fascism were not under his orders. And although he had ruled with such an iron fist in the colonies, he did not intend to do so at home among Italians.

The fourth entry is personal: '14 November, morning. Before leaving I go to the head notary to leave documents and issue a power of attorney'.

On 13 October 1943, a month before, Badoglio's government had declared war on Germany, and subsequently had decreed the confiscation of all the goods and property of those who collaborated with them. This decree included, of course, the confiscation of 'the property and the treasures of the former Marshal of Italy Rodolfo Graziani'. When Graziani heard the words 'treasures', he went into a fit of rage. As we know, he could not stand doubts or conjectures regarding his honesty, which was and had always been beyond question. The marshal had even excluded himself from the Republic's salary increase for officers. During his trial, he would exclaim: 'I can be accused of many things, but not of taking advantage of a situation'.

On 19 April 1945, with the collapse of the Republic now imminent, Graziani was concerned about a small box 'given to me by Col. Callegaris, commander of the engineers' corps of Pavia, containing ten kilos of platinum in sheets and wire along with rough, white and black diamonds'. He entrusted this precious case to the Benedictine Abbot Carlo De Vicentis so that he would 'hand it over intact to the Ministry of War of the legitimate Italian Government'. The three copies of this official document are kept in the Central State Archive, with a letter of acknowledgement enclosed (24 January 1946) from Manlio Brosio, a politician.

Given the above, it is understandable that the marshal, on 14 November, considered it a matter of honour to deposit at the office of the solicitor Carlo Capo, via Uffici del Vicario, number 18, a detailed list of 'houses and holdings in my name, and that, in my absence, will be legally administered by the same notary'. Even this list, which ended with the words 'I do not own anything else, no shares, no Italian or foreign bank accounts', can be found in the Central State Archive. Alongside it, there is a little small piece of paper, a postscript written by Graziani: 'After the war, the confiscation of my goods even included a consolidated document with a cheque of 200,000 lira in my daughter's name. Plus, an annuity for my two spinster sisters who reside in Affile. Presently, I do not own anything'.

He was not exaggerating. His house in Filettino had been ransacked, the furniture of Villa Liotta had been thrown out of the windows, his holding at Arcinazzo had been given as lodgings to an American diplomat, and the cases which had been hidden in the catacombs of the basilica of Saint Agnes had been found and sent to Washington by the US intelligence service. In 1946, from the penitentiary of Procida, Graziani would barrage Admiral Ellery Stone, chief commissioner of the Allied Commission for Italy, with letters asking to 'at least return my documents and family mementoes'. Stone did not reply, the cases would one day return to Italy, but without the jewels and silver. In 1950, Graziani was so deep in debt that he had to sell his medals and awards to Petochi the jeweller's in Piazza di Spagna.

The Ministry of the Armed Forces of the RSI had its seat at Polpenazze, near Manerba del Garda and Desenzano, in two commandeered hotels. It was a chaotic and not fitting as a military establishment. A hall was transformed into a waiting room, lounges and dining rooms were turned into meeting rooms, and bedrooms were used precariously as archives and administrative offices. Graziani received visitors in an elegant suite overlooking the lake while his chief of staff, Dr Bocca, worked in two rooms that were connected by a bathroom. The biggest problem were the beds. No one knew where to put them, as the basements and the attics were overflowing. The beds were mostly left where they were, but it was clearly not very dignified for a general to give audience sitting on a bed cluttered with papers.

By arriving at the ministry early in the morning, the marshal surprised the sentries slovenly lounging on the sofas. They quickly rose to attention when they heard him angrily shouting 'Damn it!' and 'for Christ's sake'. Fuming, he then went up to his suite and when he heard the sound of showers coming from the other offices, he complained: 'It's as if we were in a brothel'. He hated this new workplace, he hated Desenzano, he hated the lake which he referred to as 'a squalid compromise between a river and the sea'. The inhabitants of Lake Garda often saw him drive past, with a scowling expression, in a camouflaged Alfa with a blue flag fluttering on top of the mudguard. They did not like him, or for that matter, any of 'the Romans'. To the people of the lake, 'the Romans' were all outsiders, party functionaries, officers, and civil servants who, after having invaded houses, hotels, and hospitals, strutted around as if they had owned the place. Justifiably, they were considered a nuisance and generally disliked. During the winter, the lake could be quite dismal, but in the winter of '43–44, it was particularly bleak. When the sun had set, the streets became silent, with the only sign of life found in the cafes, or around the pool tables. During boring evenings in the heavy blackout tents, civil servants and officers tried in vain to pass the time. As a curfew was in place, the last film at the cinema was shown at 5 p.m. and Christmas midnight mass was celebrated at 4 p.m.

The effect this caused on the general mood of everyone was altogether negative. In their homes, residents spent their time playing *ponte* (the Fascist version of bridge), they gossiped and haggled with dealers from the black market, or with the Germans on whom everything depended, fuel, coal, and basically life itself. The wives and mistresses of the party officials sought escape in the world of sin, to forget about the boredom of today and the fear for tomorrow. Would there even be a tomorrow? People lived as if they were about to die. Salò was the last Thule, the atmosphere was that of a band of desperate survivors, however, lacking the style of Vichy France.

Graziani wanted no part in all this misery. When the sun had set, he walked home with Concitella to his assigned abode at Villa Tassinara and shut himself in. He told his wife that they would live only on the ration card like everybody else, with 'no favouritism'. Lady Ines did all she could for him. She made tasteless minestrone seasoned with 'Sapidina Galbani' stock cubes or 'Cilindretto' used for tomato sauce. Before placing the glue-like 'Roma' cheese on the table, she served 'Madrid style aubergines' and rabbit 'cooked in my own special way', recipes which were recommended by 'Il Gastronomo', a column in the *Corriere della Sera*. Embaie helped her with all the domestic chores and would even shake the bottled milk to try and make, if not butter, something similar. He prepared and dried balls of wet paper which burned better than peat in the stove. The ration card gave one the right to a kilogram of rice, 2 kg of pasta, 5 kg of potatoes and 150 grams of meat a month. However, at times, in the shops there was not even that and Lady Ines, behind her husband's back, resorted to the black market. Contraband goods could be bought via little men from the countryside who made rounds on bicycles with bags full of flour, prosciutto, and portions of butter.

Graziani now had little appetite; he would eat distractedly without uttering a word. He had also quit smoking, as it was too difficult to choose between the noxious 'Milit' and the sweetish 'Ambrosiane' cigarettes. As a former man of distinction, these plummeting standards of even basic living were taking their toll. In addition, he was also suffering from vision impairment. To read, instead of using a monocle, he wore a large pair of glasses which he regularly forgot and left wherever he went. His *shumbashi* carried a second pair and was always scurrying about searching for the first pair, which had got lost beforehand. If he was not suffering from indigestion, he was suffering from the cold in his poorly heated villa. His only small comfort from this bleak existence was consuming quantities of cognac, 'my only treat,' he justified. To protect him from the flu and colds which he often got, his wife had made him a very long field-grey woollen scarf, similar to the one which Alec Guiness wore in the film *Ladykillers*. Unkempt hair, his dog in his arms and his scarf jutting out from his uniform covering his jacket collar embellished with the gladiuses (the gladius had replaced the royal stars on 29 January 1944), the marshal looked more like a dishevelled film star than a general. However, he could not have cared less. He had more pressing concerns as matters were becoming worse each day.

On 12 February, Graziani had received an indignant letter from Kesselring. According to the *Feldmarschall*: 'The situation is intolerable', as the Republican army was rife with desertions. He read out the statistics of the most recent cases with teutonic accuracy: '1,340 men have fled from the *Siena* Battalion and 3,500 from various units in Northern Italy, even at the troop depot in Vercelli. During their transfer, 548 men disappeared from the Workers' Battalion Number 105'.

Kesselring's conclusion from all this: 'I would appreciate it if Your Excellency could tell me what steps have been taken to remedy the situation'. Graziani's response was firm and dignified:

> The cause of these desertions is well known.... Propaganda has thrived thanks to the numerous difficulties ... caused by the total disorganization of our services ... and by the delay with which some peripheral German commands have issued uniforms and lodgings. In such a state you cannot be amazed if, in full winter, men without warm clothing in cold, inhospitable barracks, could not resist the urge to escape. Given the above, I have deemed it unnecessary and wrong to take action against the deserters and their families...

In his autobiography (page 441), this reply was reproduced in full. With his trial looming, the marshal thought that his reply would help to exonerate him. He had never thought of inflicting punishment on his fellow countrymen, of pitting Italians against Italians. He had always tried to mitigate the harshness of the Germanic diktats. It was the Germans, with Mussolini's consent, who were responsible for any violent action. Again, from his autobiography:

> At the same time, the German authorities were pressing the *Duce* to apply harsher methods. Since November, Mussolini, on the occasion of the call up of those born in 1924–1925, had written two or three articles which formed the basis of a decree which would extend capital punishment for draft dodgers, equating them to cowards in the face of the enemy. I was opposed to this and I kept the decree draft dormant for three months.

This is only partially true. Graziani was initially opposed to these measures, but it is also true that on 18 February 1944, he ceased opposition and signed Legislative Decree Number 30, known as the 'Bando Graziani', which called up those born in 1922 and 1923 and read:

> The conscripts and servicemen on leave, who in the present state of war and without justification, do not present themselves three days from the prefixed date, will be considered cowards in the face of the enemy pursuant to article 144 of the military penal code and punished with death, via execution by firing squad. The same punishment will be dealt to those who, in active service, leave their unit for three days without authorization.

During his trial, the marshal would claim that 'It was an exceptional measure imposed by exceptional circumstances', and that in the decree, which was approved by the entire Council of Ministers, his signature came third, after those of Mussolini and Pisenti, the Minister of Justice. 'As far as I'm concerned,' he added, 'I tried to soften its effects by advising clemency to the military judges and in March, I recommended the promulgation of new "reductionist" decrees.'

Also, only partially true. In actual fact, from 11 March onwards, two 'pardon' decrees were passed. 'No matter which year the individual is born in,' it stated, 'deserters and those missing from the draft will be exempt from punishment if they present themselves before the 9th of March.' Alternatively, 'The deserters and draft dodgers arrested before 9 March will be exempt from any punishment if they agree to volunteer. Those who will present themselves after this date will be punished with ten days of isolation rather than death.' It is also true that Graziani, in agreement with Col. Vitali of the military judiciary (and in complete disagreement with the Fascists and the Germans), sent out a series of circulars which accommodated for many extenuating circumstances. Nonetheless, in those very same days, Graziani wrote to Kesselring in a reassuring tone that 'today we have the necessary judicial tools to dish out harsh lessons.' In addition, Gen. Gambara, after being urged by the Germans and certainly not unbeknownst to Graziani, ordered that 'Should the serviceman not present himself.... Those who will be subjected to the immediate consequences are the heads of the families.' There are those who objected that Graziani could not have acted in a way which displeased the Germans. It may be so, but to give a balanced opinion one would have to have lived in the dramatic and uncertain climate of 1944.

The fact remains that after Graziani's decree there were young people who were executed in public squares in front of horrified crowds. Fathers, often wrapped in black peasant cloaks, were dragged to barracks and threatened with arrest, deportation, and with the prospect of losing their job, pension and ration card. Desertions halved, this ignoble step of involving the parents of soldiers was very effective. Consequently, Rodolfo Graziani's name was cursed all over Italy in those days.

The marshal was conscious of the growing hatred towards him. He was nervous, almost to the point of being hysterical, and even developed a tic of constantly running his right hand through his hair. He was thinner and to his colleagues he appeared more threatening.

Lady Ines struggled to console her dishevelled and grumpy husband. Graziani recognised that everything was slipping away, including his prestige and credibility, yet he still refused all calls to moderation. In April, he approved the draft of those born in 1914, 1916, 1917, and 1918, and in June, he signed another draft, this time calling those of 1920, 1921, and the first quarter of 1926. The recruitment was a medley of threats of execution and promises of clemency. While the latest recruits headed off to the Third Reich in worker battalions, Pavolini would form the Black Brigades. As time passed, Graziani lost any real power, all that remained was his right to complain, which he used and abused frequently.[18]

On 22 April 1944, during a meeting between Hitler and Mussolini at Salzburg, the marshal, who was part of the *Duce*'s entourage, had a row with Gen. Hans

Above: The identity card of a militiamen of the 'Aldo Resega' Black Brigade of Milan. In 1944, Alessandro Pavolini created the Black Brigades, a Fascist military formation made to fight the partisans.

Below: On the back of the same card, a validation stamp from the German security forces. In fact, it was the Nazis who coordinated the round ups and reprisals conducted by the RSI's forces.

Leyers, head of the German mission for war production in Northern Italy. He said:

> Every day we produce 1,500 rifles, every month thousands upon thousands of rounds and more than 76,000 Beretta machine guns are made. All of this goes to Germany. The Italian army only receives 1,500 revolvers, 300 machine guns and twenty-five mortars a month. Leyers, who has already commandeered 45,000 horses, also commandeered the entire daily production of FIAT—fifty lorries—despite knowing that our trains are for the most part immobile due to lack of coal. Out of fifty lorries they leave us three which are used for troops, civilian transports and the harvest, which this year is meant to be

plentiful...

On 12 May 1944, Graziani was in Rome. Hunger and fear reigned in the city, the notorious German officer Herbert Kappler ruled supreme, the deportation of Jews and the Ardeatine massacre remained terrifying nightmares.[19] The marshal embraced his daughter and grandchildren, he then went to Montini, inspected the *Nembo* and *Barbarigo* battalions fighting on the Anzio front, and then spoke with Gen. Crimi, commander of the Finance guards in the capital. Daringly, the guards continued to wear the royal stars on their collars, and because of this gesture, they came to blows with the men of the Italian SS. Graziani suggested a cunning strategy to Crimi: 'Put the gladius on your collar and the stars below them, the Allies will be here in a few days anyway...' In mid-March, in the caves of Monte Soratte, the marshal met Kesselring and began complaining once again: 'We are indignant and sad that we must see Italian soldiers working as gardeners in the villas occupied by the Germans, cleaning cars, throwing out the garbage and being used for other similar duties'. Kesselring did not reply. He simply promised him that his villages, Affile, Filettino, and Trevi, 'despite having given refuge to escapee Allied prisoners', would not be burned to the ground.

On 9 June 1944, when Graziani was in Gargnano, he expressed his feelings to Mussolini, venting:

> At the Adriano I promised to bring back Italy's youth to the fight. After nine months everybody is asking themselves: where are our soldiers? Why haven't these famous divisions come back from Germany to defend Rome? Is the Republican army an illusion or a reality? All Italians know that our boys, after enthusiastically rallying to the call, were left for weeks without uniforms and without weapons. They asked to fight, but instead, they were sent to work under strict German supervision. This strict control has humiliated our men and stripped them of their confidence.

On 28 June 1944, in response to a letter from the *Duce* ('I ask you to coordinate the anti-guerrilla operations, the time has come for the Republic's march on the Vandée'), aided by Gen. Sorrentino, head of the ministry's military secretariat, Graziani prepared a twenty-one-page report. It was not an operational report, it was a litany of recriminations regarding the army, which did not exist, and the rebels, 'who on the contrary receive arms from the Allies and help from the clergy and population'. In the sixth paragraph, the marshal attacked the Fascist formations, he wrote: 'We must recognize that the good Fascists, even having faith in the *Duce*, deprecate the existence of a Republican Fascist Party and its methods, considering it an element of discord and absolutely counter-productive to the resurrection of the Nation'. The result of this was a violent row with Pavolini. Tired of all this quarrelling, Mussolini ended the dispute with this Solomonic decision: Graziani would command the regular divisions, the large ones being trained in Germany for conventional warfare while Pavolini would take charge of the fight against the rebels. An unexpected gift for the marshal. During his trial, he could say that he never ordered reprisals, and that these, and the anti-partisan operations, were orchestrated by the Germans and the Fascists. Finally, even the military units which took part in them (the X mas, the Hunters of the Alps, the CARS, the RAP, the COGU units, and the *Tagliamento* Regiment) did not receive orders from him, but from SS Gen. Karl Wolff.

On 8 July 1944, Graziani reiterated his protests against those Fascists who stupidly and ferociously, 'play the game of the enemy'. 'The Black Brigades are hated,' he repeated to Mussolini, 'and the vigilante police forces need to be suppressed by the government, starting from the Italian *Sicherheitdienst* which operates in Broni and in Pavese.'

On 21 July 1944, the marshal was at Rastenburg with the *Duce*. Together they visited the new Italian divisions which were being fitted out (*San Marco, Monterosa, Littorio, Italia*). Later on, they were Hitler's guests, as he had just miraculously survived von Stauffenberg's assassination attempt. It was now possible for two divisions to immediately return to Italy. However, Keitel started playing for time. To keep the German front calm, he would have preferred to send these divisions to other fronts. An angry Graziani shouted in protest: 'No! This would mean the end of everything, a total collapse'. His disappointment was such that Keitel ultimately abandoned his project. In August, the *San Marco* (15,325 marine infantrymen) and the *Monterosa* (19,000 *alpini*) repatriated; then in September, it would be the turn of the *Littorio* (18,500 grenadiers), and on 5 December, the *Italia* (14,000 *bersaglieri*).[20]

On 6 October 1944, at Lucca, the new seat of Kesselring's command, Graziani demanded: 'the baptism by fire' for his soldiers. 'Too many desertions,' Kesselring replied, and from his point of view, one could not blame him. After returning to Italy, the Italian divisions were crippled with desertion: all threats were in vain, the men and even the sentinels who were on guard escaped. The marshal saw red: 'Of course they flee! Where are the weapons which they have been promised? Without anything to do, the divisions crumble'.

On 20 January 1945, Graziani illustrated the state of the Republican armed forces to Rahn:

> We know that the German slogan is that Italians mustn't be deployed as soldiers, only as labourers ... I have a certain feeling that some have tried to prevent the reconstruction of the Italian armed forces. In the beginning we put 500 to 600,000 men into action. These men have fled because at the mobilization centres they did not find uniforms, weapons or board. Having fled, these men went to swell the rebel ranks. It's not our fault. All our requests fell on deaf ears. We sent enough men to Germany for four divisions. Today we ask that these divisions be able to operate. The visits that I can make, which I have made and will keep

making, those that the *Duce* has made will serve only to raise the morale of the troops, nothing more. I have sent the embassy many reports regarding the futile attempts made to obtain the necessary equipment from Gen. Leyers. Leyers is leading us by the nose. I do not hesitate to say that one of those responsible for hindering Italy's rearmament is indeed Leyers. The divisions are in part unarmed. The *Italia* Division has 25% of its men without weapons. What can a soldier do without weapons? I consider those who have stayed at their post to be heroes. Whilst I was talking to the troops during my recent visit to the *Italia* Division, a one-armed volunteer raised his stump to talk, he told me that both of his arms were unusable. When I asked him for what reason he could not use his other arm, he said that a soldier without a weapon has no arms. I asked if he had a pistol at least. He said he did not. So then I gave him mine. Shall I continue? A unit of the same division has moved its position. They are artillerymen, they have no means of carrying their heavy ammunition. Attacked by the rebels the soldiers use up all their individual rounds, they are overwhelmed and captured. Immediately afterwards, the Germans declare that the unit has gone to the rebels. This news is false. Is it the soldiers' fault, if after finishing their rounds, they had to surrender? Can they honestly be called cowards? This is what the Germans say, but it's not true. There was no desertion...

The ambassador lost his temper: 'Marshal, the desertions are real, they're not made up'.
A row started.

Graziani: 'five thousand men deserted, that's less than ten per cent'.
Rahn: 'I was told it was ten thousand'.
Graziani: 'Anyway, you all predicted that it would be twenty per cent. And don't forget that the *Brescia* and *Intra* battalions, the artillerymen and the *bersaglieri* sent to Garfagnana fought valorously against the Brazilians and the American negroes. They suffered many casualties...'
Rahn: 'Don't talk about deaths. Yesterday, during an aerial bombardment of my city, twenty-five thousand Germans died'.

If moaning and bickering were Graziani's main occupations during the final days of the RSI, they were not the only things he engaged in. On 10 June 1944, 'alarmed by rumours of an imminent partisan attack', the marshal changed offices and moved to a villa near Manerba owned by a Mr Omodeo. Aside from his wife, and the service staff, there was Col. Heinz Heggenreiner, a friend from his time in North Africa whose job was also to keep an eye on him. Like Mussolini, Graziani could do anything as long as it pleased the Germans (although he did not do much).
In the State Archive, the 'Graziani-RSI' shelf is full of documents. However, they are all well-wishing telegrams. The marshal remembered the feast day and

birthdays of everyone, including Hitler and the emperor of Japan, to whom he often wished 'fortune and prosperity'. The secretaries made sure they sent thank you letters, and the Führer's translator continued to address him as 'Minister of the Armed Forces of the Italian *Socialist* Republic'. Telegrams aside, Graziani ceased going to Desenzano, preferring to work from home. Every day at four in the afternoon he went to say hello to the *Duce* at Villa Feltrinelli in Gargnano. What the dictator and the general with the dog on his lap talked about, is unknown. The journalist Carlo Silvestri, who was present at many of these meetings, said that while Mussolini spoke, the marshal remained silent. Mussolini would read aloud extracts from the 'Corrispondenza Repubblicana', his rubric for the newspapers of the RSI, and the marshal would listen. As usual, the visits ended with a walk in the garden down to the lakeshore. The lights of the town of Limone sul Garda, could be seen in the background, outlining the border with the land of South Tyrol—annexed by the Germans after 8 September.

According to Silvestri, Mussolini had now discovered the marshal's human qualities and considered him an honest man of high esteem. However, the journalist's testimony has to be taken with a grain of salt. Silvestri was a bizarre socialist. He had been persecuted and exiled by the regime, but after the creation of the RSI, he had joined Mussolini in the hopes of accentuating the socialist character of the Fascist Republican experiment. Nonetheless, in this case his testimony should not be discounted either, as it has been corroborated by many others. For example, when the *Duce* was warned about Graziani's supposed

An anti-American propaganda cartoon published in the Fascist newspaper *Sveglia!* in August 1944. It was entitled 'The Liberators!' The caption read: 'Ford unloads and makes a killing whilst Italian workers emigrate into a life of slavery'.

contacts with Badoglio, he refused to hear any more of it: 'I don't believe it, Graziani is an honest soul, he could have asked me for a hundred favours, he hasn't asked for anything'. A second time, as the RSI was a nest of vipers, the *Duce* was informed of 'the activities of Marchioness Graziani in favour of antifascists and suspected partisans'. Mussolini, who had just had the Grazianis over for dinner, swiftly vetoed his informant's testament: 'Even if it were true it's irrelevant. The Marchioness is a woman of good heart. When I talked to her, I noticed that she is very shrewd'. Mussolini's wife Rachele also felt much sympathy for Lady Ines. With her peasant common sense, she considered her 'a well to do lady, not a tramp like many other women'.

After the war was over, Lady Ines recounted that the *Duce* received packages of anonymous letters at Gargnano regarding Graziani. He did not place any importance in them and handed them over to the marshal. Nevertheless, other letters concerning the marshal's wrongdoings reached the Germans, in particular Rahn and Kesselring. They often quarrelled with Graziani and rejected all his requests, but despite this, they did not harbour any grudges against him. They had become more acquainted with him and considered him a sincere and passionate individual. Rahn wrote of Graziani that he was 'a loyal man and a strategist of considerable skills'. Albert Kesselring declared: 'he was an Italian whose hand you could shake'. The Germans had nicknamed him 'that terrible old man' and 'the wailing wall'. Nonetheless, his rages amused Kesselring. According to Dollmann, who often acted as the marshal's interpreter, Kesselring enjoyed making him drink and hearing him ramble. After dinner and a few glasses of liquor, Graziani loved to wax lyrical over the battles of the past. His obsession was the battle of Cannae, won by Hannibal in 216 BC. He would arrange the bottles and glasses on the table to illustrate the opposing armies, then explain that the Romans were defeated because they attacked the Carthaginians in the centre, leaving their flanks undefended. 'A tactical move still feasible today,' he would say, then enthusiastically insist: 'If we lured the Allies to our centre and then, went for their flanks with new divisions…' At this point, Kesselring felt he must intervene and cut him short: 'what new divisions?' Graziani was taken aback, and Kesselring concluded: 'So no Cannae dear Marshal. Time to go to bed'.

On 15 July 1944, as we know, Graziani and Mussolini embarked on a 6,000-km trip to Germany to inspect the new Italian divisions being trained in the camps of Heidelberg, Grafenwöhr, Münsingen, and Sennelager. In his autobiography, the marshal recalled that trip as one of his most triumphant moments. Seeing Germany made a great impression on him 'A Nation fighting its utmost, despite its destruction'. He was amazed by the size of the training camps and reflected: 'Grafenwork [Grafenwöhr] alone measures 35,000 hectares and allows for the manoeuvring of three entire army corps, putting our Piedmontese style barracks built right in the city centre to shame'. Above all, he was impressed by the appearance of the Italian soldiers: 'unrecognizable, a true spectacle, German care has licked them back into shape...' Though Graziani was mistaken in that respect. 'German care' merely consisted of a loaf of black bread, a pat of margarine, barley or oat soup, and a handful of pickled cucumbers a day. If the recruits were looking healthy, it was because of the food packages sent by their mothers, who had scrimped and saved.

Mussolini delivered a clear and simple speech to the troops, emphasising the nation's gratitude. However, Graziani came close to making a historic *gaffe*. He was at Sennelager, not far away from Teutoburg forest, and so, he was swept away by classical history, he said: 'Since the times of ancient Rome we have faced challenges, and sometimes we have been defeated. It was around these parts in 9 AD that the Germanic tribes of Arminius slaughtered the legions of Varu...' Rahn energetically pulled on Graziani's coat, and he, muffling his words, ended his history lesson with: 'and now Germany has given us back our legions'. Nevertheless, he received his fair share of applause. As he was not used to it anymore, it moved him. After the order to fall out was given, he hugged the soldiers who crowded around him. '*Duce*,' he exclaimed, 'here is the army for our comeback.' However, all this turned out to be just words and illusions, destined to be blown away with the cold winds of the Po Valley. On their return to Italy, three divisions (*San Marco*, *Monterosa*, *Littorio*) would be incorporated into Army Group *Liguria*, an Italo-German force operating in the Piedmontese and Ligurian alps, quite far away from the Gothic line. On 2 August 1942, Graziani was appointed commander of this army, 'the only Italian', he would claim, 'who commanded Germans'. Yet another illusion. The marshal, being responsible for an Italo-German unit, had to receive orders from Kesselring and his successor, Heinrich von Vietinghoff. He did not command the Germans; it was, in fact, the opposite.

Not much followed. In the summer of 1944, Graziani made brief appearances in Venice, the capital of the Republic's high society, and in Milan, the 'royal' capital. Apart from brief trips to the Alps, with stops at Villa Lomellina-Raggio in Novi Ligure, he would spend most of his time between Manerba and Gargnano bickering with Rahn ('I propose the formation of a fifth division commanded by Enzo Grossi'; '*Nein*! Grossi's wife is Jewish') or rereading Tacitus (underlined passage: 'Tis an unfair law of war for which, if things go well, it is everyone's merit, however, if they go sour, then it is the fault of one man alone'). He lived like a retired general, powerless and ignored. However, he was a fearful general, always under the protection of a sizeable armed escort. As always, he suffered from a persecution complex and still believed he was 'the target of Partisans and the Allied secret services'. The truth be told was that he was essentially irrelevant and no longer an important target. In the furious post-war years, it would be said that the marshal, behind his Caesarean look, hid a fearful heart. What is certain is that during the 600 days of the RSI, Graziani was by no means a hero. Various episodes prove this.

The first amusing recount is from Eugen Dollmann in his book *With Hitler and Mussolini* (p. 319). It was October 1943 in Rome. Graziani, unaware of the failed attempt on his life at the Adriano theatre, telephoned Dollmann during the night.[21] He had been hearing strange noises from the cellars of Villa Liotta. Who knows? Maybe it was partisans, maybe Allied agents? Dollmann woke up Gen. Stahel, together, standing in their pyjamas they quickly found a solution—better send someone to have a look. It was 4 a.m.: twenty-five heavily armed paratroopers arrived at Graziani's house and descended to the cellar. The sound of creaking, the howling of the wind, and other various noises could be heard. They were convinced, most certainly, someone was down there. The paratroopers switched on their electric torches, then stormed in and began firing in all directions, wine bottles shattered, and terrified rats scurried away. Mission accomplished. Dollmann would call it 'Operation T.' as in *topi* (mice in Italian). The assault complete, the marshal returned to his bed while the Germans enthusiastically consumed the remaining bottles of wine, their war booty.

A further episode was recounted by Graziani himself in his autobiography (p. 244): '... from our radio interceptions we learnt that the Anglo-Americans knew the location of Villa Omodeo and had flown thousands of aircraft over it, all day every day'. It was common knowledge that the American flying fortresses flew over Italy exclusively to get to Germany. But the marshal was in denial and not pleased. He really did think that Allied bombers, fighter planes, and even 'Pippo'—the airplane which threw cluster bombs at random—were all there trying to take him out. Because he had no adequate air-raid shelter, when the siren went off, he would run into the garden and hide under a plane tree. When travelling by car, he insisted that his *shumbashi* stand on the running board and check that no enemy fighters were waiting for him at the next bend.

The third episode took place in Venice, in the autumn of 1944: The city was an oasis of peace, the Germans and the Allies agreed that one cannot wage war in a museum. In Venice, life went on almost as before, with a stroll through the Liston, shopping at Le Mercerie, an aperitif at the Café Florian and the pretty ladies with pathetic pretences of elegance parading themselves in St Mark's Square. Also, in this period the hotels were full of film stars. *Cinecittà* had come back to life at the Giudecca and the theatres were always sold out. However, the enchantment ended abruptly on 21 October. At the Goldoni theatre, as they were about to perform Pirandello's *Vestire gli ignudi*, to the audience's horror, the stage curtain rose to reveal three partisans pointing their machine guns directly at them. The crowd were ordered to rise, make a clenched fist salute, and sing *Fischia il vento, urla la bufera*. Fortunately, nothing happened, it was but a show of force and the partisans left, undisturbed. Not surprisingly, Graziani who had been to Venice and to that theatre a week before, was certain that it was not just a show of force. He summoned Gen. Archimede Mischi, commander of the GNR, from Brescia, 'the rebels were there for me', he insisted, 'they wanted to get me'. For protection and peace of mind, he ordered increased surveillance around Villa Omodeo. For months, the marshal avoided going to Desenzano ('alarmed by rumours of a possible partisan attack'), and from the theatre incident onwards he avoided Venice.

The fourth episode is narrated by Ildefonso Schuster, the cardinal of Milan and an important figure in the negotiations between the Fascists and the Partisans. It was February 1945, Graziani had asked for an audience in the archbishopric, he informed the cardinal that a British captain called Tooker and a priest, Don Barbareschi, had been captured at the Swiss border by the Black Brigade of Lecco: 'They have declared that they are bearers of a message from Field Marshal Alexander for me. A message which needs to be given to me via Cardinal Schuster'.[22] Was His Eminence aware of all this? Graziani was hesitant and suspicious. He preferred to entrust the British officer to Lt-Col. Di Leo, head of the RSI's intelligence services, and to Gen. Haster of the German information service of Verona. Schuster would write in his book *Gli ultimi tempi di un regime* (p. 136): 'We then learnt that it was fortunate that Graziani did not take the bait. In fact, it was a German trick to find out whether the generalissimo had given in to temptation and sent feelers out to the enemy. It was in fact the German authorities who ordered the Englishman and the priest be sent back to Switzerland'. The marshal, who would envision plots and conspiracies everywhere, had actually got it right. Apart from this, there was Graziani who tried to hand himself in to the Americans while suffering heart palpitations and sweating profusely, and the Graziani at San Vittore prison who was unanimously described as being 'terrorized' (which will be discussed further). Despite having witnessed the bravery of the marshal during the Great War and in Libya, we do not know why he was much less so at Salò. Was this due to his age, or to the nervous breakdown he had suffered after the assassination attempt at Addis Ababa from which he never recovered? Or perhaps, like most men, he was full of contradictions.

In the spring of 1945, the Allies were on the offensive, the Gothic Line had been smashed, the wind was blowing from the north, and the partisans were preparing for a mass insurrection. Graziani spent New Year's Eve in the Alps with the soldiers of the *Monterosa* Division, and Easter in Savona with the men of the *San Marco*. On 16 April, he was at Gargnano for the last council of ministers, in which total chaos ensued. Pavolini raved about turning Milan into the Italian Stalingrad to which the marshal coldly replied: 'Enough of these lies! I'm going where I ought to be, the headquarters of Army Group *Liguria*'. The headquarters were based at Vidigulfo, between Pavia and Milan. Despite being feverish, Graziani departed for Milan on 20 April. On the evening of the 19th, he had been to dinner with Rudolf Rahn, and the ambassador, with little diplomatic tact, had given him a brand-new chromed pistol. A tacit invitation to suicide, no less.

On Saturday 21 April, Heinrich von Vietinghoff, Kesselring's successor, entrusted Graziani to a delicate mission. He was to send feelers throughout the church in Milan to the *Corpo volontari della libertà* (CVL).[23] The Germans would spare Lombardy from destruction if they were not attacked during their retreat.

On Sunday 22 April, before relaying von Vietinghoff's message, the marshal recounted his life story to Cardinal Schuster, from his time at the seminary onwards. Schuster, who was impatient, wrote mercilessly in his book: 'Like all southerners, he never got to the point'.

On Monday 23 April, the Allies broke through the German lines, they were at Bologna. Graziani ordered the *Liguria* to fall back 'into the artificial fog'. It was a coded order: it meant that the troops were to deploy to the Prealps.

On Tuesday 24 April, Lady Ines sought refuge in the nuns' convent of the archbishopric. In the prefecture, the marshal had yet another clash with Pavolini who proposed taking the Black Brigades to Valtellina. Graziani: 'It's ignoble to keep lying like this'. Pavolini: 'Marshal, the respect I have for your age and for you as a person is one thing, being insulted is another'. Graziani: 'It's every man for himself. Why keep up this charade any longer?!'

On Wednesday 25 April, the mass insurrection began. There was fighting in Genoa, in Turin and shooting in the suburbs of Milan. Mussolini met the representatives of the *Comitato di Liberazione Nazionale Alta Italia* (CLNAI) at the archbishopric.[24] This famous meeting has been described in countless books, films, and news articles.

He arrived late, and while in the antechamber, he wrote a letter to his wife. 'My dearest,' he wrote, 'I am with the *Duce* and the Cardinal. Matters of prime importance are being discussed, including my work on behalf of Mussolini in the last few days. Perhaps a ray of sunlight will finally shine into the darkness which has engulfed us in this tremendous period'. Also present in the antechamber of the archbishopric was Don Giuseppe Bicchierai, Schuster's assistant. While speaking with the priest, the marshal learnt that for months the Germans had been negotiating the surrender of their army. He ran to Mussolini to inform him. The *Duce* jumped to his feet, 'we've been betrayed!' he shouted before storming out to go to the prefecture. Graziani followed him and promised the cardinal he would dissuade Mussolini from further rash decisions. When the *Duce* departed the prefecture of Milan for Como, the marshal accompanied him. He wanted to reach Mandello Lario, between Como and Lecco, where the HQ of Army Group *Liguria* had been moved to. It was 7:30 p.m. Mussolini fled Milan never to return. The final hours of Italian Fascism were lived in Milan like this: at the Ars theatre, they had just finished playing *Ba-bi-bo*, a variety act with Carlo Dapporto and the De Rege brothers; the poster for the next film coming up at the Astra cinema was *Si chiude all'alba* (We close at dawn).

On Thursday 26 April, Graziani slept on a couch in the prefecture of Como, while Mussolini set off at 4 a.m. on a journey which would end in Dongo. Those who decided to go along with him were ministers, party officials, and his armed escort. No one remained at the prefecture. 'To Mandello,' the marshal told the driver as he got into an Alfa Romeo. Little Concitella was in his arms and next to him were Embaie Tekle-Haymanot and the generals Rosario Sorrentino and Ruggero Bonomi. Along the way, they came across Buffarini Guidi's car and he

A mass insurrection was being prepared by the partisans and the Allies were about to take Bologna. However, for the *Corriere della Sera*, the war was a distant thought. All that is talked about is Germany's 'extreme resistance' against the Soviet invasion, 15 April 1945.

convinced them to go to Cadenabbia. The *Duce* was there at Villa Bonaventura, so perhaps he would cross the border into Switzerland through the Porlezza pass. In Cadenabbia, Mussolini was resting, not wanting to be disturbed. Villa Bonaventura was like a mad beehive, with Fascists quarrelling over whether to go to Switzerland or not, wasting precious time. At midday, as he returned to Como, Graziani found out that the partisans had blocked the road to Lecco. He did not know where to go, so he went back to the prefecture. 'Get out of here!' the doorman told him; upstairs Celio, the Fascist Prefect, was handing over power to the CVL. The Alfa drove around Como in increasingly narrower concentric circles. There were roadblocks everywhere and armed civilians at every turn. The marshal was trapped. The only road still open was the one to Cernobbio. At Cernobbio, there were 200 Germans stationed in houses surrounding Villa Geltrude Locatelli. They were the SS of the frontier police commanded by Capt. Voetterl from South Tyrol. Voetterl was understandably embarrassed when he welcomed Graziani—Karl Wolff, head of the SS in Italy and the man who had negotiated the German surrender, was also hiding there. There were shouts and insults. The marshal accused him of 'treachery', Wolff tried to justify his actions, saying that he had to negotiate the surrender separately.

However, there was no time for arguing. At midday, the partisans started taking up their positions on the nearby heights. There was a flurry of desperate phone calls to Milan, including Gen. Wolff who implored Cardinal Schuster so that he could have safe passage to Chiasso, near the Swiss border. He needed to sign the act of surrender. His Eminence knew the ways of the Lord, and so he probably knew the way to go to Switzerland. In fact, he did know them. Schuster phoned the US consulate in Lugano and assured Wolff that a car with agent Donald Jones of the OSS on board would pick him up during the night. As the cardinal was a man of his word, at 2 a.m., Wolff escaped by car to Switzerland with a briefcase full of documents. One of them was given to him by Graziani: it was a mandate to negotiate the surrender of the Republican armed forces on the same conditions as the Germans.

On Friday 27 April, Graziani turned himself in. In his autobiography, the marshal glosses over the details of this momentous day. It is therefore necessary to compare his account with the correspondence of the journalist and writer Ferruccio Lanfranchi who led an impromptu inquiry ('the pitiful odyssey of Marshal Graziani') for *il Nuovo Corriere della Sera*. Graziani's account and Lanfranchi's articles (later published in the book *La resa degli ottocentomila*) give us the full picture. There are only a few slight, but significant differences between these two versions. The marshal claims: 'I slept in fits and starts'. Ferruccio Lanfranchi says: 'He didn't sleep at all, he felt ill, his heart was playing up. Capt. Voetterl, whom I interviewed in Alto Adige, had to come to his aid by administering medicine and tonics'.

That Graziani felt ill is understandable. He was ashamed of being found among German soldiers and was afraid the Germans would take him hostage and 'use him as a bargaining chip at a fitting moment'. He ran to the telephone and, unable to talk with the cardinal, dictated a seven-point message to Don Bicchierai who had the task of relaying it to Schuster. In Lanfranchi's opinion, this message was totally brazen. The marshal quite often used expressions such as 'I have decided', 'I am ready to', 'My general staff', etc. as if he still had an ounce of power left. He also told a few white lies, as he transformed his casual encounter with Gen. Wolff into 'My mission to Gen. Wolff', and claimed that Wolff was still in Villa Locatelli, reasoning that if the cardinal was concerned about Wolff's fate, then he should be concerned about his.

The message reads:

1. My current situation. I am no longer in contact with members of the RSI. Since yesterday my sole position is that of Commander of Army Group *Liguria* made up of Italian and some German divisions. My duty as a Commander is to safeguard the Republican troops…
2. My mission to Gen. Wolff. With him I sorted out the agreements regarding the treatment of the Italian troops according to the ongoing conditions of surrender

with the Allies. I issued the following statement: 'I, Marshal of Italy Rodolfo Graziani, in my capacity as Minister of the armed forces, give full powers to Gen. Wolff, Supreme Commander of the SS and general plenipotentiary of Germany's armed Forces in Italy, to negotiate on my behalf the same conditions applied to the German armed Forces in Italy, with binding agreements regarding the Army, the Air Force, the Navy, and also the Fascist military units.'
3. I am currently with Gen. Wolff in Villa Geltrude Locatelli, headquarters of the SS in Cernobbio.
4. The CLNAI has set up its base in Como, but until now, I have not deemed it necessary to make any personal contact with them.
5. The attitude of the local populace and the partisans might become hostile towards me, as they might think I am either fleeing to Switzerland or hiding under the protection of the SS, when, in fact, I have come here of my own accord to the carry out the afore-mentioned mission to Gen. Wolff.
6. Given that there is still no Allied command in Milan, I have decided to hand myself over to General Cadorna, only on the condition that no harm will come to me, and generals Bonomi (Air Force) and Sorrentino (Army), who are part of my General Staff. I also ask that we be allowed to keep our personal firearms. I am therefore ready to move to Milan and to remain there at the disposal of General Cadorna. I ask Your Eminence's personal guarantee in order to continue my work which can still be useful given my position as Commander of the troops.
7. My trip from Como to Milan, as a result of the condition of the roads, cannot be made without an escort. I therefore deem it necessary, and I hope Your Eminence will convey this, to confer by telephone with General Cadorna.

His bluff was ineffective. When Don Bicchierai phoned back, it was 11 a.m. Raffaele Cadorna's response was blunt: 'the only competent body which can accept the surrender of His Excellency is the CVL. General Command Northern Italy will make sure it warns the command of Como of the possible surrender of Marshal Graziani and his escort'. Graziani was sweating profusely. Surrender to the partisans? Ferruccio Parri had always declared that 'We will never negotiate with Graziani', and Radio Milano uninterruptedly transmitted the order to 'execute the highest officials of the RSI'. Those were distressing hours. The ultimatum of the partisans surrounding Villa Locatelli would end at 6 p.m., after which they would attack. At 5 p.m., unexpectedly, *a coup de theatre*, an officer in khaki uniform with the royal stars on his collar and a tricolour badge on the sleeve of his tunic, appeared at the gate.

Graziani (from his autobiography): 'It was Lieutenant Bonetti of the *Folgore* Division. I asked Bonetti, "Did you know I was here?" "No," he replied, astounded.'

Lanfranchi (from *La resa degli ottocentomila*): 'Nothing of the sort. Lt Vittorio

Bonetti, hero of El Alamein and valiant soldier of the Italian Liberation Corps, initially didn't even recognize Graziani and Graziani didn't even address him with "*tu*." On the contrary, he addressed him abruptly, anxiously crying out: "Lieutenant, I am Marshal Graziani, please I beg you, accept my surrender," "But this can only happen within a regular military command," Bonetti replied. Graziani implored him: "Lieutenant, you are Italian, I am Italian as well, get me out of this predicament." Vittorio Bonetti, an old-school Milanese gentleman, was touched by this. "Can I take him away?" he asked Capt. Voetterl. "Please do," said Voetterl.'

Here, Ferruccio Lanfranchi gave the floor to Lt Bonetti, whom he interviewed:

In the midst of all that confusion, we split up into two groups. I let the Marshal keep his pistol instead of giving it to the partisans, just in case he needed it. And so I went out into the open towards the besiegers. After a few steps I bumped into an open car driven by a civilian and with an American soldier on board, standing up. He was wearing the same uniform as me, but without the stars and the tricolour badge, and a United States flag was wrapped around the car's bonnet. The car stopped and all was quickly explained. The man at the wheel was Doctor Carlo Peregrini and the soldier introduced himself as Captain Emilio Daddario of the High Command of the US 5th Army.[25] The son of Italian immigrants, Daddario spoke perfect Italian. We understood each other immediately. He said he would assure Graziani's safety; we then went back into Villa Locatelli to organize the Marshal's escort along with the generals Bonomi and Sorrentino. A column of four vehicles was formed. I drove the first car, Graziani's Alfa Romeo, he got in together with his *shumbashi* and Capt. Daddario. In the second car driven by Peregrini there was Gen. Bonomi. In the meantime, many Partisans had arrived in the area including the engineer Mario Borletti and my brother-in-law Pino Fiocchi. The third automobile was filled with Partisans, the fourth was driven by naval Lt Borletti and carried Gen. Sorrentino, Pino Fiocchi and Mr Nagel, an engineer.

At this point, one can imagine Graziani's relief. He had a prestigious escort, the industrialists Fiocchi and Borletti who were the *crème de la crème* of Como's resistance, and a perfect shield: the banner of the stars and stripes. On top of that, Emilio Daddario was a *paesano* from Ofena in Avezzano. He spoke to Graziani in Abruzzese dialect and slapped him heartedly on the back. While the American officer handed out chocolate, cigarettes, and chewing gum, the cheerful Graziani also gave out 1,000 lira notes to the SS soldiers of Villa Locatelli and handed the change to Embaie.

The drive on the motorway went smoothly, the only hiccup was caused by the appearance of straggling soldiers yelling, 'the Americans are here!' running towards the column to surrender. Unfortunately for them, only one American had arrived, Daddario. Even if he had been the Pied Piper of Hamelin, he could not have taken hundreds of prisoners with him. In Milan, on via Rovello, the column was attacked

The map of the Italian campaign published by the Allied High Command in May 1945.

by machine-gun fire. The motorcade stopped, perhaps they were Fascist snipers. The Como partisans exited their cars and prepared to fight. A photographer immortalised the scene: on either side of the pavement there were armed men engaged in a rigid standoff, while the marshal huddled against a wall without his hat.

In the meantime, summoned by the gunfire, Col. Rauff and his SS men bolted from the nearby Regina Hotel. The comedy commencing once again. The Germans began shouting, 'the Americans are here!' attempting to surrender. Capt. Daddario had no time for this: he explained again that he could not take any prisoners, but that they should be patient as Gen. Bolty and the 34th US Armoured Infantry Division were on their way. On the evening of 27 April 1945, Daddario was the toast of Milan (he would be given honorary citizenship of the city). He placed Graziani and his escort in the Regina Hotel and ordered that he be given a good room. Embaie smiled while Concitella wagged her tail. The American officer was a real friend. Graziani wrote in his autobiography 'I will always retain a fond memory of his well-behaved and understanding manner'.

On Saturday 28 April, Graziani finally got a good night's sleep; on Cadorna's orders, he was moved to The Milano Hotel on the corner between via Manzoni and via Monte Pieta. Daddario accompanied him and he was then settled into an apartment on the first floor, already occupied by the industrialist Donegani, president of the Montecatini company. 'Okay?' Daddario asked the marshal.

'Not really,' Graziani replied. The hall of the hotel was filled with partisans of the *Matteoti* brigades, and the situation had become ugly in the city. Saying the wrong thing could very easily get you killed.

The captain made sure the American flag was hanging from his room's window. 'Now it's ok,' he said while he walked away. However, as soon as Daddario left, everything went downhill. A waiter came in and made a clenched-fist salute, and then, four partisans with machine guns arrived and they meant business. From the marshal's autobiography:

> I was sitting on the couch, I was calm, my soul was already in a higher realm. The one who seemed to be in charge shouted at me: 'You know, Graziani, they call me the executioner of the company. I've killed twenty-three Fascists and you will be the twenty-fourth.' The others egged him on. 'In half an hour we'll end you, we'll bust your heart, we'll open up your stomach.' They continued to threaten and insult me. I did not react; all I said was: 'Do what you must, you have the power to do whatever you like.' Finally, by the grace of God, the four men left. I telephoned the receptionist about what had happened, I asked her to inform the officers who I was being held by. Immediately, a naval officer and the commander of the Partisan unit arrived: they apologized and said it would not happen again. And so, the 28th of April ended.

On Sunday 29 April, Graziani spent the entire night at his desk. He wrote a letter to his wife with his final goodbyes and jotted some notes down in his diary.[26] At 9 p.m., the apartment door opened to a partisan who threw a newspaper at the marshal's feet. The front-page headline read: 'Mussolini executed'. Graziani was halfway through reading it when new guests entered. Gen. Cadorna, Col. Faina, and Ferruccio Parri arrived along with Daddario who told the marshal that he was being moved to San Vittore prison, 'you'll be safer there, hand me your pistol'. The marshal grabbed his things: his glasses, the letter to his wife, a fountain pen and his wallet 'containing photographs of my family and my two late parents, plus the relics of Saint John Bosco'. He entrusted everything to Daddario so that he may pass it along to Lady Ines Graziani at the archbishopric. Although Daddario promised he would, he did not keep his word. He also swore that he would look after his *shumbashi* and his dog. As they left the room, Graziani told Professor Parri, 'All I ask for is a normal trial.' 'You will have one,' Parri assured him. 'A trial preceded by a proper investigation,' Graziani insisted. 'Of course,' Cadorna replied. Generals Bonomi and Sorrentino joined Graziani in leaving the building, but while the group descended the stairs, an explosion shook the hotel. Some extremists had planted explosives in the marshal's Alfa Romeo, which had detonated in the outside car park. Lt Bonnetti, who at the time was starting the engine, suffered serious injuries to his eyes, sadly causing him to become blind.

Graziani reached San Vittore in another car. The prison entrance was guarded by partisans of the *Garibaldi* brigades, causing the new guests to feel tense and afraid. People could be heard shouting 'shoot him', 'kill him'. Cadorna and Parri had to place themselves between the marshal and the guards to prevent any bloodshed. Inside, the hospitality was even worse. Graziani and the two generals were pushed and dragged all the way to the inmate reception office. 'Take your clothes off,' said a partisan. The prison commandant was Dr Giardina, 'a real gentlemen', the marshal later admitted. However, not even Dr Giardina could stop the excesses of the more brutal partisans. The partisans laughed as Graziani, Bonomi, and Sorrentino were forcefully undressed and made to bend over for a thorough inspection. In his autobiography, the marshal declared that he proudly told the partisan who was frisking him, 'In my flesh you will only find the 350 scars from Addis Ababa.' It could be that he said this, but it is doubtful. It really was not the time for Graziani's particular style of verbal grandeur. After the inspection and inventory of the inmate's items, Tonino threw the 'new guys' into their cells, Graziani was in number 65, Sorrentino and Bonomi were in numbers 67 and 69. The fact there were no shutters on the barred windows caused the marshal, wearing only his underpants and a shirt, to feel quite cold. He knocked on the small window of his cell door, 'something to cover myself up with please.' He was given back his coat—missing two buttons—his pyjamas, and a communist-style beret. In the afternoon, things seemed to improve. The guard was an old prison hand, he addressed Graziani as 'Your Excellency' and gave him a piece of bread, a metal net, a mattress, and clean sheets. He even brought in a priest, however, here is where the versions differ. The marshal stated: 'In the morning, I had expressed the wish to see a priest. When I saw it was Don Bicchierai from the archbishopric, I couldn't believe my eyes'. Don Bicchierai, interviewed by Ferruccio Lanfranchi, stated: 'When Graziani saw me, he jumped up and said: "What do you want from me?" He was restless, he obviously thought his time had come. He begged me to inform the cardinal'.

Be that as it may, Don Bicchierai did much more. He informed Gen. Cadorna and Capt. Daddario of the situation, just in the nick of time. Sandro Pertini had ordered that the marshal be executed post-haste.[27, 28] The firing squad was ready, and it was commanded by Corrado Bonfantini of the *Matteoti* brigades. At 7 p.m., Daddario swooped into San Vittore. 'Quickly,' he told Graziani as he threw his overcoat onto his shoulders, 'we have to escape.' It was an adventurous getaway. The halls were deserted and the doors to the prison were wide open. Embaie and a barking Concitella were outside, as were Cadorna, Don Bicchierai, and three American officers. Two olive green US Army vehicles with their headlights turned off pulled up: 'Everyone in,' Daddario ordered, 'we're going to Ghedi, to the Allied Command.' Graziani, Bonomi, and Sorrentino jumped in; Cadorna accompanied them for part of the journey in order to get through the checkpoints. During the night, they drove towards Bergamo and then Brescia. 'How are you?' Graziani was asked by one of the American officers. It was Col. Norman E. Fiske, former US military *attaché* to Italy, he had known Graziani since the Ethiopian campaign. 'It's a small world isn't it?' a warm embrace followed. From Graziani's autobiography: 'When we arrived at Ghedi, in the Brescia region at two in the morning, we were freezing. Gen. Crittemberger, Commander of the 4th US Armoured Corps, greeted us courteously and offered us a bottle of fine cognac'.

It was finally over; despite this, he was still in his underpants.

The following day, Graziani signed the official act of surrender. He was taken to Florence on a military aircraft, and there, on 1 May, he read the proclamation on the radio:

> This is the Commander's order to the Italo-German troops of Army Group *Liguria*. In this, Italy's last battle, you have behaved with the usual discipline and valour, even when our numbers were heavily inferior to those of the enemy. Any further resistance would be not only futile, but inhumane—and I, your Commander, would be guilty of unnecessary bloodshed. The German High Command in Italy has stopped sending out orders and its location is unknown. Given these circumstances, I have taken upon myself the responsibility of signing the unconditional surrender in the American High Command on the day of 29th April, as has been relayed to you through leaflets dropped from aeroplanes.[29] Obey this order and lay down your weapons, it guards your honour as soldiers.

This proclamation was necessary due to the general chaos reigning at the time. Some had continued to resist. Among these was the commander of the *San Marco* Division, Amilcare Farina, who was encamped with 12,000 men in the countryside of Alessandria. Farina, after hearing the marshal's words, surrendered to the CLNAI of Alessandria.

For the Allies, Graziani now became a prisoner of war, POW number AA-252433. This designation made a significant difference, a prisoner and not a war criminal. During his trial, this detail would be crucial.

7

A Sentence Which is More Like an Acquittal

In the trial a mood of courtesy, indolence and amiable tolerance reigned: it was almost like being in an English country club where an old former colonial governor, with a rough character and a short temper, recounts the exploits of his career whilst often pouring himself a drink. Every now and then, sounds of applause broke out and the old gentlemen of the club looked irritated because it's not good manners to clap in a club. Or, during a pause in the debate, the old governor caught sight of an old acquaintance in the crowd, and a lively exchange of gestures, jokes and handshaking ensued.... The *Carabinieri* smiled, they found the whole thing quite exciting. Then, the narrator got back to his story: battles, wars, deserts, dust, vices, miserable slander from the metropolis, from the government in Rome, and again with war, with its triumphs. Outside the autumn was quite pleasant, the most pleasant Roman autumn which had been seen for years. Even inside one could feel its pleasantness. The old governor was exalted by his reminiscences. Some had fallen asleep. It was hard to believe that this was a court of law…

Sandro De Feo, a born writer and journalist, was the man describing the special court of assizes where, for more than a week, Rodolfo Graziani was being tried.[1] His reports captured the mood of that period perfectly. It was 23 October 1948: there was no television and these big trials—like the one of Rina Fort, Countess Bellentani, and the former marshal's one—were like the television series of their time. People went to the courts as they would to the theatre, the newspapers published the shorthand reports of the hearing and made millions. For the public, which was split between the pro- and anti-Grazianis, entertainment was assured: the accused's rages, the flitting of robes, the ire of the judges for not being able to maintain order, were a true spectacle. Graziani was dressed in blue; he was pale and handsome. He arrived every morning from Forte Boccea on the *Carabinieri*'s transport van with a stack of books, a flask, and a metal tin full of pills. At the second hearing, he unbuttoned his shirt and took off his tie, 'Excuse me,' he shouted, 'I feel like I'm suffocating.' 'Poor man,' the ladies in the court murmured, 'He's suffered so much…'

'Poor Graziani' was an opinion that was beginning to take hold. The only ones calling him 'murderer', 'fascist scum', and 'the criminal of all criminals' were *Unità* and the left-wing press. On 18 April, the Christian Democrats made a killing at the elections, and in the eyes of the common man the new baddie was '*Baffone*' ('Mustachio'), aka Joseph Stalin. Things had changed. This was exactly what Graziani's lawyers were hoping for, they had fought long and hard to halt, delay, and push back the start of the trial. Irked by these dilatory tactics Palmiro Togliatti, leader of the Italian Communist Party, asked the Minister of Justice for a parliamentary inquiry to know when the trial against 'the traitor Graziani' would commence. It was all to no avail. The lawyers had been fighting on two fronts, they were trying to calm down their client who was impatient to defend himself, and at the same time, were bombarding the magistrature by way of procedural objections and requests for further medical examinations. They succeeded, mainly because, more than a nation of justice, Italy is the nation of the legal loophole. Professor Francesco Carnelutti smugly told the judges that Rome had waited patiently. He meant it as a compliment, but it was an accurate observation: to live in Italy, one must know how to wait.

Unlike his lawyers, Graziani was restless, he wanted to be heard. He had been waiting for three years: first, in a POW camp, then in the penitentiary of Procida, in a clinic in Naples, and, finally, in the military prison of Forte Boccea in Rome. 'A calvary', the marshal wrote to his wife. Perhaps he was exaggerating, considering that for him every restriction was an ordeal. What is certain is that the British had treated him well, and at Procida Arturo Galatola, the very humane Neapolitan prison warden had gone out of his way to alleviate the afflictions of prison life.

We left Graziani in Florence, where he was intent on reading the surrender proclamation of the troops of the RSI on the radio. On 10 May 1945, he was in the Cinecittà refugee camp, and on 12 June, he was sent to Algiers, to the British POW camp number 211. The British treated the marshal like a gentleman: they gave him a tent in the officers' quarters, they allowed him to eat in their mess where the food was better; they gave him an adjutant, Capt. Marchesi of the *Decima Mas*, and an orderly, Giuseppe Bonfanti, a marine infantryman. However, Graziani did not feel at ease: he looked over to the nearby camp for the Italian soldiers and he felt guilty, they looked like 10,000 scarecrows. After a brief stay in the military hospital to have his enflamed gall bladder treated, he asked to be moved. 'I want to be with my soldiers,' he explained. The British were happy to oblige and so the marshal was given a new number, AA-252533, and a new tent, number twenty-one. When he met his fellow countrymen, he became emotional. He told Col. Bassi, the head of the prisoners: 'we have lost everything, except our honour. Let us show them that we are men even as prisoners'. The days were monotonous, filled with mundane tasks: roll calls, mealtimes, and yard time. Graziani preferred being alone. He wore an Italian army uniform without rank slides or badges, on his head he donned the famous 'communist' beret from San Vittore. During the cold Algerian nights, he covered himself with his famous greatcoat with the buttons ripped off, a coat which he would wear in Procida, at his trial, and to his grave. He ate little and did not talk much; he did not confide in anyone. In vain, the other prisoners invited him to the little theatre they had built with cardboard and metal sheets. Once he got angry. It was November 1945, five officers had tried to escape, two had been captured and taken back to camp. The marshal ordered a general assembly, he yelled at the soldiers before him: 'Escapes are only gymnastic exercises, they're useless'. He was livid, he went on: 'they've kept us standing up for whole days, with roll calls and searches. Where are the bastards to whom we owe all this fun and games?' Pushed gently by their comrades, the two failed fugitives took a step forward. Surprisingly, Graziani concluded by saying: 'Anyway, good job. A little more luck and you would have outwitted the English'.

On 8 February 1946, camp 211 demobilised: it was time to go back to Italy, the POWs were taken on board the *Liberty* bound for Naples. Everyone except the marshal. For him, things were different. The Italian Government accused him on the basis of article 51 of the military penal code of 'acts which favour the military operations of the enemy or, otherwise, harm the operations of the State's armed forces'. The punishment for this was demotion and death. Between 8 and 16 February, the British moved Graziani to the Bir Kadem fort on the outskirts of Algiers. On the morning of the 10th, they changed his serial number to AA-253402, and they took him by plane to Pomigliano d'Arco, near Naples, and handed him over to the *Carabinieri*. Maj. H. C. Edwards of the RAF, Graziani's flight companion, seemed embarrassed: 'Sorry,' he said as they took leave of one another. Even the *Carabinieri* seemed embarrassed, how should they address the prisoner? Graziani was not anything anymore, not His Excellency, not a marshal, not even an officer. In the end, a captain of the *Carabinieri* decided to call him by his number and invited him to sit down in a lorry. Security was tight, and so the lorry was escorted by vans and motorbikes. The journey from Pomigliano d'Arco to Procida was short, but it seemed even shorter to Graziani whose head was buried in the papers of his arrest warrant and other judicial documents. In his absence, Minister of War, Alessandro Casati and Mario Berlinguer, high commissioner for the sanctions against Fascism, had been very busy. On top of his accusations of treachery, Casati expelled him from the army 'in accordance with the legislative decree of 26 April 1945 number. 249, which entails the removal of rank and role as an officer to all those who, after 13 October 1943, given Italy's declaration of war against Germany, collaborated with the forces fighting against Italy'. Berlinguer, Enrico's father, had instead penned a long and detailed report on Graziani whereby 'The Magistrate's jurisdiction justifies the High Commissioner's request for Graziani's referral to the High Court of Justice'.[2]

The report specified:

> After the declaration of the armistice and after seeing Rome fall into German hands, Mr Graziani, instead of taking charge of the forces engaged in defending the capital after the fleeing of its rulers—as should have been his duty as a soldier and an Italian—joined the Germans and the Republican Government of which he soon became Minister for National Defence. Graziani was the organizer and the animator of the Fascist Government's new army, inciting the people to a fratricidal war, and continuing the fight alongside the German invader. Graziani was principally responsible for looting, deportations, and the murder of citizens and patriots who fought and obstructed the enemy to save Italy. The capture and subsequent deportation to Germany of almost 7,000 Carabinieri, which occurred in Rome on 7 October 1943, was ordered by Graziani. He gave numerous speeches inciting the young to join the Republican army, the most famous being the speech at the Adriano Theatre in early October 1943, to the capital's numerous officers. In order to reach his goal, Graziani tirelessly enacted martial laws and proclamations ordering death sentences. Graziani was loyal to the Fascist Republican Government until the end, offering his services as Minister for National Defence and Commander of Mussolini's army.

To cut a long story short, there was not much to be happy about. With accusations like these, there was a high chance of him either being executed or getting a life sentence.

Given the above, when Graziani arrived at Procida in the afternoon of 16 February 1946, he felt troubled. He arrived at the island on a *Carabinieri* boat and struggled to walk up the steep slope which led to the prison. In the fortress prison there was a general sense of unease. The 'politicals' and the common criminals were uneasy, they had all been informed by the prison's loudspeaker that an important guest was arriving. Arturo Galatola, the prison warden, was also uneasy—he had received strict orders: 'Always keep an eye on prisoner Graziani, constantly move him from his cell in order to prevent any possible escape'.

Initially, the former marshal was lodged in dormitory number six with Junio Valerio Borghese, Gastone Gambara, Emilio Canevari, and Baron Alessandro Sardi. He stayed there for less than a fortnight. He himself asked to be moved because, as he would later recall: 'It was an impossible arrangement. Gambara snored, Borghese was restless, pacing up and down like a lion in a cage. Canevari read all night by candlelight, coughing and commenting as he did so. I, resting on my bunk which was too short and too narrow, could not get a wink of sleep'. An attentive Galatola decided to move Graziani into a single cell. It was 2.5 metres by 3 metres, and the warden added a desk, a chair, paper, and a bigger mattress. 'Be careful with the desk,' said Galatola, 'It's an antique. In 1799 it was used by the patriots of the

Neapolitan Republic imprisoned by the Bourbons.' Graziani's cell was next to the ones of the common criminals, thieves, gangsters, and murderers of the worst kind. But the criminals seemed to be caring towards the former marshal: they washed his clothes, they wiped the floor of his cell, and they gave him a canary in a cage and a geranium. Peppino La Marca, a notorious Neapolitan bandit, made it his duty to personally protect Graziani from any rude behaviour. He called him 'Your Excellency', and despite Graziani's protests, he told him: 'You're a Lord, when you were born you were already His most Excellent Excellency'. In exchange for his protection, La Marca barraged Graziani with religious and philosophical questions which seriously tested the former marshal's knowledge. Years later, Graziani would say: 'Peppino always brought up his woman, Marì Marì. The others were delinquents sentenced to thirty, forty and fifty years: and yet, I learnt much from them and I started to see life in a way which I had never contemplated before'.

These episodes from Graziani's life in Procida come from his dear friend Alessandro Sardi. After Graziani's death, he cowrote a favourable biography on the recently deceased marshal.[3]

Here is an excerpt:

I remember he seemed troubled, whilst he made his bed, while he moved his chair, his suitcase, the table and his few personal belongings. I remember him intent on writing page after page. In prison, he even had three books published, *Libia redenta*, his autobiography, and his account of the unfortunate campaign in North Africa. When the sun set, to avoid having to walk up and down the 137 steps which divided the cells from the inner courtyard, the director allowed Graziani to spend his yard time on the prison's terrace. On the terrace he whistled an Arab tune, always the same one, and he would look over to the sea and the lights of Ischia. He was on the terrace even on 20 February when his wife arrived at Procida to see him. The director was worried, the Marchioness did not have a regular permit, goodness gracious, now what? She apologized as she stood in front of the prison gates, waving to her husband who waved back from the terrace. Doctor Galatola was quite a strange fellow. Once, in May, Lady Ines arrived on the island by fishing boat. The ferry wasn't working—back then nothing worked—and despite the weather, she asked to stay with the boatman. We saw her walk up the slope all drenched and shivering from the cold. The director insisted that she make herself comfortable and warm herself up, and the politeness of the prison guards was beyond compare.

Colourful episodes of Neapolitan prison life. Obviously, life in prison is not that colourful. In June, Graziani's health took a turn for the worse. On the morning of the 20th, while getting up from his cot, he complained of stabbing pains in his abdomen. Appendicitis was what prison Dr Bormioli diagnosed. Graziani wanted to be operated on by Professor Vittorio Puccinelli, the doctor who had treated him in Addis Ababa. There was no time to lose, they feared it could be peritonitis, and so Bormioli decided to operate immediately. In the absence of an operating table, the surgery took place on a wooden plank in the prison clinic which was also utilised for the barber shop. The hygienic conditions were not the best, the only assistant Dr Bormioli had was 'Totonno the gun', a serial killer serving a life sentence. He was only given local anaesthetic, surgical appliances were disinfected as best they could, and there was bad lighting. Despite all this, the operation was a success. Graziani went back to his cell carried in a blanket by two convicts. Professor Puccinelli, who had arrived from Rome just in time, said: 'You made it, I don't know how but you made it'.

The former marshal's convalescence was difficult, he needed proper medical care in a normal hospital. Lady Ines began filling in forms for his hospitalisation, and after fifty-six days of bureaucratic delays, she managed to have her husband transported on an Italian navy motorboat and then an ambulance escorted by thirty *Carabinieri* to the 'Elena of Aosta' clinic in Naples. It was 28 August 1946. The people of Naples had not lived through the tragedy of the civil war and so the city was remarkably friendly. The staff at the clinic made the marshal's stay as comfortable as possible; in fact, he made a full recovery. His room was like an open port, visitors would come and go while the sentries standing at the door turned a blind eye. In the corridor, Concitella and Embaie stood guard, Emilio Daddario made sure he provided them with food and treats, both of them were cheerful. Graziani kept himself incredibly busy: he wrote downs memos for his lawyers, he filed lawsuits against journalists who had written 'lies and slander', he contacted countless publishers. 'With this autobiography,' he told his family, 'I will demonstrate that I acted in good faith, putting the interests of the Nation before my own. For this reason, I have entitled it *Ho difeso la Patria* [*I Defended the Nation*]. What matters now is that it's published as soon as possible before the trial.' This rush to justify his actions explains why Graziani's autobiography is of such limited scope: it is clear at first glance that it is a personal defence of oneself where much is explained, and much is omitted. The arguments and disputes in the book are almost incomprehensible to today's reader.

However, in 1946, *Ho difeso la Patria* had a certain pertinence, and in 1947, when it was published by Garzanti, it sold out (nineteen consecutive editions) and created a pandemonium. Extracts were published in various newspapers. Palmiro Togliatti was outraged and put forward another request to the Minister of Justice to know 'what measures you intend to take to stop the scandalous publication of Rodolfo Graziani's memoirs, a prisoner awaiting trial for the crime of treason and who has not yet been tried due to supposed ill health.'

Those who claimed that the former marshal could not attend the hearing due to his state of illness were his three expert lawyers. Francesco Carnelutti and Giacomo Primo Augenti had been anti-fascists and Giorgio Mastino Del Rio had even been a partisan decorated with the Gold Medal of Military Valour. Together they formed an excellent defence team. Their leader was Carnelutti, an eloquent and experienced orator; Augenti had an eye for detail, he was an inveterate shyster and an expert in finding loops holes in the law; and Mastino Del Rio was the court's bloodhound, he gave the prosecutor no quarter with his booming Sardinian accent. Journalists called them the 'Three Musketeers'.

The opening round went quite smoothly. Graziani would not be judged by the Supreme Court and its unappealable verdicts, but by an ordinary magistrature. The pretext for this was found by Augenti in a legislative decree of October 1945, which, when a trial is not taking place, imposes 'the deferment to the judicial authority of the legal proceedings which are pending before the High Commissioner for the sanctions against Fascism'. Once the high commission had been dodged, the procedural duel went on uninterruptedly from 1946–47, and most of '48. Graziani was called to the stand on 24 May 1946. 'He's ill,' objected Del Rio. He was recalled on 23 June. 'He is unable to travel,' his lawyers informed. At his hearing of 3 December, he was absent. 'He has angina,' Carnelutti explained, showing a medical certificate. At the next hearing of 9 December, only Professor Augenti was present, and he asked for 'the terms of the defence to be given as we still need time to confer with our client.' Dr Spagnuolo, the general prosecutor of Rome's Court of Appeals, exhausted, gave up. With one delay after another, the date for the hearing was pushed forward to 1947, but that year passed without anything happening as well. It seemed that 1948 would go by too. A disheartened Pertini wrote in *Avanti!* 'Perhaps it will never happen'. However, on 11 October 1948, finally, it all began.

The judge presiding was Dr Luigi Marantonio, a seasoned magistrate with a firm hand, the prosecutor was Viscount Ugo Guarnera, a shrewd and implacable accuser. However, the defence were not as fearful of him as they were of Graziani's fits of rage. The former marshal hated half-measures, either he sat down quietly or he went on long tirades. 'Keep calm,' Carnelutti implored during a recess. 'Keep calm my foot!' Graziani replied, 'I'm here to establish the truth.'

The court pundits wrote down all these amusing exchanges:

Carnelutti: 'It's not wise to tell the whole truth now, we need to water it down with time to seize the right opportunity'.
Graziani: 'If it's the truth then why be afraid of it?'
Carnelutti: 'Because this is a trial, things can get misinterpreted'.
Graziani: 'Oh, who cares'.

A pointless endeavour.

The trial began quietly with the reading of the indictment. It was along the same lines as the Berlinguer report:

After the 8th of September 1943 and until May 1945, in Rome and Northern Italy, the defendant committed crimes against the State's military honour. He is

A Sentence Which is More Like an Acquittal

accused of being the animator, organizer and Chief of the army of turncoats and traitors on the payroll of the Fascist Republican Government; of having taken the post of Minister of National Defence of the aforementioned Government; of issuing proclamations and recruiting orders with terrorist threats; of having ordered round ups; of having used military repression against the Patriots who were fighting against the German invaders; and so, of ordering his troops to take part in a fratricidal war of Italians against Italians.

Graziani became enraged. He rose to his feet and shouted: 'Lies, nonsense. I was never responsible for the conduct of the internal war. Yes, I was responsible for Anzio, Senio, and Garfagnana. I was responsible for the fact that Italians of the north were never put against Italians from the south'. The judge shut him up, the public started grumbling: there were former partisans and former fascists in the crowd. To avoid any fisticuffs, Dr Marantonio rang his bell and ordered the *Carabinieri* to clear the hall. The tension eased in the following days. The lawyers went mad applying procedural exceptions to everything, the trial seemed to be dragging its feet. The left-wing members in the crowd murmured 'It's all a joke', and then walked out of the hall. Only the right-wing spectators remained, they were all ladies and distinguished gentlemen in double breasted suits, those described in Sandro De Feo's articles.

A drawing from 1948 which appeared on *Travaso delle idee* entitled 'Cunningness of the Condemned'. Caption: '"What is your last wish?" "I want to see the end of Graziani's trial." "Damn it, he got us."'

On 20 October, it was the defendant's turn. 'Take a seat,' the judge told Graziani, pointing to a chair at the centre of the chamber. Graziani refused, he preferred to testify from the dock. 'I'll be brief,' he said, and then went on for six hearings. Mr Ruffolo, a book publisher, seeing a hit in the making, published the trial's stenographic record. A book of three volumes and 150,000 words. In the preface, Ruffolo distanced himself from the accused and warned the unfortunate buyer that 'Graziani's speaking style is uneven and sometimes convoluted. His words do not obey the rules of grammar. He would use a preposition, then a second and then a third, all suspended in the air like fireworks. The same goes for his ideas which appear, disappear and then reappear like karstic rivers.'

The economist Antonio Repaci was of the same opinion.[4]

Graziani's testimony was disorganized, muddled, and interspersed with vehement statements and violent tirades against his enemies and adversaries. His speech was pervaded by his passionate, strong and impetuous temperament, which sounded quite self-centred with its excessive militaristic emphasis. In this, he found his own style which was closer to his being, a style which was certainly original and effective. The former Marshal's oratory was not only concerned with defending himself from the judge's accusation, but also, in giving an open and impassioned apology of his own work. To demonstrate once and for all that he, Graziani, was right and everyone else was totally wrong.

On 24 October, Dr Marantonio tried to take the bull by the horns. Graziani was explaining how and why he had joined the Italian Social Republic, and that his wife had tried to stop him from making hasty decisions, 'Poor woman,' he exclaimed, 'I condemned her to a life of suffering…' 'please,' the judge intervened, 'keep to the facts and do not digress.' Graziani was cut to the quick and came back with 'you must understand what type of person I am' and started off again.

A duel began.

Marantonio: 'Let's try to understand then. Did you intend to live a quiet life, or did you intend to defend the Nation?'

Graziani: All worked up. 'Before I intended to stay in the shadows. What did Pirzio-Biroli do, what did hundreds of other generals do? They did nothing. Then, when all these emotions started building up inside me…'

Marantonio: 'So before you didn't but afterwards you did. Why did you change your mind then?'

Graziani: even more worked up, 'Because the Nation was facing disaster'.

Marantonio: 'But before you weren't thinking about the Nation at all'.

Graziani: banging his fist on the balustrade 'I'm sick of this. I repeat that until 23 September 1943 I was only thinking of leading a quiet life. However, when I saw the truth, when the enemy himself revealed to me what would happen to

Italy.... Your Honour, what would you have done in my shoes? Would you have gone into a monastery?'

Marantonio: 'I'm not you'.

Graziani: 'I was just saying'.

Marantonio: 'Don't "just say." Answer the question: why did you change your mind?'

Graziani: 'Because I am sensitive to these things, I am a soldier and a patriot ... and because of the German threats'.

Marantonio: 'Now it's all clear'.

Graziani: 'Your Honour you're killing me'.

It was a drama. The former marshal sank down on to his bench, the crowd cackled, the lawyers protested, Dr Marantonio adjourned the hearing.

And then came 30 October 1948. On that day, the court received a letter from 'Maurizio', *nom de guerre* of Ferruccio Parri, second-in-command of all Partisan forces:

> I have learnt from the press that, on request of the defence, the court allowed for a witness who tried to prove that the forces of the Italian Social Republic were not deployed to fight other Italians. I would like to say that this was not due to Graziani but to the German army's mistrust towards him; and also, because the Allies only deployed a few Italian contingents on the front line. For these reasons, Graziani's army could not fight against the regular army formations of the Government of Rome.... However, given that the Partisans who fought north of the Gothic line were Italians and were recruited in regular battalions, there are tens of thousands of Italian citizens who can say that they fought against General Graziani's forces. Other crucial testimonies include the thousands who were tortured and killed by the RSI's military formations.... The Army of Salò, which deployed more than 200,000 men equipped with a sizeable number of weapons, was sent by the German army exclusively to fight the Partisans. And it was the CVL that faced the brunt of these forces, wore them down and defeated them. All of Graziani's units, without exception, were used in anti-partisan actions and in round ups conducted with ruthlessness and cruelty.... All of those in charge of the fight against the Partisans can testify that they never received orders urging them to soften their stance.

With 'Maurizio's' letter, the entire *Associazione Nazionale Partigiani d'Italia* (ANPI) joined the fight.[5] On 2 November, fifty-eight-year-old Ferruccio Parri repeated his accusations in court. Carnelutti interrupted him, 'Sir,' he complained, 'you're going beyond the charge, you're taking the prosecutors place.' 'I am the civil party,' Parri replied. He then listed about a hundred former Partisan commanders, 'all trustworthy witnesses'.

Augenti: 'If that's how we're doing it then, we want the following to come here and testify…' he then listed about a hundred former officers and civil servants of the RSI.

Parri: 'Your witnesses are notorious criminals'.

Mastino del Rio: 'This is unprecedented. Witnesses which haven't even been heard yet are already being judged and denigrated. I'm aware that the Hon. Parri went to a technical college and law is a bit challenging for him, but…'

With shouts of 'Enough' and 'Shame on you!', the bickering got out of control. To make matters worse, Graziani was railing against 'Maurizio': 'I never deployed the army against the partisans. It was Gen. Wolff who wanted the round ups and the reprisals, I had nothing to do with them. Your Honour, let me out, let me out by God…'

Marantonio: 'Please spare us these blasphemies'.

Graziani: 'What blasphemies? I invoke the Creator before such lies'. He sank back down yet again.

The witnesses were brought in by both sides, but none of them were to any avail. Graziani was either a 'swine' or 'the man who always tried to mitigate the fatal consequences of that situation'.

Carnelutti, Augenti, and Del Rio went on the offensive: 'The facts, where are the facts?' they insisted, 'show us a piece of paper, an order, a document signed by Graziani which supports the anti-Partisan war.' Either the document did not exist, or no one could find it, and so, the lawyers had an easy job sustaining that 'the regular forces of the Republican army only reacted to partisan attacks'. With a mandatory injunction of 6 November, the court agreed with the defendant's argument and

A drawing by Verdini from 1949 which appeared on *Vie Nuove*, entitled: 'The fascists on trial'. The caption reads: 'Excuse me, Mr defendant, may I also question the witness?'

decided that only those witnesses able to testify with regards to the anti-partisan war should be admitted in the court. Skilfully, Del Rio reminded the court of how the former marshal was opposed to 'sending RSI units to the front against the British 8th Army, in which the Italian Liberation Corps fought'. Graziani: 'If something like that had happened, I would have killed myself'; Augenti bamboozled the judges by citing various military regulations of war and peace; Carnelutti, with a sly smile, mentioned his client's contacts with emissaries of the Kingdom of the South. However, here Graziani drew the line. He told Carnelutti: 'Sir, if anyone doubts my honesty, I'll start shooting'. He was worn out and had fallen ill again.

From January 1949, the trial stopped once again. The former marshal was absent 'due to ill health'. The defence tried to get the court to 'declare its incompetence and refer the case to a military tribunal, as only it is competent to assess questions on military affairs which have sprung up during some of the testimonies'. The request was granted. On 4 March 1949, after seventy-nine hearings, the court of assizes of Rome transferred the proceedings to the Military Tribunal of Rome:

> In light of the contrast which has arisen between the statements of the defendant, who declares he deployed the troops under his orders to protect the alpine and maritime frontiers, in so doing avoiding any conflict with Partisan forces and with the regular forces of the Italian Liberation Corps—with the exception of purely defensive actions which took place at the rear of his army—and the depositions of Ferruccio Parri and numerous others who took part in the Partisan war.

The months passed and it started all over again. On 8 October 1949, Maj. Gen. Florindo De Renzis ended the investigation, and on 23 February 1950, Gen. Beraudo Di Pralormo, the presiding judge of the military tribunal, opened the hearing. Even this time—given that Graziani was a marshal of Italy when these events took place—it was a special tribunal, formed precisely for the occasion and made up of officers of the highest rank.

What followed was the interrogation of the accused, examination of the testimonies. interventions of the prosecutor Gen. Galasso and counter interventions of the defence. Graziani looked at ease, Carnelutti was delighted: 'A soldier must be judged by soldiers'. With the army magistrates, Graziani was frank and to the point: he reneged nothing, he paid homage to 'the fallen soldiers of the south who like the ones of the north gave their lives for the common Nation'. He talked about Germany and its secret weapons. 'Today we know that they were not made up,' he said, 'and so, I ask you: if Germany had won, who, if not I, could have stood between the Germans and the Italian people?' The judges were struck as they listened in silence. Gen. Galasso 'with infinitely profound sadness' asked for twenty-four years in prison, the defence took three days to read their final statement. Carnelutti pronounced his final deeply moving words: 'May your decision, oh magistrates of the court, not end at the procedural papers, but reach beyond into eternity. God bless you!' On 2 May, after thirty-five hearings, the sentence came:

> The Military Tribunal of Rome recognizes Graziani to be guilty of collaboration with the Germans and sentences him to nineteen years in prison, recognizing the existence of mitigating factors in favour of the accused, set forth under article 26 of the military penal code of war. 'In consideration of acts of valour and severe wounds sustained in war'; recognizing the existence of mitigating factors set forth by article 61, comma 2 of the civilian penal code, 'of having acted morally in favour of social valour.' It absolves the accused of the crime of having deported the officers resident in Rome to the north; it absolves the accused of the accusation of having ordered the disarming of the Carabinieri of Rome on October 1943 because, despite the court having ascertained that the facts took place, it has been excluded that this act was committed with the intent of favouring the Germans ... it absolves the accused due to 'insufficient evidence' of having conducted anti-partisan operations through fighting and round-ups against the Patriot forces, deploying troops under his direct orders, precisely units of Army Group *Liguria*; it absolves the accused for not having committed the crime of having conducted anti-partisan operations through fighting and round-ups against the Patriot forces and through the deployment of other units under his command; it absolves the accused 'for not having committed the act' of having recruited thousands of Italian labourers to be sent to Germany.

In short, the military judges only considered Graziani to be guilty of those things which he himself had declared himself to be guilty of (collaboration with the Germans—note, not the 'German invader'—being Minister of National Defence and Commander of Army Group *Liguria*, creating the Republican army, and issuing the proclamations, decrees and recruitment orders). As expected, for the former partisans, it was a scandalous sentence, and for Graziani's supporters, a sentence 'which was like an acquittal'.

If this was not enough to infuriate the former partisans and those on the left, the reasoning behind it made them go berserk, especially where the court justified the concession of the mitigating circumstances:

> The containment of the more violent Fascist extremists, the softening of the Germans' repressive methods, defending social values, defending groups and individuals, favouring work interests, his attempted and successful interventions to avoid or reduce damage and danger to individuals, to cities, to goods, in a tragic situation which befell our country after the proclamation of the armistice, all these are considered to be mitigating factors for the crime of collaboration.

To the other collaborationists, he was often an obstacle in the fulfilment of their objectives, given that deeply engrained in the defendant's conscience were sentiments of devotion to the people of his Nation and his land.

Besides this, the supreme military tribunal also asked that 'the law on collaborationism be declared unconstitutional and therefore obsolete'. This appeal was refused, but on the topic of treason, it had this to say:

> History is filled with innumerable facts which are qualified as treason, even though those who took up arms against the legitimate state did so for love of the Nation, even if it was a misguided conception of its being. Looking back on history, one should duly remember the sentence handed out nearly a century ago by the Supreme Military Tribunal on 19 February 1863. The tribunal sentenced that: 'The soldier who deserts the banner of the Nation to which he has sworn loyalty to go and join Garibaldi's bands in Aspromonte[6] commits high treason. These bands were in open rebellion against the State, against the powers which represent the State, and so replacing the Sovereign, tried to wage war against other powers and, in so doing, compromised the security of the State, and caused the southern regions to be placed in a state of siege and declared in a state of war. And finally, of having fought against the National army which fought against them in the name of the State.' Such sentences entailed serious penalties which were almost always carried out. Garibaldi was never put on trial because he was given amnesty. Even recently, in 1920, regular soldiers deserted their regiments to serve under Gabriele d'Annunzio, until they were dispersed in the tragic Bloody Christmas of Fiume and Zara, a battle fought against Government troops commanded by the then General Caviglia.[7] All this demonstrates that the word 'treason' is not necessarily connected to contemptible acts originating from despicable sentiments. The law ... has made sure that the Marshal of Italy Rodolfo Graziani does not feel that he has been declared guilty of treason.

For Rodolfo Pacciardi, MP for the Italian Republican Party and Minister of Defence, the Graziani-Garibaldi comparison was 'an insult to Garibaldi's memory'. Pacciardi decreed that the former marshal 'be deprived of the faculty of wearing his decorations and his war wounded medal'. A vengeful measure which eventually boomeranged back at him: the Federation of Combatants of the RSI struck a special medal 'of recognition' for Graziani; José Millán Astray, founder of the Spanish Legion, sent him his own war wounded medal. Meanwhile, Graziani had been released from prison. After amnesties, reductions, and the commutations of his sentence and the time he already spent in jail, his nineteen years were reduced to thirteen years, then five, then eight months, and then nothing. On 20 August 1950, at 6 a.m., the great door of Forte Boccea closed behind Graziani. He was free to go back home, his wife was waiting for him in via Monti Parioli 51, a small, rented apartment. He would go there, but not before posting three insulting letters to a few journalists. Just so he could show them that Graziani was still Graziani, a grumpy old man.

Affile, 22 September 1952: Graziani was seventy years old; he had lost some of his vigour, he had wattle cheeks, he was watering the grapes on his balcony. Baron Alessandro Sardi came over from Rome to see him, the old man told him he did not like the capital anymore, he was a nineteenth-century man, he did not fit in in the modern world. 'Is Affile better?' Sardi asked, 'A lot better,' Graziani replied:

> Everyone loves me here, even the Communists. They're all agreed: we'll look after him they said, he's a *paesano* who's suffered and all he wants now is to live in peace. Nearly every week they send me a gift, a sweet, a basket of fruit, or some pecorino cheese. To them I'm the Marshal. Even for the *Carabinieri* I'm the Marshal. Poor fellows, they don't know what to do when they see me. When I walk by they stand to attention. How funny!

In truth, since his release, Graziani had had little to laugh about. The year 1950 was one of sadness. His prodigal grandson, Rodolfo, Jnr, heir to the family and its name sake had caught polio. The parents and grandparents were ever vigil at the boy's sick bed, they consulted specialists, and went on journeys of hope to Florence, Switzerland, and Germany. They were counting every penny.

To pay for Rodolfo's hospitalisation in a physical therapy facility, the marshal (we will continue to call him by his title to make things easier) had sold his medals and decorations, his very last possessions. He would have liked to sell a piece of land, but this was impossible as his properties had been confiscated. The echo of his economic troubles had gone beyond Italy's borders. Graziani received letters and parcels from Argentina, Brazil, and North America. In the autumn of 1950, they amounted to 4,000. Those who wrote to him were nostalgic fascists who had escaped abroad: they offered him work, money, and the chance to start a new life abroad. The marshal refused any charity and declined those invitations with dignity, he did not want to start a new life, he was tired—he wanted to finish his life where he was born, in Ciociaria.

In 1951, things on the economic front took a turn for the better. Mr Fausto Calvosa, the new official in charge of the confiscation of Graziani's property, was a dynamic and honest professional. Steadily, Calvosa managed to obtain the release from seizure of the farm at Arcinazzo, the houses in Affile, Filettino, and the vineyard in Piglio. All these had not been obtained through the Fascist regime, there were plenty of documents proving that. Graziani returned to Arcinazzo, his property was derelict, the stables were empty, poplars cut off at the roots, and weeds everywhere. He then returned to Affile and Filettino. The Minister of the Interior Mario Scelba ordered the *Carabinieri* to constantly keep an eye on him 'to prevent any possible public disturbances'. A useless precaution. In his hometown, the only time the marshal caused public disturbances was when groups of townsfolks welcomed him. To thank the people of Filettino, Graziani gifted them the first floor of his house 'so it may be turned into a pharmacy and local clinic'. To the people of Affile, he promised that he would restore the Meridiana tower, a medieval building that is the pride of the town. In 1952, feeling uncomfortable in Rome, he settled permanently in his father's house in Affile.

Alessandro Sardi often went to see him; the following words are from his memoirs:

> He had recuperated part of his books and twenty six of the seventy-six volumes of newspaper cuttings. He was proud of them, he kept rearranging them neatly and orderly in his drawers. He had a thousand projects: to enlarge the house at Affile, to make Arcinazzo great again, or alternatively, turn the farm into a hotel for tourists, with a playground, a swimming pool and stables. He seemed calm, he was only bothered by a quarrel which had come up with some of his relatives concerning an early division of his assets: 'a miserable and vulgar affair about money,' he said. On his desk in his office, engraved on two wooden shutters was Gabriele d'Annunzio's 'Table of Bitterness.' He insisted on reading it to me: 'He who conducts an enterprise of faith and ardour amongst uncertain and impure men, must expect to be disavowed before the cock crows twice. And he must not take any notice or be offended by this. For a spirit to be truly heroic, it must go beyond treachery and repudiation.' It was the only indirect reference to the past. For the most part he didn't not talk about it.

However, the past which Graziani tried to blot out continued to pursue him. For the party members of the far-right *Movimento Sociale Italiano* (MSI), the marshal was a living symbol, he had no right to stand aside.[8] On 7 October 1952, a few hundred neo-fascists of the Association of Republican Combatants of Milan arrived by bus at Piani di Arcinazzo. They set up camp in his farm and started singing, shouting, and praising Mussolini. Pandemonium broke out with eleven parliamentary hearings, a court investigation, strikes in Lombardy, and a speech by Scelba on 'The Fascist hydra rearing its head once again'. On 15 October, a defiant Graziani joined the MSI, and on 19 March 1953, he was made president of the party. Honorary president, of course, since he lacked an electorate. The MSI organised meetings and rallies for him with thousands of people in Perugia, Frosinone, Caserta, and Catania. The marshal's speeches were good enough, he talked about peace, of an end to hatred—'we are all Italians'. He went to Montecassino, he went to Montelungo to lay a wreath on the tomb of the soldiers of the Italian Liberation Corps and their commander, Gen. Utili, 'a homage of the soldiers of the north to the soldiers of the south who fell in the name of our Italy, our motherland.' Being among the people galvanised him and the crowd liked his colourful oratory. He was always talking about the past, as often happens to those who want to ignore the present, knowing full well that their time is coming.

The meeting between Graziani and Andreotti in the spring of 1953 caused an uproar. The left talked about a 'clerico-fascist conspiracy'. It was the last time that the marshal's name was featured on the front pages.

Even though the MSI saw Graziani as a figure head, they also saw that politically he could not be trusted. He was too old and too often refused to obey the party's directives. They were right. The embrace with Giulio Andreotti cost the MSI thousands of votes.[9] Andreotti denied ever having embraced the marshal, 'I was happy to shake his hand,' he explained. This is not correct, he hugged him in public for a few very good reasons. Regarding this, a note written by Graziani is held in the State Archive. Let us try to summarise: It was the spring of 1953, elections were afoot and a young Andreotti, then undersecretary to the prime minister, headed up to Arcinazzo in search of votes. Among those present was Graziani, Andreotti waved him over, the meeting turned into a friendly chat between the two. Andreotti boasted about the government's works, 'we have completed the Filettino–Capistrello road,' he declared, 'The Abruzzo and Ciociaria have finally been connected.' The marshal replied: 'I must concede that De Gasperi's Government has worked for the country's revival. One must only look at our mountains to see how much is being done'. Andreotti could not believe what he was hearing, Graziani, honorary president of the MSI, recognising the government's merits, it was like finding gold—and votes. The marshal insisted, he gave credit to the Christian Democrats for 'having worked towards national pacification, with the recently proposed law which should provide pensions to the wounded and the families of those who fell for the RSI'. 'But what about Fascism?' Andreotti asked. Graziani replied: 'I joined the MSI because it mirrors my beliefs and convictions. However, it would be absurd to think that a new Fascist dictatorship could be set up today. History teaches us that dictatorships don't spring up like mushrooms'. At this point an embrace was obligatory. Obviously, it was an aseptic political embrace; much like the kisses exchanged by Soviet leaders.

Graziani resigned from the MSI in the summer of 1954. In parliament, they were debating whether or not Italy should join the EDC, the European Defence Community: the MSI was against it, 'we need to settle Trieste first.'[10] The marshal, on the other hand, was in favour. On 8 August 1954, he gave an interview to *Il Tempo*, a Roman newspaper. It was more like a spiritual statement than an interview. After having explained the reasons for his resignation, he said: 'I fought for Italy, the idea of a Nation has always been close to my heart. However, I'm not blind to the point of denying today's reality, which is European. There's no doubt: either we join a flowering European Federation through the EDC or shut ourselves away in a foggy neutrality which will make us servants of Russia'. Today everyone thinks like this. But then, coming from Graziani, it left people speechless. It seemed impossible that a poor old man (he would often fall asleep on the sofa and, sometimes, wake up thinking he was still viceroy at Addis Ababa) could, in moments of lucidity, be sharper than many young people on the right and the left.

In the autumn of 1954, the marshal did not have much time left. Sardi recounted: 'He was losing strength; his eyes lacked that brightness which they once had. We, his friends, were all worried. He tried to put us at ease, "I'm only sad because Concitella has died," he kept repeating. The truth was that he was not well at all, his stomach was bloated and painful. Perhaps it was a tumour, no one ever found out for sure'.

In late November, Graziani went to Rome. Tests needed to be done, a cholecystography and a check up on his digestive tract. Despite some paleness on his gallbladder, nothing serious came up. However, after a few days, the pain became more acute and so Dr Frugoni recommended he be taken to the 'Sanatrix' clinic in via Trasone. At Christmas, before going into the clinic, the marshal wrote a letter (it would be found in a drawer). A warning against his greedy relatives and a final statement of love to his dear wife. 'I intend,' he wrote, 'that no one dare disturb the tranquillity of the companion of my life who has sacrificed so much and worked tirelessly for our family, especially in the most tragic period of my existence—giving a noble example of how much one woman who remains loyal, for better and for worse, can do.'

On Boxing Day, Graziani was operated on by Professor Pietro Valdoni. It all went well. He started recovering. On 6 January, to celebrate the dodged bullet, he toasted with champagne. However, on 10 January, suddenly, the situation worsened. He felt too hot, too cold, he was delirious. Doctors and family members came to his sick bed, his pulse was weak, and his heart trembled. Ines told her husband the white lies which are told in these cases: 'Don Vincenzo Cufalo is here,' she said, 'he wants to say hello, can I let him in?' Don Cufalo was the military chaplain of Forte Boccea. The marshal understood, he confessed and received absolution. At midnight he went into a coma, at 4 a.m., as he briefly regained consciousness, he murmured: 'If my time has come, I'll go calmly to be judged by God'. His last breath was at 6 a.m., he appeared not to suffer, he was holding his wife's hand. It was 11 January 1955. *Il Secolo d'Italia*, mouthpiece of the MSI, printed an extraordinary edition with this sensational title: 'His last words were: "Courage, onwards!"' Perhaps not. It was simply the rhetoric of the *bella morte*: anyone who has been someone in life cannot go in silence, he has to say a historic phrase: '*Tête d'armée*' like Napoleon, 'Light! More light!' like Goethe.

Rodolfo Graziani wanted a simple funeral. Instead, it was grand and spectacular. Around 100,000 people attended the ceremony in Piazza Ungheria in front of the church of Saint Bellarmino, the very heart of the Parioli district. Traffic was blocked—in the 1950s this was unheard of—fascist salutes, banners, hymns, a real show. One of his wishes was respected. He was laid in his coffin wearing his bush jacket with his field-grey great coat on top. It was his old threadbare coat that he had worn on 25 April 1945, the one with the buttons ripped off.

8

What Remains?

Today, Filettino is the richest village in the Lazio region. Its 669 inhabitants, centenarians, and new-borns included, possess, according to the annual survey on the income of Italian municipalities 'a yearly income of thirteen million lira each'. All this is thanks to tourism and winter sports. On the roads that lead up to Largo Martino Filetico, there are a variety of small shops, some selling sports clothing and others local food. The biggest and most well supplied is the 'Bottega del Maestro', which is situated right in Graziani's birthplace, next to the post office. One enters among winter coats and mountain boots, and there is also a bust of the marshal which is used as a coat hanger. The house's architecture still retains a certain nobility. It is spacious, there are three floors, the main entrance surmounted by the heraldic coat of arms with *Ense et Aratro* written at the bottom. The first floor houses the pharmacy and the clinic, the other rooms are closed.

Romano Misserville, the MSI mayor of Filettino, hopes to turn the house into a museum. The town's councillors, including the Communist and Socialist ones, are all in favour. Going ahead with this project has been a struggle, the controversy it has caused even reached national newspapers. Should a museum on Rodolfo Graziani be created? What should be put in it? The Negus's throne? Not possible, Badoglio took it and used it as a kennel for his dog. Menelik's drum? Sorry, it was given back to Ethiopia after the war. Miserville says: 'The museum will be divided into two sections, one dedicated to local history and traditions, the other to the memory of the General, with his writings, medals, and the banners of his battalions'.

It is not much, but there really is not much to keep the memory of the marshal alive. In the village, there is only a stone tablet dedicated to him in a small green space between Largo Martino Filetico and Giuditta Tavani Arquati square, near the stone fountain where the source of the Aniene river gushes out from. The stone tablet honours: 'the sacrifice of the *paesano* Arcangelo Caraffa, fallen at Adwa'. On its side is written: 'His unburied ashes were returned in 1936 by Rodolfo Graziani, undefeated Commander of the Italian armies in Africa'. On the rear, Menelik's drum is mentioned, brought to Italy by the 'Filettinian Rodolfo Graziani'. For the young people of Filettino Graziani is the name of the communal park. They know next to nothing about the 'undefeated Commander' and they do not seem to care either.

The same thing goes for Affile. The Graziani family home is situated in the lower part of the town, behind the Meridiana tower, and it lies next to the small chapel of la Madonna del Giglio. On top of the little entrance of the tower, there is a coat of arms covered in dust and cobwebs. The house is in dire need of repair. Alberto Gualandi's Spanish wife, Ondina Canibano, occasionally lives there with their daughter, Ethel Romana. The marshal is laid to rest in the small cemetery of Affile. It is an imposing tomb, a rectangle of travertine stone, 3 by 6 metres. Nearly all the Grazianis are here, from the grandparents Benedetto Graziani and Domenica De Caesaris, the parents Filippo Graziani and Adelia Clementi, the sisters Ilda Graziani and Maria Graziani, to brother Goffredo and uncle Peppino.

Rodolfo Graziani's grave is right next to his wife's, who died in 1979, it can be spotted immediately because it is the only one covered in flowers. All done by the *camerati*, members of the MSI who, each month, go on a pilgrimage to Affile to lay a wreath on his gravestone.

Even the villa at Piani di Arcinazzo smacks of abandonment and death. The windows are closed, doors nailed shut, and the whole building is falling apart.

The farm, inherited by Rodolfo Gualandi Graziani and Alberto Gualandi, is for sale and some parts have already been sold. The Salesian monks bought the cowshed and transformed it into a social centre for young people, instead of the farmhouses there are now villas and holiday homes. Coming from via Paolucci de' Calboli you can see a poplar laned avenue which the marshal had planted, and further up—amid the fields with grazing horses—the fir trees where Graziani's dogs Quoncit and Topolino were buried. Only Alberto Gualandi occasionally comes up here. His father, Count Sergio Gualandi, lives elsewhere. He resides in Rome near the via Cassia with his first-born Rodolfo, who is gravely ill. His mother, Vanda Gualandi Graziani, passed away on 16 October 1985 and was buried at Viareggio, in the Gualandi family crypt.

That is all that remains. Of Rodolfo Graziani there is very little, he is like a ghost, a shadow now long forgotten. He was certainly an important general, not a second-tier individual in the history of Italy. Now and then his name comes up when speaking of Badoglio. Italians like rivalries: Nuvolari or Varzi, Coppi or Bartali, Graziani or Badoglio.[1] But about his great rival Pietro Badoglio, books, essays, and monographs have been written; about Graziani nothing has been printed and no images have been shown on television, as if he were the bad copy of the same photo. And yet, like Badoglio, Graziani enjoyed immense popularity, in the years of the war in Africa the youngsters who cheered for him were numerous.

Was he a good general? This is difficult to say. He was surely an efficient colonial officer, a master of counter-insurgency more than strategy. Towards the Abyssinians, he was certainly a cruel and merciless soldier. In Africa, during the Second World War, he lost an entire army and the whole of Cyrenaica. It was not all his fault, but at the end of the day, it is the facts that count. Napoleon rightly preferred lucky generals to good ones. The facts speak against the marshal during the RSI, a decision he took against his own will and which overwhelmed him. This reckless behaviour, acting on impulse and against everyone, was Graziani in a nutshell. On a personal level, Rodolfo Graziani was a tormented soul with the pros and cons of the people of his time and his land. He was hard working, fond of his family, stubborn, and imbued with peasant suspiciousness typical of mountain people. On the other hand, he committed violent acts and he lacked those qualities of coherence and cunningness that, even for the worst people, are what set men apart from great men.

Postscript

After his death in January 1955, Rodolfo Graziani was mostly forgotten.

People who could have said a few things about him had either already passed away or would do so shortly afterwards.

In 1950, Archibald Wavell died. After his victory in the desert, Wavell had been sent to India as viceroy, his job this time was to push back the Japanese invasion of the Raj. He would be quite distraught when, in 1947, he was replaced as viceroy by Louis Mountbatten, believing that London had not given him enough time to prepare India for independence. He died of liver cancer a few years later, perhaps never having given a second thought to that irate Italian general whose armies he destroyed.

Pietro Badoglio died a year after Graziani. Unlike his rival, who in his final years enjoyed the political support of the MSI, Badoglio lived out his final years surrounded only by his daughter (his wife and his three sons had all died during the war), a few close friends, and some old collaborators from the army. His hometown is still called Grazzano Badoglio.

Haile Selassie was overthrown in a military coup and later secretly executed in 1975. He did attempt to have Graziani and Badoglio tried as war criminals in Ethiopia, but due to British and French pressure, he was forced to abandon this idea. He would leave them to God's judgement.

Idris as-Senussi became king of an independent Libya in 1951. He was a tolerant ruler who did not persecute the many Italians who had remained in the country. In 1969, King Idris was overthrown by army officers led by Col. Muammar Gaddafi. The young colonel had not forgotten the killing of his hero Omar al-Mukhtar, and in 1974, he enacted the 'day of revenge', deporting all Italians and Jews from the country. Only after the overthrow of Gaddafi in 2011 did portraits of Idris reappear in the streets of Libya.

As for Omar al-Mukhtar, after the war, he became Libya's national hero. His life-long struggle for the freedom of his country inspired the world. Streets and monuments have been dedicated to him from Saudi Arabia to Venezuela.

In the years that followed the end of the war, historians started putting pen to paper and the history of Italian Fascism was written. And so, Graziani's name came up once more.

In 1964, the British historian William Deakin wrote *The Brutal Friendship*, a history of Italy at war from 1942 to 1945. In this book, Deakin gave an in-depth analysis of Graziani's attempt to create a new army for the RSI. In 1974, the Italian historian and journalist Silvio Bertoldi wrote *Salò*, a history of the Italian Social Republic. Alongside Mussolini, Graziani is presented as one of the most crucial characters in the final period of Fascism. In the 1970s and early '80s, the historian Angelo Del Boca wrote a series of volumes entitled *Gli Italiani in Africa orientale* (*The Italians in East Africa*). This was the first attempt by a historian to critically analyse Italy's colonisation of the Horn of Africa. The third volume of his work, *La caduta dell'Impero*, dealt with Graziani's tenure as viceroy and the atrocities he committed after the failed assassination attempt in 1936.

Del Boca was to be engaged in a long-heated debate with the journalist Indro Montanelli; the former insisted that Italy had used poison gas in Ethiopia, with the latter denying it, claiming that Italy had been kind and generous to the Abyssinians. Only in 1996, when the then-Minister of Defence Domenico Corcione told the Italian parliament that poison gas had actually been used in Ethiopia would Montanelli apologise and retract his previous statements.

However, the book which you are reading was the first to publish documents proving the use of poison gas, nine years before Corcione's statements. It was released in 1987 by the Italian publishing house Newton Compton, with the title *Rodolfo Graziani, un generale per il regime* (*A General for the Regime*). The author of the book would later be sued by Graziani's grandson, Alberto Gualandi. Gualandi had no issue with the book's content but was unhappy with the title. In his opinion, 'A General for the Regime' implied that Graziani had gained his promotion only thanks to the Fascist regime, and not thanks to his skill as an officer. The author defended himself, explaining that it was the publishing house which had chosen the title. Mr Gualandi would win the case and have Newton Compton change the title in all future editions. However, despite receiving resounding praise from various historians and both the left- and right-wing press, the book was not reprinted until 2019 (this was mostly due to the tense political climate which reigned in Italy at the time, where an objective book on a Fascist figure was deemed as too controversial). Then, it was it republished by the newspaper *Il Giornale*, with the new title *Vita di un discusso generale* (*Life of a Controversial General*).

Two more biographies would follow: *Graziani l'africano* (La Nuova Italia, 1997) written by Giuseppe Mayda, gives an in-depth look at Graziani's career, utilising interviews with the marshal's nephew, Giulio Cesare Graziani, who after the war became a general in the Italian Air Force. Subsequently, *Graziani* (Oscar Mondadori, 2004), written by Romano Canosa, drew on previously classified documents held in the 'Fondo Graziani' of the Central State Archive.

As we have seen, the mayor of Filettino, Romano Miserville, attempted to create a museum in the home where Graziani was born. However, this never came to anything. Almost three decades later, in 2012, the mayor of Affile, Ercole Viri, had a mausoleum-monument to Rodolfo Graziani erected in a one-acre park just outside the town. The monument was unveiled during a public ceremony which was attended by civil and military dignitaries. The mausoleum is a square brick building with the words '*Patria—Onore*' ('Nation—Honour') written over the entrance. Inside, there is a bust of the marshal surrounded by photographs and other memorabilia.

When this story became known, it caused an uproar and made the rounds of the world's newspapers, including *The New York Times*, which questioned 'whether Italy … has ever fully come to terms with its wartime past'.[1] Ethiopian and Libyan cultural organisations around the world expressed outrage; protests were staged in front of Italian consulates and embassies from New York to London. In Addis Ababa, veterans of the Ethiopian resistance gathered in front of the *Yekatit 12* monument with placards demanding the dismantling of the mausoleum.[2] The Italian press denounced the fact that the monument was built using the Lazio region's public funds.

In Italy, under the 1952 Scelba law, the glorification of the Fascist period is a crime. And so, legal action was taken against the mayor of Affile and a few of his colleagues. In 2017, a court in Tivoli sentenced Mr Viri and two councillors to eight months in jail for the crime of 'championing Fascism'. Following this, Mr Viri gave an interview to *la Repubblica* where he indignantly declared: 'The problem in Italy today isn't fascism, it's politicized judges'.[3] However, this was just a temporary sentence, which meant nothing would happen to the mausoleum itself. Meanwhile, in 2018, Mr Viri was re-elected mayor, and in September 2020, the court of appeals absolved the three accused men. The magistrates did not deem the building of a monument to Rodolfo Graziani as the glorification of a fascist figure. It would seem that the monument is here to stay.

Apart from the scandal regarding the mausoleum, Graziani's name is only mentioned infrequently from time to time, and always with condemnation. His actions in Libya and Ethiopia have relegated him to the darkest corner of history.

James Cetrullo
Pescara, 2021

Endnotes

Chapter 1

1. Report by Gen. Richard O'Connor to Col. Fiske, US military *attaché* in Rome, written on 24 April 1941 while O'Connor was a prisoner in a POW camp in Sulmona, Italy. The translated Italian version was attached to Rodolfo Graziani's defence statement, p. 308 onwards, and also in his book *Africa Settentrionale 1940–1940*.
2. Archibald Wavell (1883–1950). During the First World War, he fought in Flanders, where he was injured and lost his left eye. He later served in Egypt under Gen. Allenby. In the interwar period, he served as a staff officer in various infantry divisions in the south of England. At the start of the Second World War, he was commander-in-chief of Middle East Command, stationed in Egypt. In 1943, after having defeated Graziani, he was sent to India, where he was later made viceroy. In 1947, he was replaced by Louis Mountbatten. He died in London. [TN].
3. Field Marshal Archibald Wavell's foreword to Chapman F. Spencer's book *The Jungle is Neutral* (1948).
4. Heinz Heggenreiner's 'Report on the North African Front for the Führer', January 1941. German collection of the Italian Ministry of War. A copy can also be found in the *Archivio Centrale dello Stato* (often referred to in this book as the Central State Archive. These are Italy's main national archives located in the EUR district of Rome). Shelf 62, file 47.
5. Franz Reicher's 'Account of my stay with Marshal Graziani's Army from 19 October to 22 December 1940', *Deutsches Nachrichten Buro*. Attached to Rodolfo Graziani's defence statement, *op. cit.*, p. 290 onwards.
6. Winston Churchill, *The Second World War: Their Finest Hour*, (1949), Rosetta books, p. 574 onwards.
7. Winston Churchill, *op. cit.*, p. 580. The song 'brought over from Australia' was actually the theme from the film *The Wizard of Oz*, based on a book written by Frank Lyman Baum. The film, starring Judy Garland, was directed by Victor Fleming in 1939.
8. This photo, like many others, is held in the Central State Archive among Graziani's personal documents; shelf 11, File 16.

9   *Shumbashi* (spelt *sciumbasci* in Italian) was the highest rank which could be reached by Eritrean and Ethiopian NCOs in the Italian army. The *shumbashi* held command duties subordinate to officers.
10 It is a custom in Italy to never use oil to season food with butter, and to always use oil to season salads. [*TN*].
11 'Dall' agenda di Graziani', *L'Indipendente*, Rome, 25 September 1945. Newspaper section of the Biblioteca Nazionale.
12 Pietro Badoglio (1871–1956). When Italy entered the First World War, he was already a lieutenant-colonel. He commanded various divisions during the conflict and was one of the generals responsible for the defeat of Caporetto. After the war, he was made marquis of the Sabotino and in 1925, he became marshal of Italy. From 1929 to 1933, he was governor of Libya, and in 1935, he replaced Marshal Emilio De Bono as commander-in-chief of the Army in Eritrea. Mussolini appointed him chief of the general staff in 1925, a position which he held until his resignation in 1940, in protest against the invasion of Greece. He conspired with the king for Mussolini's removal from power on 25 July 1943, after which the sovereign appointed Badoglio chief of state. He signed the armistice with the Allies and, on 8 September, escaped with the king to Brindisi to form the new Italian Government in the south. In 1944, after the liberation of Rome, he ceded his position to Ivanoe Bonomi. He died in his hometown of Grazzano Badoglio. [*TN*].
13 Rodolfo Graziani, *Ho difeso la Patria*, (1947), p. 182.
14 Titta Madia, Emilio Faldella, *Graziani, l'uomo e il soldato*, (1955) p. 78.
15 *Ho difeso la Patria*, p. 224.
16 Emilio Canevari, *Graziani mi ha detto*, (1947), p. 42.
17 The accusation of 'recklessness' against the general staff was published by Roberto Farinacci on his newspaper *Regime Fascista*, on 23 November 1940. The article, entitled '*Petit bourgeois* dead weight', was a scathing attack against Badoglio. Source: newspaper section of the Biblioteca Nazionale.
18 Rodolfo Graziani, *Africa settentrionale 1940–1941*, p. 239.
19 This note and the ones that follow are in: *Destruction of an Army* (1943). His Majesty's Stationery Office. In this book and in Graziani's autobiography, *Destruction of an Army* is referred to as being written by Wavell, however, this is not the case. [*TN*].
20 This quote was written in Graziani's first report (12 December 1940) sent to the general staff. It is also in the aforementioned *Africa Settentrionale 1940–41*.
21 An anti-fascist and republican political party which operated during and after the collapse of the Fascist regime. [*TN*].
22 *Responsibilitá di Graziani nel 1940 in Cirenaica*, edited by the Party of Action, p. 21, 23, 26, (1944).
23 The *Carabinieri* are Italy's national *gendarmerie* who primarily carry out domestic policing duties. Being part of the armed forces, they are also deployed to war zones and operate as a military police force. [*TN*].
24 *Ente Italiano per le Audizioni Radiofoniche* (EIAR) was Fascist Italy's public service broadcaster. Minculpop was the humorous abbreviation used by the Italians for the omnipresent *Ministero della Cultura Popolare* (Ministry of Popular Culture). [*TN*].
25 Many books have published this abridged version of Graziani's telegram, which makes it seem as if he was ready to retreat to Tripoli as soon as the British entered Libya. In the complete telegram, Graziani explained how he would only go to Tripoli if Bardia and Tobruk fell first. [*TN*].
26 *Responsibilitá di Graziani nel 1940 in Cirenaica*, p. 29.

Endnotes

27 Rommel had actually already arrived in Tripoli by plane on 11 February 1941, the day after Graziani departed. But this had been a secret trip.
28 Cf. *Il deserto della Libia*, by Mario Tobino, (1964).

Chapter 2

1 Ciociaria is the folkloristic name given to the rural territories south-east of Rome which border on the Abruzzo region. Today, Ciociaria is mostly applied to the area held within the province of Frosinone. The name derives from the *ciocie*, a type of footwear worn by shepherds from the mountains. [*TN*].
2 Memo number 6, Central State Archive. With slight variations, the same version is repeated by Graziani in *Ho difeso la Patria*, p. 241 and 295.
3 This and other small episodes from his family life have been collected from Graziani's personal papers in the Central State Archive, shelf 14, file 20; shelf 72, file 59.
4 The photo in question was also published (photo number 43) in *Libia Redenta*, (1948). Col. Stevens was an Anglo-Italian British Army officer, known for his broadcasts to Italy during the Second World War where he incited the people against Mussolini's dictatorship.
5 Scopa and Briscola are Italian trick-taking, Ace-Ten card games. [*TN*].
6 A Federal (*Federale* in Italian) was a provincial Fascist Party secretary. [*TN*].
7 Bartolomeo Colleoni was a famous medieval Italian warlord. [*TN*].
8 *Raccomandazione* is the Italian custom of helping friends or relatives to obtain jobs or other positions, regardless of their qualifications or credentials. [*TN*].
9 Titta Madia, *Pezzi di mondo e Umanita' di Graziani*, (1937).
10 Ciro Poggiali, *Diario AOI, giugno 1936-ottobre 1937. Gli appunti dell'inviato del Corriere della Sera*, (1971), p. 240.
11 In Italy, it is commonplace to use '*lei*' when addressing someone in a formal manner. However, during the Fascist period, for nationalistic reasons, it was decided that the second person plural '*voi*' should be used instead. [*TN*].
12 Cf. *L'esercito italiano nella grande guerra* (the Italian army in the Great War), edited by the historical archive of the general staff. Biblioteca Militare Centrale.
13 Graziani asked the very same question in *Ho difeso la Patria*, p. 25.

Chapter 3

1 The *Hijrah*, also spelt *Hegira*. This word is commonly used to refer to the journey of the Islamic prophet Muhammad and his followers from Mecca to Medina in the year 622. [*TN*].
2 A *Fantasia* is a traditional exhibition of horsemanship in the Maghreb performed during celebrations. [*TN*].
3 *Dor*, the plural of *duar*, means dwelling, village, or encampment. When Omar al-Mukhtar was alive, each *dor* was governed by its own *Kamaican* (the equivalent of a mayor) and a *cadi* (judge). For more information on the life and organisation of the Cyrenaican peoples during this period, go to shelf 9, file 12 in the Central State Archive.
4 This information appears to be incorrect. According to various news articles, Muhammed Mukhtar, Omar's only son who died in 2018, was the son of Nizla al-Gilani. She was not repudiated; Omar simply sent his wife and their son to Egypt so that they would avoid being captured by the Italians. [*TN*].

5 These documents are held as copies in the National Archives in Washington, DC. [*TN*].
6 The document in question (like many others in this chapter) is preserved in the Central State Archive, shelf 8, file 12.
7 In 1939, Graziani gifted the banners of the Libyan campaign and the items which Omar al-Mukhtar had on him when he was captured to the Colonial Museum in Rome. Here are some of those items in a list written by Graziani (currently held in the Central State Archive): three wallets, two pairs of glasses, a fine edition of the Koran, a Mauser rifle and some photos of his hanging. These items (like the relics taken to Italy after the Ethiopian campaign) went missing. In 1945, the Colonial Museum was closed, and its belongings were given back to the Libyan and Ethiopian governments. However, most of the items were lost or went into private collections.
8 *Revolt in the Desert* was written by Lawrence of Arabia in 1926 and published in 1927. Meanwhile, *Seven Pillars of Wisdom*, the book which brought Lawrence world fame, came out posthumously in 1935.
9 Mario Missiroli. An Italian stage and film director of the 1960s and '70s. [*TN*].
10 Then Prime Minister Silvio Berlusconi finally allowed the film to air on June 11, 2009, in occasion of Muammar Gaddafi's state visit to Italy. [*TN*].
11 The article by Amintore Fanfani, 'Cinquant'anni di preparazione per l'Impero' ('Fifty years of preparation for the Empire'), was also republished in the magazine *Colonialismo europeo e Impero fascista*, p. 27-33, edited by the Fascist Colonial Institute, (1936). Source: newspaper section of the Biblioteca Nazionale in Rome. Amintore Fafani later joined the Christian Democrats and would become prime minister of Italy. [*TN*].
12 The book of Giuseppe Bedendo's poems is called *Le gesta e la politica del generale Graziani*. Subtitle 'Canti in dialetto romanesco' ('Songs in Roman dialect'). It was published by Edizioni generali CESA, in 1934.
13 Giuseppe Gioacchino Belli and Trilussa were two famous Romanesco poets. [*TN*].
14 The poison gas bombing of the oasis of Tazerbo on 31 July 1930 is not mentioned in this book. At the time of writing, the documents regarding this episode were barred to historians. [*TN*].

Chapter 4

1 There was a legal battle between Graziani's descendants and the State Archive. The Grazianis complained that the archive holds the deceased marshal's intimate family letters, which they want back. The diaries of 1942 and 1943 were given to the Central State Archive by the Benedictine monk Don Marino Marsili, of the Abbey of Santa Maria della Scala di Noci in Bari. Don Marsili, who was the RSI's military chaplain, was given the diaries and the documents in accordance with Rodolfo Graziani's will.
2 The minutes of the Investigative Commission set up by Mussolini to evaluate Graziani's conduct in North Africa are currently held in the Biblioteca militare centrale and, as a copy in the Central State Archive.
3 This has been quoted from the book *Caesar in Abyssinia* by George L. Steer, (1936).
4 A hint to the use of poison gas can also be found in *La campagna al fronte sud* (an official report with three volumes attached to it), which was published a few months before *Il fronte sud* by Rodolfo Graziani.

Endnotes

5 Indro Montanelli (1909–2001). In 1935, he fought in the Italo-Abyssinian War where he commanded an Eritrean battalion. After the establishment of the RSI, he was imprisoned for anti-Fascist activity but later managed to escape to Switzerland. After the war, he became a popular journalist, interviewing many of Italy's famous historical and political figures, also writing books on Italian history. He was also the founder of *Il Giornale*. [TN].
6 The interview with Pietro Badoglio can also be found in *Pantheon minore*, the first collection of Indro Montanelli's interviews, (1954).
7 During the petrol crisis of 1973, the Italian Government decided to prohibit all circulations of vehicles on Sundays. [TN].
8 Arturo Labriola was a Socialist politician who fled to France after the March on Rome in 1922. Vittorio Emanuele Orlando was prime minster from 1917–1919 and represented Italy at the Paris Peace Conference. He retired from politics in the 1920s, an opponent of Fascism. [TN].
9 *Ras* Desta Damtew (1892–1937). *Ras* Desta was part of the noble Addisge clan. In 1924, he married Tenagnework Haile Selassie, daughter of future Emperor Haile Selassie I. During the Italo-Ethiopian war, his armies were defeated by Graziani at the battle of Ganale Doria. After Ethiopia's occupation, he went into the countryside to organise the resistance against the Italians. He was executed after being caught in the village of Goggetti. [TN].
10 *Ras* is an Ethiopian aristocratic title roughly equivalent to duke or lord. Meanwhile, *Dejazmach*, *Grazmach*, *Balambaras* are Ethiopian military ranks: *Dejazmach*, commander of the gate; *Grazmach*, commander of the left-wing; *Balambaras*, commander of the fort. [TN].
11 The Ministry of Popular Culture (divided into six sections: Italian press, foreign press, propaganda, cinema, theatre, and administrative services) did not exist back then. In 1935, this sort of work was carried out by the Ministry of the Press, born from the undersecretariat of the press with a 1933 royal decree.
12 Courbash: A whip made of hippopotamus hide. [TN].

Chapter 5

1 These same considerations were made in *Ho difeso la Patria*.
2 Among the Abyssinian notables who wished to submit was Berhane Marcos, the Ethiopian *charges d'affaires* to Turkey. His request was accompanied by a friendly letter, dated 23 August 1936, signed by *Monseigneur* Angelo Giuseppe Roncalli, who would become Pope John XXIII. At that time, he was the Apostolic Delegate to Istanbul. Source: Central State Archive.
3 *Ras* Hailu Tekle-Haymanot (1868–1950). Son of Tekle-Haymanot Tessemma, King of Gojjam. Before the Italian invasion, *Ras* Hailu refused to pay taxes to Addis Ababa and was later imprisoned because of his plotting against Emperor Haile Selassie. During the Italian occupation, he was a loyal collaborator of Rodolfo Graziani. When the British invaded Gojjam, he switched sides and swore loyalty to the emperor. When he died he was given a state funeral. [TN].
4 Amedeo of Aosta (1898–1942). Son of Duke Emanuele Filiberto of Aosta. After the First World War, he took part in many expeditions exploring Sub-Saharan Africa. In 1938, he replaced Rodolfo Graziani as viceroy of Ethiopia. He was highly critical of Graziani's harsh methods and ruled the Empire in a humane manner. At the start of the Second World War, he tried to counter the British invasion of the colony but was eventually defeated at the battle of Amba Alagi in 1941. He died of malaria while a POW in Kenya. [TN].

5 The thaler was a silver bullion coin used as the currency of Ethiopia before the Italian invasion. [*TN*].
6 The telegrams and the transcriptions of the radio-communication can all be seen in the Central State Archive: shelf 41, file 33.
7 In 2020, Antonio Di Dato, son of Capt. Di Dato, gave an interview denying that his father had ever killed these two individuals. His father was one of the men who carried Graziani to Mr Birindelli's car which then took him to hospital. Therefore, Capt. Di Dato could not have been in the Ghebbi killing those two Ethiopians. [*TN*].
8 *Tukul*. A traditional round thatched Ethiopian village hut. This term is used mostly by foreigners. [*TN*].
9 The article of French journalist Boccara, 'Graziani en justice', is partially reproduced in Graziani's autobiography (p. 148) and the original is to be found among Graziani's personal papers in the Central State Archive. At the bottom of the newspaper cutting, the marshal wrote: 'It seems I already had the atomic bomb but didn't know it'.
10 After Gen. Maletti's death at the battle of Nibeiwa, roads were named after him in a few towns in his native province of Mantua. Maletti's daughter, Ginevra, even became mayor of Cocquio-Trevisago, in Varese. However, because of Maletti's role in the massacre of Debre Libanos, these roads have recently been renamed. In 2017, his name was removed from a road in his birthplace of Castiglione delle Stiviere. In 2018, another was removed in Mantua, and in 2020, in Cocquio-Trevisago. [*TN*].
11 The perpetrators of the assassination attempt were two Eritreans: Abraham Debotch and Mogus Asghedom. Ian Campbell (in his book, *The Addis Ababa Massacre*) claims they were executed by the Italians in northern Ethiopia. [*TN*].
12 The correspondence of Graziani's presumed evisceration is held in the Central State Archive: shelf 48, file 422; shelf 49, file 42.
13 *Ras* Hailu had been told that the Kassa brothers would have their lives spared. He was incredibly distraught when he found out they had been executed. [*TN*].
14 Victor Emanuel III made Rodolfo Graziani marquis of Neghelli on 6 December 1937. Subsequently, with the sovereign's *motu proprio*, the title was made transmissible to the first born of Mrs Ethel Vanda Graziani, the marshal's daughter. Coat of arms. Break off: the first half is red, with a flying eagle holding a Roman gladius in its claws; the second half is gold with a plough between two palm trees on a green field. On the truncation: a shield with a crowned Savoyard eagle. Motto: *Ense et aratro*.
15 Seventy-nine suitcases may seem a lot, but it was actually further proof of Graziani's honesty. Pietro Badoglio left Ethiopia with 300 packing cases. And as for Attilio Teruzzi's 'baggage', it was more like war booty: two train coaches were needed to carry all of it and Lessona rightly protested.
16 The dedication to Pietro Badoglio which appears on the frontispiece of Graziani's book *Il fronte sud* is particularly deferent and friendly. It says: 'To His Excellency Marshal of Italy Badoglio, whom I served with honour for the reconquest of Libya and the conquest of the Empire'.

Chapter 6

1 Rudolf Rahn (1900–1975). He was a career diplomat, and in the first years of the war he was sent to Vichy France, Syria, and then Tunisia. He was appointed German ambassador to Rome in August 1943, and after 8 September, plenipotentiary of the Third Reich in Italy. After the war, he was tried at Nuremberg but then acquitted. He died in Düsseldorf. [*TN*].

2 The Italian Social Republic, also referred to in Italy as the Republic of Salò, was Germany's puppet state created after Italy's capitulation on 8 September. Salò was not the capital of the RSI. Many of the dispatches published in the newspapers by the Ministry of Popular Culture based in Salò, started with the phrase 'Salò announces...' and so this became the popular name for the RSI. [TN].
3 Cf. Friedrich E. Mollhausen, *La carta perdente*, (1947).
4 The Kingdom of the South was the state formed by the king and Badoglio in the southern region of Apulia in September 1943. This was the government which joined forces with the Allies and declared war on Germany. [TN].
5 Umberto I was assassinated by the anarchist Gaetano Bresci in the town of Monza while riding in his carriage. [TN].
6 *Corpo Italiano di Liberazione*. A military unit of the Kingdom of the South which fought alongside the Allies during the Italian campaign. [TN].
7 Umberto II (1904–1983). He was the son of King Victor Emanuel III. As heir to the Italian throne, he was given the title of prince of Piedmont. In 1930, he married Marie José of Belgium. After his father's abdication, he briefly became king in 1946, but soon afterwards the Italian monarchy was abolished in a referendum which took place later that year. He died in exile in Portugal. [TN].
8 Mussolini had called for a meeting of the Grand Council of Fascism to take place on 24 July 1943. The main topic of discussion was the Allied invasion of Sicily, and the meeting went on past midnight. Near the end, the fascist official Dino Grandi issued a vote of no confidence in Mussolini which was approved by the majority of those present. Mussolini then left the meeting. On the afternoon of the 25th, as he visited the king, Mussolini was arrested. The king then appointed Badoglio as chief of state. [TN].
9 The diary he kept in 1943 and parts of his 1942 diary remained in Graziani's possession. He often used these for his autobiography, but only to cite the passages which were useful for his defence.
10 Cf. Rudolf Rahn, *Ambasciatore di Hitler a Vichy e a Salò*, (1950).
11 Karl Wolff (1900–1984). At the beginning of the war, he was stationed in Poland where he organised the mass deportation of Slavs and Jews. In September 1943, he was made Supreme SS and Police Leader in Italy, and by 1945, he was the effective military leader of all German forces in the country. He was tried in 1948 and imprisoned for four years. He was convicted again in 1964 for having organised the deportation of Italy's Jews and was sentenced to fifteen years but was released in 1971. He died in Rosenheim. [TN].
12 These same considerations were made, on 27 September 1943, in Enrico Caviglia's April 1925 to March 1945 diary which was published posthumously in 1953.
13 Ettore Muti was Italy's most decorated soldier of the Second World War. In August 1943, after Badoglio seized power, he was mysteriously killed by the *Carabinieri* who had come to arrest him. [TN].
14 Nicola Bombacci (1879–1945). He was one of the founders of the Italian Communist Party and had been acquainted with Lenin during the Russian Civil War. He was not persecuted during the Fascist regime because of his childhood friendship with Mussolini. He joined the RSI and was one of Mussolini's advisors. He was executed by the partisans, alongside other high-ranking government officials of the RSI, in Dongo, on Lake Como. [TN].
15 Alessandro Pavolini (1903–1945). He was made Minister of Popular Culture in 1939, in charge of Fascist Italy's propaganda during the war. After Badoglio's coup, he fled to Germany and later joined the RSI, becoming secretary of the new Fascist Republican Party. He was executed by the partisans in Dongo. [TN].

16 Before the armistice, the *Decima Flottiglia MAS* was a commando frogman unit of the Italian Navy, commanded by Prince Junio Valerio Borghese. After the armistice, Borghese sided with the Germans and turned the *Decima* into a marine infantry unit. [TN].

17 In the book *Qui non riposano*, which came out soon after the war, Indro Montanelli painted an unfavourable portrait of Graziani, calling him a 'picturesque braggart'. Only afterwards did Montanelli learn that his life had been saved thanks to the help of Lady Ines and the marshal. He kindly made sure to let them know of his gratitude by writing the following: 'I declare that during my imprisonment and soon after my death sentence, my mother asked Lady Graziani to intercede on my behalf to the Marshal. She was kindly and humanely received. I then learnt that it was largely due to the Marshal that my death sentence was never carried out. Seven months later I escaped to Switzerland, all of this was unbeknownst to me when I wrote about him in my book *Qui non riposano*. I must retract the opinions which I expressed then. Milan, 16 April 1946'. Indro Montanelli also wrote the preface for a reprint of Graziani's autobiography, published in 1986 with the title *Una vita per l'Italia: Ho difeso la Patria* published by Mursia. As for Gen. Emilio Faldella (whom Graziani accused of ingratitude in his autobiography), his thank you came late but that does not make it less relevant. Faldella was arrested during the RSI and freed on Graziani's orders and later appointed commander of the garrison of Milan by Raffaele Cadorna on 26 April 1945. He later became a noteworthy military historian. In 1955, after the marshal's death, together with Titta Madia, he published an essay on Graziani as a soldier. For obvious reasons, the essay ends with the unfortunate North African campaign. Faldella's judgement as a military historian on that campaign was: 'For the first time in his life as a commander, Marshal Graziani had to act against his beliefs, with a military force which was not appropriate for the special type of war that he had had to fight'. (Titta Madia, Emilio Faldella, *Graziani. l'uomo e il soldato*. (1950), p. 408).

18 Graziani's *cahiers de doléance* and the following pages have been taken from the minutes of Italo-German meetings and secret reports from the *Ufficio Situazione*. Many of these documents can be found in the *Istituto Nazionale per la storia del Movimento di liberazione*, in Milan.

19 The Ardeatine massacre was a mass killing of Italian civilians perpetrated by the Germans on 24 March 1944, in retaliation for a partisan attack against German troops which had occurred the day before. [TN].

20 The *bersaglieri* are Italy's light infantry soldiers. The *alpini* are the mountain infantry. [TN].

21 On 1 October 1943, when Graziani was going to speak at the Adriano theatre, Fabrizio Onofri, a member of the Rome's resistance, placed a bomb in a fire extinguisher inside the building. The bomb, prepared by a young chemist called Giorgio Labò—later killed by the Nazis—was hidden in the prompt box. The bomb did not go off and the marshal learnt about the failed attempt in 1945, from a pamphlet on the Partisan war.

22 Cardinal Alfredo Ildefonso Schuster (1880–1954). He was made archbishop of Milan in 1929. He supported Italy's invasion of Ethiopia, however, he would later distance himself from Fascism after the introduction of racial laws in 1938. He helped bring about negotiations between the Fascists and the Partisans during the RSI. He continued to be archbishop of Milan until his death. He was beatified in 1996. [TN].

23 The Volunteers of Liberty Corps. An organisation which coordinated the operations of Italy's resistance movement. [TN].

24 National Liberation Committee for Northern Italy. An organisation which included all the anti-fascist movements fighting in German occupied Italy. [*TN*].
25 Emilio Q. Daddario (1918–2010), OSS agent and politician. He enlisted in the US Army in 1943. As an OSS agent, he was attached to the US Consulate in Lugano from where he entered Italy to rescue Graziani. Because of his actions he was awarded the Legion of Merit and the Bronze Star medal. After the war, he joined the Democratic party and served as a member of the US House of Representatives. He died in Washington, DC. [*TN*].
26 By his own admission, Graziani did not keep a diary in 1944 and 1945. He did, however, (according to his autobiography, p. 533) write down important events in a small notebook. However, this notebook was never found, perhaps it was mislaid, perhaps it was destroyed. Embaie Tekle-Haymanot, whom the marshal wanted to give it to, would say that he never saw it. In the hectic days of April 1945, even Graziani's personal bag which had been entrusted to his wife disappeared, as Lady Ines had left it in a car. 'The documents in there were dynamite,' journalists would later write, looking for a hit piece. The marshal would deny it: 'The only things in that bag were maps, orders, and family photographs'. In 1988, Graziani's 1945 diary, which spans the time period from 23 April to 22 December, was found by a Mr Rosario Angotti. [*TN*].
27 Sandro Pertini (1896–1990). He was imprisoned by the Fascist regime on the island of Santo Stefano, only being released after Badoglio seized power. He was a prominent member of the Italian resistance during the Partisan war. In the post-war years, he was a leading Socialist politician, and in 1978, Pertini was elected president of the Italian Republic, a position he held until 1985. He died in Rome. [*TN*].
28 Pertini himself admitted to this in an article called 'The ignominy and flight of the Fascists', published by *Rinascita* in April 1955. 'I considered the interference of Daddario, the American officer, to be inconsequential,' Pertini wrote, 'Therefore, in compliance with the order given out by the CLNAI, I ordered the former Marshal to be shot'. Graziani dodged the firing squad only because Corrado Bonfantini, the man charged with executing the order, wavered due to 'weakness'. It was only a question of minutes. Years later, Bonfantini would say he regretted such 'weakness'.
29 The act of surrender of the Italo-German army was actually signed by Lt-Gen. Max Joseph Pemzell, chief of staff of Army Group *Liguria*. As we have seen, the marshal perfected the act of surrender, and Pemzell wrote down the following footnote: 'As chief of staff of the Army Group *Liguria*, I confirm, without any reservations, what my Commander Marshal Rodolfo Graziani, has just stated. German soldiers, obey his orders'.

Chapter 7

1 This article was written by Sandro De Feo for *Europeo*, number 43, October 1948. Source: newspaper section of the *Biblioteca Nazionale* in Rome.
2 Enrico Berlinguer, leader of the Italian Communist Party from 1972 to 1984. Alongside Palmiro Togliatti, he was the best-known leader of Italian Communism in the post-war period. [*TN*].
3 The book in question is called *Graziani* and it was published by *Rivista Romana*. It is a book 'of history and remembrance' which was written by Alessandro Sardi, in collaboration with: Fausto Belfiori, Magno Bocca, Emilio Canevari, Paolo Gasparri, Pierre Pascal, Piero Pisenti, Mario Ramperti, Vanni Teodorani, and Luigi Villari.

4 *Cf.* 'Il processo Graziani' by Antonio Repaci can be found in the journal *Movimento di Liberazione in Italia*, (1952), numbers 17-18. pp. 27 and 28.
5 National Association of Italian Partisans. This association was founded in 1945 by the veterans of the Italian resistance. Today, ANPI mainly organises events and lectures on the Partisan war and acts as a charitable organisation for veterans of the resistance. [*TN*].
6 In 1862, Garibaldi had formed an army in Sicily with the intent to march up the peninsula and occupy Rome, which back then was part of the Papal State. Fearing repercussions from France, the Italian government sent in the army to stop Garibaldi and defeated him at the battle of Aspromonte in Calabria. [*TN*].
7 In 1920, Gabriele d'Annunzio, in defiance of the Italian government, occupied the city of Fiume in Istria with a band of legionaries. This was done in protest to the Paris Peace Conference of 1919 which had not assigned this city to Italy. [*TN*].
8 The Italian Social Movement. It was founded in 1946 by neo-fascists and would remain Italy's main far-right party for the entirety of the Cold War. Its most recognisable leader was Giorgio Almirante who led the party from 1969 to 1987. [*TN*].
9 Giulio Andreotti (1919–2013). Italian political figure. During the war, he wrote for dissident newspapers associated with the Christian Democrats. In 1946, he became undersecretary to Alcide de Gasperi, the first prime minister of the Italian Republic. He held many political positions throughout his career and was prime minister on various occasions in the 1970s and '80s. In 1993, he was put on trial for his supposed association with the mafia, but later absolved. [*TN*].
10 In 1947, the UN established the free territory of Trieste. The city was garrisoned by US and British troops in order to prevent any territorial clashes between Italy and Yugoslavia. Back then, it was uncertain as to which country the city would be handed over to. Finally, in 1954, the city was given back Italy. [*TN*].

Chapter 8

1 Tazio Nuvolari and Achille Varzi were two Italian race car drivers. Fausto Coppi and Gino Bartali were two famous road cyclists.

Postscript

1 'Village's Tribute Reignites a Debate About Italy's Fascist Past', *The New York Times*. Article by Gaia Pianigiani. 28 August 2012.
2 *Yekatit 12* is a date in the Ethiopian calendar which refers to the massacre which followed the failed assassination attempt on Rodolfo Graziani.
3 'Affile, parla il sindaco del sacrario a Graziani: "Pentirmi io? Alle elezioni prenderò l'80%"' *La Repubblica*. Article by Mauro Favale. 8 November 2017.

Bibliography

Algardi, Z., *Processo ai fascisti* (Florence: Vallechi editore, 1973)
Anfuso, F., *Roma Berlino Salò* (Milan: Garzanti editore, 1950)
Armellini, Q., 'I piani di campagna del Negus,' in *Rassegna Italica* (Rome: 1938. Source: newspaper section of the Biblioteca nazionale in Rome)
Assan, G., *La Libia e il mondo arabo*. (Rome: Editori Riuniti, 1959)
Autodifesa di Graziani davanti alla Corte d'Assise straordinaria, (Rome: Edizioni Mediterranee, 1948)
Badoglio, P., 'Rapporto al Duce sull'Etiopia,' in *Italia Imperiale* (Milan: 1937. Source: newspaper section of the Biblioteca nazionale in Rome)
Barnes, J. S., *Half a life left* (London: Eyre Press, 1937)
Ben Amir, S., 'A series of articles on the Gran Senussi in Cyrenaica' in *Majallat Umar al Mukhtar* (Benghazi: 1934)
Benedetti, A., *La guerra equatoriale con l'armata del Maresciallo Graziani* (Milan: Zucchi editore, 1937)
Benelli, S., *Io in Africa* (Milan: Mondadori editore, 1937)
Bertoldi, S., *La repubblica di Salò* (Milan: Compagnia generale editoriale, 1980)
Bing, A., 'I resistenti alla guerra,' newspaper cutting (translated from English and held in the Biblioteca nazionale in Rome, 1948)
Bocca, G., *Storia della guerra partigiana* (Bari: Laterza editori, 1966)
Bollati, A., *La campagna italo-etiopica nella stampa estera* (Rome: edizioni del poligrafico dello Stato, 1938)
Bosco, G. N., *Il colonialismo nella storia d'Italia* (Florence: edizioni La Nuova Italia, 1975)
Campiglio, G., *Storia dell'Africa bianca* (Milan: Pan editore, 1980)
Canevari, E., *Graziani mi ha detto* (Rome: Magi & Spinetti editori, 1948); *Comando delle forze armate in Somalia* (edited by the ufficio supremo militare) (Addis Ababa: Tipografia Same, 1937)
Ceva, L., *Africa settentrionale 1940–1943* (Rome: Bonacci editore, 1982)
Curotti, T., *Libia, dalle immigrazioni preistoriche fino ad una ambigua nazionalita' in regime di dittatura* (Borgo San Dalmazzo: edited by the Istituto geografico Bertelli, 1973)
De Agostini, E., *Le popolazioni della Cirenaica* (Benghazi: edited by the Istituto Italiano di cultura di Bengasi, 1923)

Deakin, F. W. D., *The Brutal Friendship: Mussolini, Hitler and the fall of Italian fascism* (New York: London & Harper and Rowe, 1962)
Depois, J., *La colonisation italienne en Lybie, problèmes et méthodes* (Paris: Gallimard ed., 1935). Del Boca, A., *La guerra d'Abissinia 1935-1941* (Milan: Feltrinelli editore, 1965); *Gli Italiani in Africa Orientale* (Bari: Laterza editori, 1979)
Di Lauro, R., *Bolletini etiopici* (Milan: Mondadori editore, 1939)
Dollman, E., *With Hitler and Mussolini: Memoirs of a Nazi Interpreter* [original title: *Un libero schiavo*, Bologna: Cappelli editore, 1962] (London: Skyhorse Pub Co. Inc., 2017); *Roma Nazista* (Milan: Longanesi editore, 1949)
Duignan, P., & Gann, L. H., *Colonialism in Africa* (Cambridge University Press, 1969)
Eric, V., *The Abyssinia I knew* (London: McMillan & Co. editor, 1936)
Evans-Pritchard, E. E., *The Sanusi of Cyrenaica* (London: Oxford University Press, 1949). Finocchiaro, M., *La localizzazione e la trasformazione fondiaria in Libia attraverso le sue fasi* (Rome: Tipografia Marchetti, 1968)
Focarile, C., *La guerra con i motori* (Rome: edizioni Ardita, 1937)
Frusci, L., *In Somalia sul fronte meridionale*, (Bologna: Cappelli ed., 1936)
Gallo, M., *Vita di Mussolini* (Bari: Laterza editori, 1967)
Garibaldi, L., *Mussolini e il professore* (Milan: Mursia editore, 1983)
Giovenco, S., *La divisione Peloritania e la guerra di Somalia* (Palermo: edizioni Priula, 1937)
Graziani, R., *Verso il Fezzan* (con prefazione di Pietro Badoglio) (Tripoli: edizioni Cacopardo, 1929); 'La situazione Cirenaica,' conference held at the Istituto fascista di cultura, Benghazi, 23 November 1931. Source: Biblioteca nazionale di Roma; 'L'avvenire economico della Cirenaica,' in *Rassegna italiana* (February-March 1933). Source: Biblioteca nazionale di Roma; *Africa settentrionale 1940-1941* (Rome: Danesi ed., 1948); *Cirenaica nuova*, (Rome: edited by the Istituto coloniale fascista, 1932); *Cirenaica pacificata* (Milan: Mondadori editore, 1932); *Ho difeso la Patria* (Milan: Garzanti editore, 1947); *Il fronte sud* (con prefazione di Benito Mussolini) (Milan: Mondadori editore, 1938); *La riconquista del Fezzan* (Milan: Mondadori editore, 1934); *Libia redenta, storia di trent'anni di passione italiana in Africa* (Naples: edizione Torella, 1948); *Pace romana in Libia (con 55 illustrazioni fuori testo e una carta geografica)* (Milan: Mondadori editore, 1937)
Il dramma di Graziani nelle arringhe della difesa (edited by: G.P Augenti, Mastino Del Rio, and Francesco Carnelutti). (Bologna: Zuffi editore, 1950)
Jansen, P. G., *Abissina d'oggi* (Milan: Marangoni editore, 1933)
Kesselring, A., *The Memoirs of Field-Marshal Kesselring* (Skyhorse; Reprint edition, 2016)
'La giornata coloniale dell'Anno XVI era fascista: parole pronunciate da S.E. il Maresciallo d'Italia Rodolfo Graziani il 22 maggio 1938 al teatro Adriano di Roma,' published by the dell'Istituto fascista per l'Africa Orientale italiana (Rome: 1938, source: Biblioteca nazionale di Roma)
La Libia in vent'anni di occupazione italiana (Authors: Pietro Badoglio, Rodolfo Graziani, Alessandro Lessona e Biagio Pace), (Rome: edited by the Istituto coloniale fascista, 1932)
Lanfranchi, F., *La resa degli ottocentomila* (Mila: Rizzoli editore, 1948)
Lattanzio, F., *Nostre terre d'oltremare: brevi cenni storici, geografici, politici ed economici* (Bologna: Cappelli editore, 1936)
'Le forze armate italiane in AOI,' edited by the Ministero della Guerra, Rome, 1936
Madia, T. & Faldella, M., *Graziani, l'uomo e il soldato* (Rome: edizione Aniene, 1955)
Madia, T., *Pezzi di mondo* (Napoli: editrice La Toga, 1937)
Majoni, G., *Guerra italo-abissina: la neutralita' americana* (Firenze: SEC editori, 1936)
Maltese, P., *La terra promessa: la guerra italo-turca e la conquista della Libia* (Milan: Sugar editore, 1968)

Mandalari, O. C., *Il Maresciallo Graziani, condottiero africano della Patria fascista* (Rome: edited by the R.G. historical archive, 1937)
Manuta, U., *La caduta degli angeli: storia intima della RSI* (Rome: AZ editrice italiana, 1947)
Mazzola, G., *L'organizzazione ginevrina e il conflitto italo-etiopico* (Palermo: edizioni Ires, 1937)
Milanese, C., 'Il Maresciallo d'Italia Rodolfo Graziani,' in *L'impero coloniale fascista*, pp. 51-54 (Rome: 1957, source: newspaper section of the Biblioteca nazionale in Rome)
Moellhausen, F.E., *La carta perdente* (Rome: edizioni Sestante, 1947)
Molinari, M., *Agli ordini di Graziani in Somalia* (Milan: edizioni scientifiche, 1940)
Montanelli, I., & Cervi, M., *L'Italia littoria (1925-1936)* (Milan: Rizzoli editore, 1979)
Montanelli, I., *Guerra e pace in AOI* (Firenze: Vallechi editore, 1937); *Qui non riposano* (Milan: edizioni Ponti, 1945)
Orano, P., *Rodolfo Graziani, generale scipionico* (Rome: ed. Pinciana, 1936)
Pansa, G., *L'esercito di Salò* (Milan: Mondadori editore, 1970)
Partito d'Azione, *Responsabilita' di Graziani nel 1940 in Cirenaica* (Rome: edizioni Sagittarius, 1944)
Pertini, S., 'Ignomia e fuga dei fascisti,' in *Rinascita* (1955: source: newspaper section of the Biblioteca nazionale in Rome)
Piccioli, A., 'La nuova Italia d'Oltremare,' in *Rivista Oltremare* (May 1933, source: newspaper section of the Biblioteca nazionale in Rome)
Pieroni, P., *L'Italia in Africa* (Firenze: Vallechi editore, 1974)
Pini, G., *Itinerario tragico* (Milan: ed. Omnia, 1950)
Poggiali, C., *Diario AOI, giugno 1936-ottobre 1937: gli appunti segreti dell'inviato del Corriere della Sera* (Milan: Longanesi editore, 1971)
Rahn, R., *Ambasciatore di Hitler a Vichy e a Salò* (Milan; Garzanti editore, 1950)
Sandri, S., *Il generale Rodolfo Graziani* (Milan: Garzanti editore, 1950); *Sei mesi di guerra sul fronte somalo: da Mogadisco a Neghelli* (Milan: ed. Torriali, 1936)
Savarese, E., *Le terre della Cirenaica* (Benghazi: edited by the Istituto italiano di cultura di Bengasi, 1928)
Schuster, I., *Gli ultimi tempi di un regime* (Milan: edizioni La via, printed at the Istituto di Arti Grafiche of Bergamo 1946)
Segrè, G. C., *Fourth shore: the Italian colonization of Libya* (Chicago: edited by the University of Chicago, 1974)
Serra, F., 'Italia e Senusiyya,' (the essay, written in 1933, has been consult from the newspaper section of the Biblioteca nazionale in Rome)
Silvestri, C., *Mussolini, Graziani e l'antifascismo* (Milan: Longanesi editore, 1945); *Contro la vendetta* (Milan: Longanesi editore 1948)
Steer, G. L., *Caesar in Abyssinia* (London: Stongton Ltd, 1936)
Teruzzi, A., *Cirenaica verde* (Milan: edizioni SPE, 1931)
Vignolo, M., *Gheddafi* (Milan: Rizzoli editore, 1982)
Volta, S., *Graziani a Neghelli* (Florence: Vallechi editore, 1936)
Vv.Aa., 'Gli esploratori e i colonizzatori sulla via dell'Impero,' in *Celebrazioni Liguri* (Urbino: 1939)
Vv.Aa., *Al comando delle forze armate della Somalia* (foreword by Rodolfo Graziani), (Addis Ababa: Tipografia Same, 1937)
Vv.Aa., *Errate previsioni della stampa internazionale sulla campagna etiopica* (Rome: edizioni Laboremus, 1938)
Vv.Aa., *Governo generale AOI, il primo anno dell'Impero* (Addis Ababa: edito dallo Stato Maggiore generale, Tipografia Same, 1937)

Vv.Aa., *Graziani e la sua terra, edito a cura del gruppo fascista E. Torriali* (Milan, 1937)
Vv.Aa., *Graziani*, (Rome: edited by Rivista Romana, 1956)
Vv.Aa., *Handbook of Cyrenaica*, (Cairo: edizioni de Il Cairo, 1947)
Vv.Aa., *Legionari universitari sul fronte somalo* (Milano: Sperling ed., 1937)
Vv.Aa., *Mussolini e gli uomini del suo tempo tempo* (Rome: Ciarrapico editore, 1977)
Vv.Aa., *Per le onoranze al Maresciallo Graziani nel suo paese di Affile* (Rome: edizioni SEC, 1938)
Wolfder, J., 'Il Maresciallo d'Italia Rodolfo Graziani,' in *Rassegna italica*, (Rome, 1937, source: newspaper section of the Biblioteca nazionale in Rome)

Index

Acquarone, Pietro 37, 152, 156-157, 159
Afarwaq, *Grazmach* 103-104, 106-107
Aftan, Shekib al 56
Agnelli, Giovanni 91
Ago, General 55, 172
Agostini, General 103
Akkad, Mustafa 86
Albertazzi, Captain 40
Alexander, Field Marshal Harold Rupert 186
Alfonsi, Giuseppe 84
Alleg, Henri 85
Allenby, Edmund Henry 8
Ambrosio, Vittorio 151
Amendola, Giovanni 65
Amey, Muhammed Ben 61, 87
Andreotti, Giulio 212-213
Andronico, Pietro 118
Aosta, Duke Amedeo of 88, 123, 143, 146, 149
Aosta, Duke Emanuele Filiberto of 53
Appelius, Mario 136
Aptewold, Bascinured 132
Arerù, Aden 56
Arminius 184
Arwilopilos, medical officer 113
Augenti, Giacomo Primo 201-202, 206-207

Babini, General 33
Badoglio, Mario 120
Badoglio, Marshal Pietro 14, 16-27, 29-30, 54, 59, 68, 70, 72-75, 77, 79, 81-86, 88, 93, 96-98, 99, 105, 108-111, 113, 117, 119-120, 140, 145, 148-152, 154, 155-156, 158-160, 163-164, 166, 173, 183, 215, 217-218
Baistrocchi Federico 96, 106, 120
Balbo, Italo 16-17, 42, 88, 145

Balcha, *Dejazmach* 126
Baldissera, Antonio 99
Banon, Cesare 131
Barbareschi, Don 186
Bardi, Gino 173
Barra, Lieutenant 144
Barracu, Francesco Maria 162
Bartolomasi, A. 149
Bassi, Mario 67
Batasso, Hagi 132
Battistella, Franco 102
Beati, pilot 79
Bedei, medical officer 135
Bedendo, Giuseppe 80, 88-89
Bellentani, Pia 196
Belli, Gioacchino 89
Belly, General 145
Beraudo di Pralormo, Emanuele 207
Beresford Pierce, General 10
Bergonzoli, General Annibale 25-26, 32-33
Berlinguer, Mario 198-199, 203
Bernasconi, General B. A. 96, 108-110, 114
Berté, Roberto 76-77
Berti, General Mario 19, 25
Bertoldi, Silvio 151, 219
Bertoloni, B. 148
Beyene Merid, *Dejazmach* 121, 137
Bicchierai, Giuseppe 187, 189-190, 194
Birindelli, Danilo 133, 143
Blandi, B. B. 148
Bocca, Giorgio 151
Bocca, Magno 37, 41, 56, 58, 93, 154-156, 162, 164, 174
Boccara, Victor M. 133
Bodard, Monsieur and Madame Pierrette 121, 141

Bolty, General Charles 192
Bombacci, Nicola 170
Bonardi, Pierre 87
Bonetti, Vittorio 190-191
Bonfanti, Giuseppe 194, 197
Bonfantini, Corrado 194
Boniface VIII, Pope 152
Bonomi, General Ruggero 187, 190, 194-195
Bonomi, Ivanoe 172
Borahil, Yousaf 77
Borghese, Junio Valerio 171, 199
Boris, tsar of Bulgaria 159
Borletti, Mario 191
Bormioli, medical officer 200-201
Borra, medical officer 135
Brosio, Manlio 173
Brunei, Riccardo 66
Buffarini Guidi, Guido 156, 161, 168, 172, 188
Buffon, Comte de 47, 65
Bugeaud, Thomas Robert 59
Burkler, Guido 119, 148
Burru, *Ras* 125
Busi, Captain 107
Busiri Vici, Clemente 161

Cadorna, Marshal Luigi 53
Cadorna, Raffaele 190, 192-194
Callegaris, Colonel 173
Calvi di Bergolo, Carlo 160-161
Calvosa, Fausto 211
Candela, Giuseppe 138
Canevari, Emilio 18-19, 169, 199
Canosa, Romano 220
Cantalupo, Roberto 67, 72, 75
Capo, Carlo 173
Caraffa, Arcangelo 216
Carnelutti, Francesco 197, 201-202, 205-208
Casati, Ettore 172, 198
Castagna, Colonel 31, 40
Castelli, Temistocle 45
Castriota, Raffaele 68
Cavagnaro, Tullio 158
Cavallero, Marshal Ugo 26, 29-30
Cavicchioli, Antonio 149
Caviglia, Marshal Enrico 86, 160, 166, 170, 209
Cecchi, Emilio 87
Celio, Prefect 188
Chierico, Colonel 168
Churchill, Winston 7, 12-13, 22, 31, 33, 40
Ciano, Galeazzo 18, 27, 29-30, 99
Cicero 54
Clementi, Adelia 43, 48, 51, 144, 216
Clementi, Muzio 43
Cobolli Gigli, Giuseppe 126-127
Colonna, Sciarra 152

Colucci, civil servant 115
Contini, Paolo 44
Coobar, al-Hadi 65-66
Corcione, Domenico 219
Cortese, Guido 124, 133-135, 137-138,
Crimi, General 179
Crittemberger, General Willis 195
Cufalo, Vincenzo 214

D'Annunzio, Gabriele 209, 211
Daddario, Emilio 191-195, 201
Daodiace, Giuseppe 77
Dapporto, Carlo 187
De Bono, Marshal Emilio 66
De Caesaris, Domenica 216
De Caesaris, Giuseppe 43
De Feo, Sandro 196, 203
De Gasperi, Alcide 172, 212
De Martini, *Carabinieri* 125
De Rege, brothers 187
De Renzis, Florindo 207
Deakin, William 151, 219
Del Boca, Angelo 98, 133, 219
Del Mastro, Sergeant 144
Del Rio, Mastino 201-202, 206-207
Delfino, Colonel 167
Dessy, Flavio 130
Desta Damtew, *Ras* 102-103, 105, 108, 110-115, 121, 129, 134, 137-138
Di Dato, Captain 132
Di Leo, Lieutenant-Colonel 40, 186
Dollmann, Eugen 168, 183-185
Donegani, Guido 192

Eden, Anthony 115
Edwards, H. C., Major 198
El-Krim, Abd 85
Embaie, *Balambaras* 104
Emiliani, Rodolfo 44
Ewotion, Tzahai 115

Facchini, Colonel 116
Facta, Luigi 62
Faldella, Emilio 172
Fanfani, Amintore 87
Fani, Bartolomeo 44
Farina, Amilcare 195
Farinacci, Roberto 21, 27, 29, 41, 61, 165, 170
Federzoni, Luigi 68, 143
Filomusi-Guelfi, Francesco 46
Finocchiaro, Cesare 148
Fiocchi, Pino 191
Fiske, Norman E. 96, 105, 194
Flamini, Elena 118
Fort, Rina 196
Freda, Franco 97
Frére, Armand 113

Index

Frugoni, Cesare 137, 213
Frusci, Luigi 96, 103, 109

Gaddafi, Muammar 82, 86, 218
Galasso, General 208
Galatola, Arturo 197, 199-200
Gallina, General Sebastiano 11-12, 126
Gallo, Max 151
Gambara, General Gastone 42, 170, 177, 199
Garibaldi, Giuseppe 209
Gariboldi, General Italo 19, 132, 134-136
Gebremariam, *Dejazmach* 121, 137
Geriani al-Kemesi, Hamedi al 69
Geronazzo, Major 42
Giardina, Prison Commandant 194
Giarratana, Mario 148
Gilani, Abdalla al 69
Giolitti, Giovanni 63
Gospodinoff, veterinary surgeon 57
Granata, Colonel 42
Graziani, Andrea 62
Graziani, Augusto 41, 118
Graziani, Benedetto 43, 45, 216
Graziani, Filippo 35, 43, 48, 216
Graziani, Giulio Cesare 152-153, 220
Graziani, Giuseppe (Peppino) 41, 87, 92, 118, 216
Graziani, Goffredo 216
Graziani, Ilda 216
Graziani, Ines 34, 41-42, 48-52, 57, 62, 78, 86, 102, 136, 172, 175, 177, 183, 187, 193, 200-201, 214
Graziani, Maria 216
Graziani, Vanda 50-52, 60, 92, 102, 144, 146, 153-154, 159, 172, 216
Grazioli, Francesco Saverio 161
Grignolo, Giacomo 149
Grippo, Commissar 46
Grossi, Enzo 184
Gualandi Graziani, Rodolfo 50, 52, 60, 92, 95, 210, 216
Gualandi, Alberto 50, 52, 95, 216
Gualandi, Ethel Romana 216
Gualandi, Ondina 216
Gualandi, Sergio 51-52, 144, 216
Guarnera, Ugo 202
Guerra, lawyer 90
Guinness, Alec 175
Guzzoni, Alfredo 26, 29-30, 33

Hailu, *Ras* 123, 127, 140-141, 145
Hannibal, Barca 44, 183
Hargia, Aisha 69
Haster, General 186
Hazon, Azolino 128, 136
Heggenreiner, Heinz 11, 25, 27, 181
Herriot, Edouard 115

Heruy, *Blattengetta* 110-111, 113
Heruy, Wolde-Selassie 113
Hitler, Adolf 87, 151, 163, 168-169, 177, 180, 182
Holmes, journalist 113
Howard, Lieutenant Henry 107
Hueber, pilot 79
Hylander, Swedish medic 108, 111, 113

Ighezu, *Dejazmach* 105
Imru, *Ras* 121, 128-129
Isawi, Muhammed Akhdar al 71
Israel, Norbert 131
Itamar, Ben-Avi 101

Janni, Salvatore 49
Jayme, Henry 41
Jella, Don Lorenzo 49, 118
Jones, Donald 189
Jorio, Domenico 92, 153, 172

Kaled, Kalifa 61, 64, 78, 95
Kappler, Herbert 179
Karl, prince of Sweden 113
Kassa, Aberra 121, 123, 145
Kassa, Asfawossen 121, 145
Keitel, Wilhelm 168-169, 180
Kesselring, Albert 160-161, 166-167, 171, 175-177, 179-180, 183-184, 186

La Marca, Giuseppe 200
Labriola, Arturo 100
Lanfranchi, Ferruccio 189, 191, 194
Lawrence, Thomas Edward 65, 84
Lessona, Alessandro 96-97, 101, 107-111, 116, 122, 126, 130-131, 135, 139-141, 143, 145
Leyers, Hans 179, 181
Liberati, Colonel 116
Liotta, Aurelio 135
Liverani, Major 144
Lontano, Captain 80
Loss, Eyat 56
Lyautey, Hubert 86

Machiavelli, Niccolò 56, 85
Mackensen, August von 162
Madia, Titta 16, 49, 135
Magnani, Aldo 148
Mahdi as-Senussi, El Sayyid Muhammed Idris al 62, 68, 70, 72, 76, 79, 218
Maitland Wilson, General Henry 22
Malcovati, Major 29
Maletti, General Pietro 10, 140
Malta, Colonel 128-129
Mannaresi, National Councillor 56
Marantonio, Luigi 202
Marchesi, Captain 197

Marchiafava, Ettore 43
Marcos, *Abuna* 135
Marinetti, Filippo Tommaso 100
Marinoni, Lieutenant-Colonel 80
Marmi, General 56
Massu, Jacques 85
Mayda, Giuseppe 219
Mazza, Giulio 149
Mazzario, Pietro 148
Mazzetti, Guido 129
Mazzi, Colonel Alberto 103-106, 116, 128, 132, 134, 137, 141
Melchiorri, Alessandro 155
Menelik, Emperor 34, 102, 126, 147, 215-216
Mezzasoma, Ferdinando 162
Mezzetti, General 153
Mieville, Roberto 128
Millán Astray, José 209
Minniti, Colonel 128
Minniti, Tito 109, 112
Mischi, Archimede 49-50, 186
Misserville, Romano 215
Missiroli, Mario 85
Mitterrand, François 86
Molinari, Giacinto 42
Möllhausen, Friedrich 150, 162-163
Montanelli, Indro 97, 172, 219
Montefoschi, painter 92
Montini, Giovan Battista 172, 179
Moroni, Captain 132
Mountbatten of Burma, Louis, 1st Earl 218
Mukthar, Ben Omar 69
Mukthar, Omar al 24, 62-63, 68-78, 80, 84-89, 219
Mussolini, Benito 8, 11, 15-20, 24, 26-30, 33-34, 36-38, 45, 55, 58, 65-66, 68, 73, 83-84, 86, 88, 90, 92-95, 98-100, 102-103, 107-108, 111, 113-117, 119-120, 122, 128-129, 131, 135-137, 139-140, 142-143, 145, 147, 149, 151, 155-156, 160, 163-166, 170-172, 176-177, 179-184, 187-188, 193, 199, 211, 219
Mussolini, Bruno 99
Mussolini, Rachele 99, 183
Mussolini, Vittorio 99
Mutanabbi, Ahmed Ibn al-Husain al 65
Muti, Ettore 168

Nasibu, Zamanuel 102, 104, 106-107
Nasser, Sef en 40
Natale, General 136
Nenni, Pietro 172

O'Connor, Lieutenant-General Richard N. 7, 9, 32
Orazi, Federal 124
Orlando, Vittorio Emanuele 100

Osvaldo, Pietro 131
Ottolenghi, Loris 131

Pacciardi, Randolfo 209
Pace, Biagio 66
Pala, Michele 135, 142
Pallavicino, Giorgio Vicino 128, 132, 137
Pansa, Giampaolo 151
Parri, Ferruccio 190, 193-194, 205-207
Paternostro, Captain 144
Pavolini, Alessandro 99, 165, 170, 177, 179-180, 186-187
Pellegrini Giampietro, Domenico 162
Peregrini, Carlo 191
Perrot, Giuseppe 55
Pertini, Sandro 194, 202
Pescatori, Armando 50
Pétain, Henri Philippe Omer 162
Petochi, jewellers 174
Petretti, Arnaldo 134
Petros, *Abuna* 123, 126
Pintus, Giovan Battista 149
Pirzio-Biroli, General Alessandro 140, 204
Pisenti, Piero 176
Pizzi, Gaetano 84
Poggialli, Ciro 49, 51, 124, 133
Pollastrini, Guglielmo 172
Pontecorvo, Gillo 86
Porta, Count Gherardo della 132-133, 141
Presti, Umberto 163
Puccinelli, Vittorio 137, 200-201
Puntoni, General 92, 157

Qerellos, *Abuna* 126, 132
Quercia, Major 132
Quinn, Anthony 86

Ragazzi, Corrado 76
Rahn, Rudolf 150, 162-163, 180-181, 183-184, 186
Rao, Mrs 153
Rauff, Walter 192
Ravasco, Alfredo 147
Reed, Oliver 86
Reicher, Franz 12
Repaci, Antonino 204
Retice, Licinio 148
Reul, Belgian officer 113
Revetria, Lieutenant-Colonel 8-9
Riccardi, Raffaele 15
Ricci, Renato 170
Rigolone, Virgilio 96, 110, 112
Rimini, Alberto 131
Roatta, Mario 18, 42
Roberts, Patrick 121
Rocchi, Federale 41
Rommel, Erwin 34, 37, 92

Index

Ronca, Roberto 172
Roosevelt, Franklin Delano 13
Ruini, Meuccio 172

Sagramoso, Colonel 47
Salandra, Antonio 46
San Marzano, Roberto di 152
Sandri, Sandro 70
Sardi, Alessandro 199-200, 202, 210-211, 213
Savoy, King Umberto I of 151
Savoy, King Victor Emanuel III of 52, 85, 144
Savoy, Prince Umberto of 132, 152, 159
Savoy, Prince Vittorio Emanuele 132
Savoy, Princess Maria José of 132
Savoy, Queen Elena of 100
Savoy, Queen Margherita of 151
Scelba, Mario 210-211, 220
Schuster, Cardinal Ildefonso 41, 100, 172, 186-187, 189
Scorza, Carlo 151, 154-156
Sebastiani, Osvaldo 142
Selassie, Emperor Haile 56, 107, 110, 129, 218
Serena, Adelchi 41, 55
Seyum Mengesha, *Ras* 123
Sforza, Federico 131
Sharif, Ahmad al 69
Shaw, George Bernard 114
Signorino, Doctor Rosario 142
Silvestri, Carlo 172, 182
Sindico, Giovanni 137
Siniscalchi, Governor 135
Soldatini, Captain 144
Soleri, Marcello 172
Soliman, Muhammed 64
Sorice, Antonio 158-159
Sorrentino, Rosario 179, 187, 190-191, 193-195
Spagnuolo, Magistrate 202
Spizzichino, Elia 131
Stahel, Rainer 160, 165, 168, 185
Stalin, Joseph 197
Starace, Achille 100, 130, 143, 153-154, 159
Stauffenberg, Klaus Schenk von 180
Steer, George L. 96, 105
Steiger, Rod 86
Stevens, Colonel 41, 86
Stone, Ellery 174
Strom, Hans 121

Tacitus 56, 87, 153
Talleyrand, Charles Maurice 85
Taranto, Alfredo 63
Tarquini, Cairoli 132, 142
Tedeschini Lalli, General 96, 117
Teghegn, Menghestu 56
Tekle-Haymanot, Embaie 14, 21, 38-39, 42, 127-128, 163, 175, 187, 191-192, 194, 201
Tellera, General 16, 31, 33
Teruzzi, Attilio 61, 145-146
Thaon di Revel, Grand Admiral 55, 93, 171
Tito, Josip Broz 166
Tobino, Mario 34
Togliatti, Palmiro 197, 201
Tooker, British army officer 186
Tracchia, Ruggero 139, 145
Trilussa 89
Tucci, Captain 138

Ungari, Mrs 56
Uorkemariam, witch 56
Utili, General 212

Valdoni, Pietro 213
Valletta, Vittorio 118
Valletti Borghini, Lieutenant-Colonel 84
Vergani, Orio 87
Vietinghoff, Heinrich von 184, 186
Villani, Ercole 50
Viri, Ercole 220
Vitali, Colonel 177
Voetterl, Captain 188-189, 191
Volpi di Misurata, Count Giovanni 61, 63, 65-66, 88, 93, 143, 145, 149, 160
Volta, Sandro 103

Wavell, General Archibald Percival 7-8, 11-14, 22-26, 29, 31-33, 86, 218
Wehib, General Pasha 102
Wilson, journalist 113
Wolff, Karl 162-163, 180, 188-190, 206

Young, General Desmond 32
Young, Henry A. 111

Zardi, Mr 41
Zingoni, Mario 41, 153, 160, 162, 168